Sports Broadcasting

SPORTS BROADCASTING

BRAD SCHULTZ

Focal Press
An imprint of Butterworth-Heinemann

Boston • Oxford • Johannesburg • Melbourne • New Delhi

Library of Congress Cataloging-in-Publication Data

Schultz, Brad, 1961–
   Sports broadcasting / by Brad Schultz.
     p. cm.
   Includes bibliographical references and index.
   ISBN 0-240-80463-5 (pbk. : alk. paper)
    1. Television broadcasting of sports—United States.   2. Radio broadcasting of sports—United States.   I. Title.
GV742.3 .S38 2001
070.4'49796'0973—dc21   2001033280

British Library Cataloguing-in-Publication Data
A catalogue record for this book is available from the British Library.

The publisher offers special discounts on bulk orders of this book.
For information, please contact:
Manager of Special Sales
Butterworth–Heinemann
225 Wildwood Avenue
Woburn, MA 01801-2041
Tel: 781-904-2500
Fax: 781-904-2620

For information on all Focal Press publications available, contact our World Wide Web home page at: http://www.focalpress.com

10 9 8 7 6 5 4 3 2 1

Printed in the United States of America

This book is dedicated to the mostly anonymous sports broad-casters who work in America's smaller television markets. Specif-ically, I would like to mention Bill Jackson, Mike King, and John Campbell. Bill taught me the basics of the sports broadcasting pro-fession in Wichita Falls, Texas. Mike taught me to think big and push the envelope when we worked together in Terre Haute, Indi-ana. And John Campbell in Cedar Rapids, Iowa taught me about planning and organization. I enjoyed working with all of these professionals, but I especially treasure John's help and friendship. He epitomizes all that's good about local sports broadcasting.

Special thanks to my wife and children, who spent many nights alone while I was off at some game. Although, on the plus side, my wife is now a serious hockey fan. And finally, I told myself if I ever wrote a book I would make special mention of my grand-parents—the four greatest people I ever met.

Contents

Foreword

Sports journalism is the greatest job in the world. Sometimes. I can tell you that from experience, and so can the author of this book. Brad and I worked together for several years at a Midwest CBS-TV affiliate, and for the most part we had a blast. The reason was simple—we loved the job. We didn't always love the conditions, or the equipment, or even some of the other people we had to deal with at the station, but we loved what we were doing. This book can't explain what it's like to spend eight or nine hours covering a college or pro football game, then condense the entire day into less than two minutes of airtime. This book can't explain what it's like to cover a city golf tournament, only to find that when you return to the station the tape is wrinkled and unusable. And this book can't explain why someone would sit in an edit bay for six, eight, or more hours trying to get a music piece on the state basketball tournament just right. This book can't explain all of the things that you're going to learn over the next few years about print journalism or broadcasting, but you can be sure of this—Brad Schultz has experienced the good and the bad, and he knows what it takes to succeed.

If you're thinking, "Man, what a great job ... going to games, easy hours, good money, no worries, no pressure ... ," then I suggest you pick another profession. I can tell you firsthand that there are plenty of people out there looking for jobs, particularly in sports radio and TV. The only problem is there aren't many good people out there. As you'll soon see, it's the innovator, the investigator, and the interviewer who thrive in broadcasting.

A good suit and good hair will never disguise a lousy broadcast journalist. I have been fortunate during the course of my years in broadcasting to work with some great journalists. I have also had to work with some people who didn't have a clue. The latter made me understand just how dangerous a poor journalist can be. You can bet you will encounter the same mix of people during the course of your career.

Brad and I have something in common and that's passion for the job. If you share that same passion (and I hope you do), you will experience some of the highest highs and some of the lowest lows that a professional can experience. It's just part of the job. This textbook can't teach you to be a great sports journalist, but it sure can help. One thing is for sure—the guy who wrote it has been there, so you can trust what he says. The passion is your responsibility.

Do a good job. A lot of people will be reading, listening, and watching.

Mike King
Indy Racing Radio Network
Radio Voice: Indianapolis, Brickyard, U.S. Grand Prix,
      and Indy Racing League

Preface

Like many millions of other young kids, I wanted to grow up to be a professional athlete. I played all the sports, especially football, basketball, and baseball. I followed my favorite professional teams and became something of a walking encyclopedia on trivial sports information (I can still recite the starting rotation for the 1969 Mets).

But it didn't take long to realize I would never be good enough to play professional sports (probably when the other kids started getting a lot bigger and faster). That's when my attention turned to sports broadcasting. What better way to stay close to the games? It all seemed so easy—just talk on television or radio about something you already like, and you get into the games for free! I was probably the only kid on my block with a tape recorder, which I used to practice my play-by-play. If you can't be the next Joe Montana, Wayne Gretzky, or Michael Jordan, why not John Madden, Howard Cosell, or Bob Costas?

In reality, it's almost as hard to become a great sportscaster as it is a famous athlete. Jobs in the industry are scarce, and most of them demand long hours at very little pay. The work is often unglamorous, unless you consider a junior high school soccer game exciting. Sportscasters often spend years in the smaller markets, burning themselves out in an attempt to "pay their dues" and move on to bigger and better stations. I like to tell people I've covered sports in some exotic places like Paris, Brazil, and Scotland. Of course, that's Paris, Illinois; Brazil, Indiana; and Scotland, Texas.

That's one of the reasons I wrote this book. Very few students who want to get into the industry understand these realities. They're completely unprepared for what they have to face, and as a result many of them drop out or change careers. Students who decide to go into sports broadcasting need to know just how hard it is to get into the business, and how hard it is to make a living at it. This is not meant to scare anyone away; rather it is hoped that all the millions of would-be sportscasters will pursue their goals with their eyes wide open.

This book also hopes to fill a perceived void in the sportscasting literature. Most current textbooks concentrate on the sportscasting industry in a theoretical sense. That is, they go into great depth about how things are done at ABC, ESPN, or Fox Sports. But how many students go to work at those places right out of school? More likely, graduates will start their careers in some small market like Florence, Alabama or Marquette, Michigan. And that's what this book focuses on: providing the necessary skills and knowledge to get that first job and succeed at an entry-level position. It also offers important theoretical concepts to help the student better understand the changing sports broadcasting industry. Major concepts are also placed within the context of society and culture as a whole, so the text is not simply just a "sports book." It takes a serious look at major cultural issues, including the role of women and minorities, and the growing importance of global communication.

But most importantly, the book offers solid, practical skills necessary to function as a modern sportscaster. There are lengthy sections on writing, photography, producing, editing, anchoring, reporting, and providing play-by-play. These are not theoretical discussions, but rather concrete and effectual skills the student can practice and learn. And they come not from some college ivory tower, but from someone with years of commercial sportscasting experience who has been in the field and covered a wide variety of events.

This book could be used by itself in a sports broadcasting course or as a supplementary text in a related course on reporting, broadcast journalism, or radio-television. In any event, it is hoped that it provides something that has been missing from other texts: a realistic and practical approach that students can use as they enter a demanding field.

Introduction

No industry changes quite as quickly as telecommunications. New technology is introduced every day, making previously accepted standards nearly obsolete. Regulations change almost as quickly, with just as much impact on the industry landscape. And perhaps even more importantly, culture continues to change and evolve, creating even more uncertainty.

As with anything else, sports broadcasting is a reflection of the culture in which it exists. As radio and then television began to develop, sports broadcasting was still very primitive, not only technologically, but also in terms of presentation and format. Now decades later, sports broadcasting has adapted to the hurry-up, instant-gratification culture of modern times, which has produced such recent advances as the Internet and digital technology. Where once sports broadcasting seemed somewhat restrained and genteel, it now delivers its omnipresent message with an "in your face" attitude. And there should be no doubt that, one day, the cultural pendulum will swing again and take sports broadcasting into another different direction.

The good news for the student is that no matter what the cultural implications, the basics of the business remain pretty much the same. Even in an age of "infotainment," good sports broadcasting still relies on quality writing, photography, editing, producing, and anchoring. You can ask different news directors to critique a story, and they'll give you different overall impressions. But all of them will demand good writing and good storytelling. These are also the things that can be learned and practiced over and over again, in the classroom and in the lab. There is simply no substitute for highly developed skills in the basics of radio and television sports. That is why this book offers "how to" chapters on the main components of sports broadcasting: writing, editing, photography, producing, anchoring, and play-by-play. Each chapter includes practical exercises that will help the student develop the necessary skills involved.

But sports broadcasting has to be more than just skills, and certainly more than just sports. Too often, today's colleges and universities teach broadcast journalism as they would in a trade school. That is, they concentrate mostly on the broadcasting skills, figuring that's what students will need most when they get into the industry. But as a result, while students learn the technical side of the business they can't put what they've learned into a larger framework. They know how to point a camera or hold a microphone, but can't connect those skills to the issues they're supposed to be covering on a daily basis.

This is a particular danger for students of sports broadcasting. There is a great temptation for such students to get "tunnel vision," where they eat, sleep, and breathe nothing but sports. Years ago, this approach worked fine. But in today's world, sports stories encompass a myriad of other issues, including crime, politics, religion, law, and race. It is impossible for today's students to ignore such issues and simply report sports scores and highlights. Anyone interested in working in the modern sports broadcasting environment should have a solid grounding on the important cultural issues of the day, and they are encouraged to expose themselves to a wide variety of topics in school.

The first three chapters of this book offer such grounding, on the topics of history, impact, and sports broadcasting style. Each issue is connected to the larger framework of the culture as a whole, in order to help the student bridge the gap between sports and society. Similar chapters concentrate on ethics, women, and minorities, with a special chapter featuring a discussion with the commissioners of the four major American sports leagues.

It is hoped that this combination of theory and practice will equip today's student to establish a solid career in the world of sports broadcasting.

History

IN THE BEGINNING

David Halberstam won a Pulitzer Prize for his coverage of the Vietnam War, but his real passion is writing about sports. Halberstam has written several books, mostly about baseball history and the game he grew up watching. One effort in particular chronicles the 1949 American League pennant race between the Red Sox and Yankees, which the Yankees finally won on the final day of the season.

That same year also marked an important milestone in sports broadcasting as television began to make its presence felt. Just two years earlier, the World Series appeared on television for the first time, seen by some three million viewers. By 1949, everyone realized that this was no fad; television was here to stay, especially in sports.

Halberstam wrote of a man named Otis Freeman who worked as a television engineer for the fledgling DuMont station in New York. In those days, engineer also meant repairman and Freeman spent much of his time making house calls to fix balky equipment. But his job also put him on the ground floor of perhaps the greatest communications breakthrough of the twentieth century.

Looking back on his career, Freeman believed that the history of television could be divided into three stages: the early engineer-driven stage, the later creativity-driven stage, and finally the accountant-driven stage. The engineer stage focused on technical developments and seeing how the new technology would work. Once the technology was worked out, there was a need for new and interesting programming in the creativity stage. And finally, once the medium became accepted, it became a profit-oriented busi-

ness. For better or worse, accountants and profits determine the future of any electronic enterprise.

Freeman showed remarkable insight into the entire history of broadcasting in general and sports broadcasting in particular. For the amazing developments of radio and television seemed to grow exactly along these lines.

RADIO
The Era of Technology: 1900–1920

The earliest radio broadcasts had very little to do with sports and hardly resembled radio as we know it today. Soon after pioneers like Guglielmo Marconi and Lee De Forest made "wireless speech" a reality, the search began to figure out how to use the new medium. Because of the uncertainty of the technology, early programming was used mainly for practical purposes, such as weather reports and ship-to-shore communication. In fact, radio first came to national attention for its role in reporting the sinking of the Titanic in 1912.

During this period, everything about radio was chaotic. The government dominated the medium under the U.S. Department of Commerce, but did not really regulate it. Stations appeared and disappeared almost overnight, often changing locations on the dial. Programming was infrequent and unreliable and focused mainly on educational programs and music. Signal pirates abounded as the entire industry seemed on the verge of collapse.

Many of the problems related to the technical limitations of the period, especially for sports. Broadcasting live from a sports event presented a peculiar set of challenges that had to be worked out almost on the spot. Pioneer radio sportscaster Harold Arlin remembers, "Sometimes the transmitter worked and sometimes it didn't. Sometimes the crowd noise would drown us out and sometimes it wouldn't. And quite frankly, we didn't know what the reaction would be—if we'd be talking in a total vacuum or whether somebody would hear us."

The only constant during this time was the steady growth of technological advancement. The first radio broadcast went out over the airwaves in 1906. By 1915, experimental stations were on the air and a few years later regular transmissions became possible. The breakthrough achievement for radio is considered the live coverage of the 1920 presidential returns by station KDKA in Pittsburgh. From that point on, the power and possibilities of radio mesmerized the nation. Technological growth had set the stage for the next era in radio development—commercialism and creativity.

The Era of Creativity: 1920–1950

A critical part of the development of radio came in 1922, when station WEAF in New York broadcast the first commercial message. Up until that time, radio had been much like public broadcasting is today. Programming was mostly educational and designed mainly to provide motivation for listeners to buy radio sets. Most of the money in radio came from the selling of the big, bulky receivers that pulled in the signals. In fact, that's how companies like Westinghouse and RCA became giants in the industry—by making and selling radio sets. But that was soon to change.

Once the first commercial got on the air, the cat was out of the bag and the money rolled in. The radio industry mushroomed almost overnight, as the number of stations grew at an enormous rate. Congress finally realized that its antiquated system of handling the industry could not keep up with the growth, and in 1927 it authorized the creation of the Federal Radio Commission (later the FCC). The FRC brought regulation and stability to radio, which included setting frequencies, issuing licenses, and limiting power. Most importantly, it created rules and regulations that favored commercial broadcasters. Intentional or not, the government made advertising the backbone of the industry.

Thus began what historians call the "Golden Age of Radio." Networks formed in the late 20s and came to dominate the industry. As profits soared, so too did new and creative programming. In 1935, a New York announcer started a show mixing commentary and music, thus becoming the first radio disc jockey. Three years later, Orson Welles panicked a nation with his "War of the Worlds" broadcast about a fictitious Martian invasion of earth, which vividly demonstrated the power of the growing medium.

More and more stations came on the air. Only five had licenses in 1921, but that number jumped to 556 by 1923, then rose to 681 in 1927. With all those stations, all that money, and all those commercials to air, advertisers began demanding more creative programming. It didn't take long for sports to jump into the breech. The first sports broadcast took place on July 2, 1921 and involved a heavyweight boxing match arranged by RCA founder David Sarnoff as a way to promote radio. Later that same year, the World Series went on radio for the first time and again Sarnoff played a leading role. Recognizing that the new medium needed programming, Sarnoff made baseball one of the cornerstones of the industry. "We had to have baseball in order to sell enough sets to go on to other programming," he later wrote. Journalist Judith Waller claims to have sold the idea of radio to the Chicago Cubs. After one season on WMAQ, Waller says the Cubs had the highest financial receipts of any club in the league and the broadcasts stimulated so much interest among women that the team added a "Ladies Day" at the park the following season. Cubs owner William Wrigley had his team's games on five different stations and reportedly said, "The more outlets the better; we'll tie up the entire city."

But not everyone was sold on the idea, especially baseball club owners. Before the era of big radio and TV contracts, owners made almost all of their money from gate receipts and ticket sales. To them, broadcasting games was like giving away the product. Why come to the game when you can hear it at home for free? In 1929, American League owners considered a proposal to ban radio broadcasting of their games. And as late as 1938, the three New York teams agreed on a five-year ban. Not until the success of the Brooklyn Dodgers in the late 1930s did owners change their minds. Dodgers general manager Larry MacPhail signed a deal with a 50-thousand-watt station, WOR, and in one year sponsors paid $113,000 in ads. And while the Dodgers struggled on the field, their attendance soared and even surpassed the more successful Yankees and Giants.

As baseball and other sports became accepted on radio, the medium looked for more creative ways to market the product. In these early days, announcers became as famous as the events they covered, primarily because of their unique styles. Graham McNamee and Ted Husing became known for their thorough preparation and reporting. Bill Stern had a more colorful style and may have been the first sportscaster to interject more personality in his broadcasts. Of the baseball announcers, Red Barber earned a reputation as a master storyteller and someone who could make the game enjoyable and colorful (see Chapter 16). All of this was important, because many historians argue that in those days the announcer *was* radio.

While broadcasters like the Yankees Mel Allen played it mostly straight, more and more announcers began to shake things up with their own particular styles. This included former pitcher Dizzy Dean, who infuriated a generation of English teachers with phrases like "slud into second" or "swang at a bad pitch." Allen worked with Dean for two seasons and appreciated the new dimension he brought to the broadcast booth. "Once he took off solo," Allen recalled, "it was show biz time. Diz had a method and a style all his own. Nothing like it before, nothing like it since."

Many announcers let their creativity and personalities show in one of the most unique forms of American broadcasting—the re-creation. To save money, many stations would not let their announcers travel for road games. Instead, the announcer would "re-create" the game as it came in on the telegraph wire. The telegraphy would supply all the basic information and the announcer would embellish it with creative narrative and sound effects to make it sound as if he was actually at the game. Many famous sportscasters experimented with re-creation, including a man who would later try his hand at movies and politics, Ronald Reagan. Byrum Saam, former broadcaster for the Athletics and Phillies, said, "Re-creations planted the seeds of our coverage—they were the nectar from which most listeners drank. It was at the very heart of radio." But by the 50s, telephone wire had replaced the telegraph, making it much cheaper and easier to broadcast on the road. The re-creation was headed down the long road toward oblivion, with much of the radio industry right behind it.

The Era of Accountants: 1950–Present

Contrary to popular opinion, television did not kill radio. But it certainly ended radio's era of dominance and forced the medium to reinvent itself. The decisive moments came in the late 40s and early 50s, when radio giants like CBS and RCA realized that television was not just a fad and would not go away. They began investing huge sums of money in the new medium, taking money away from radio. The same thing began to happen with advertisers, who quickly saw television's commercial potential. It wasn't so much that radio lost advertising money; television just began cutting into the pie. In 1949, advertisers spent $571 million for radio compared to $58 million for television. In just five short years, television advertising expenditures jumped to $809 million and eclipsed radio for the first time (see Table 1-1).

The Mutual Network broadcast a "Game of the Day" every day for nearly a dozen years. But by the early 60s, a combination of television games and dwindling radio markets killed the package. Al Wester did play-by-play for the "Game of the Day," and said, "It became a case of there being fewer stations every year available to carry our games." Faced with this drastic situation, radio changed to meet the changing economic times. Once the dominant electronic medium of mass communication, radio had to become more secondary, more local, and more specialized in order to survive financially.

Two developments helped save radio during this dark period: the emergence of FM and the production of the transistor. The FCC finally removed restrictions on the development of FM in 1961, which drastically improved

Table 1-1 Comparison of Advertising Revenue in Millions of Dollars

Year	Radio	Television
1949	571	58
1950	605	171
1951	606	332
1952	624	454
1953	611	606
1954	559	809
1955	545	1,035
1956	567	1,225

Source: Robert J. Coen, McCann-Erickson, Inc. (as cited in Sterling, 1984)

signal quality and allowed stations to broadcast in stereo. The introduction of the transistor in the 50s finally made radio portable, which meant listeners could take it to the beach, the store, or the ballgame.

Both of these developments pointed radio in the direction of specialized or "niche" programming. Instead of catering to national audiences, which had all seemingly defected to television, radio marketed itself to smaller, segmented groups of listeners. The first major breakthrough came in the 50s with the birth of rock and roll, which appealed to teenagers and young adults. Soon "format" radio dominated the industry with programming such as country-and-western music, urban, ethnic, talk, and ultimately all sports. By 1969, WABC in New York promoted its "Top 40" music format as the most listened-to station in the country.

The lessening impact of networks and the localization of radio also impacted sports. As television grabbed more and more sports programming, radio became a secondary medium: a way to kill time on a long drive or something to listen to if you can't see the game on TV. Network radio still aired the big events, like the Super Bowl and the World Series, but the money those events generated was dwarfed by corresponding revenues from television.

Like the rest of the industry, radio sports had to make changes in the face of economic reality. And like other programming, radio sports survived because it became local and interactive. The niche that sports found on radio was the local sports audience. Because of technological improvements and the nature of the medium, radio found it was the perfect venue to broadcast local high school and college games. The development of telephone lines for radio use and later the emergence of the Marti portable broadcasting system, made broadcasting games easy, quick, and relatively inexpensive—especially compared to what it would cost for a local television broadcast. The only major cost is the talent, which still doesn't add up to much because most of the announcers already work at the station in some capacity. Thus, broadcasting live sporting events has become the bedrock of local radio sports. WTMJ-AM in Milwaukee promotes itself as the only station in the country to flagship three local sports teams—the Packers, Brewers, and Bucks.

The other major staple of local sports broadcasting is talk—and lots of it. Talk radio began in California in the 60s, but really didn't hit its stride until the late 70s. By the mid-80s, radio talk exploded with the emergence of Larry King, Rush Limbaugh, Tom Snyder, and Sally Jessy Raphael. By the end of the 90s, talk radio had become a solid force in radio broadcasting, with millions of listeners tuning in to talk about politics, current affairs, pop psychology, and sports.

The appeal of talk radio is simple—listeners can voice their opinions and become active rather than passive users of the medium. Sometimes people call in to vent their frustrations or to comment on a certain topic. But many times, people just want their voices heard. In a highly fragmented society, many people want to know that their opinion counts, no matter what the topic. And if there are any doubts about the importance of interactivity and active participation in a medium, witness the phenomenal growth of the Internet.

Sports talk and call-in shows really boomed in the mid- to late-80s. In 1987, Emmis Broadcasting started WFAN, an all-sports talk format. WFAN operated in the red for a couple of years, but by the 90s had become one of the most profitable radio stations in the country. In 1991, Infinity Broadcasting bought WFAN for $70 million—at that time a record for a stand-alone AM station. By the mid-1990s, 28 stations in the nation's 100 largest markets ran a sports talk format, with total revenues worth almost $140 million. Since 1992, ESPN Radio has grown from a part-time programmer to providing 8,000 hours of annual content on more than 620 affiliates, reaching an estimated 16.5 million people (see Figure 1-1).

The success of WFAN and ESPN led to a rising tide of competition. Other sports-oriented programmers, like One-On-One Sports, soon began delivering national talk and call-in shows. But the beauty and simplicity of the format remains its local orientation. Any small station in any market can build a loyal audience simply by opening the phone lines and asking fans what's on their minds. "I think the biggest thing to remember about local sports talk radio is that local is what works," says veteran sports talk show host Mike Gastineau of KJR-AM in Seattle. "I can go on this afternoon and

Figure 1-1   Andy Pollin (L) and Tony Kornheiser of ESPN Radio (Courtesy ESPN)

talk ad nauseum about what is going on nationally, but I've got to somehow relate it to the people here in Seattle. That's a key, finding the local angle that will provoke calls."

As radio moves into the twenty-first century, the problems of the 50s and 60s seem like distant memories. Advertising revenue, profit margins, profit ratios, and station values keep rising into the multi-millions of dollars. And the future looks even brighter, thanks to new technology. Radio has now tapped into the Internet and other digital technology to create new markets for its products, especially sports. With the click of a mouse, Internet users can now listen to their favorite radio program via their home computer, including a wide variety of live sports events.

This convergence of old and new technology promises more growth and profit for radio in the years ahead.

TELEVISION
The Era of Technology: 1920–1960

Work on television began in the early part of the twentieth century, but ran into several delays. In the beginning, television pioneers engaged in a great race to see who could make the medium a reality first. John Baird invested a lot of time and money in the development of "mechanical" television—a means of transmission similar to motion pictures. But the real promise lay in electrical transmission, or "radio with pictures." Two giants of the early days, Vladimir Zworykin and Philo T. Farnsworth raced each other for technological advances. A combination of their efforts led to a workable model in the 1920s and finally a public demonstration of television at the 1939 World's Fair in New York. It seemed like television was ready to explode on the country, just as radio had 20 years before. However, 1939 also marked the beginning of the war in Europe, an event that stalled television's development. The government needed all its manpower and resources concentrated on the war effort, which meant further research in television development would have to wait. But not for long.

With the end of the war in 1945, television development once again took center stage. Communications industries well understood the promise of the new medium and rushed to pour money in equipment and development. So many companies wanted on the air, that the television industry was headed towards the mad chaos of radio's early days. The FCC finally had to step in and issue a temporary freeze on licenses, starting in 1948. Even so, the number of television stations jumped rapidly—from 6 in 1946, to 98 in 1950, and then to 234 after the freeze finally lifted in the mid-1950s.

Television went through much the same growth pattern that radio did. At first, most of the financing came from the sale of receivers, but eventually advertising would propel and dominate the new mass medium. And, at least in the beginning, television borrowed much of its programming and formats from radio.

Technology limited much of what could go on the air, including sports events. The first telecast of a major league baseball game occurred on August 26, 1939, but featured only two cameras. Reception was fairly poor, but hardly anyone seemed to notice—only about 400 sets existed in New York to pick up the signal. The *New York Times* noted, "Television set owners as far away as 50 miles viewed the action" between the Reds and Dodgers from Brooklyn. Other sports programming suffered similar handicaps. WBAP-TV in Fort Worth, Texas broadcast the 1948 college football game between Oklahoma and Texas, but the bands that performed at halftime had to stay in between the 35-yard lines so as to remain in range of primitive cameras. Pro football also televised its first game in 1939, which consisted mostly of fuzzy camera shots of the player with the ball. Cameramen were frequently faked out, and on several occasions announcers had to invent intricate lateral passes to explain why the home viewer could not see the ball. Long-time football director Harry Coyle remembers that "the equipment always kept breaking down. There were always hot smoldering irons laying around for repairs. You could recognize a television guy by the burn marks all over his clothes from those irons."

On August 26, 2000, Fox Sports broadcast a special edition of its Saturday game of the week. To commemorate the sixty-first anniversary of the first televised baseball game, Fox broadcast the Cubs–Dodgers game to highlight the advances in television sports technology. Fox broadcast the first few innings as they would have looked to viewers in different television eras. Thus, the game started off in black and white with only two cameras, and ended with sophisticated modern technology. (See Table 1-2.)

As technology improved in the 50s, sports programming began to branch out. Wrestling and boxing became popular attractions because of their relative ease in shooting and their location in primarily larger cities with better production facilities. Some boxing matches were actually shot in television studios using just one camera. It was also during this time that stations first began to realize the appeal of sports violence on television.

The first television sets were a complicated mass of wires and tubes and did not produce a very good picture. That and the expense made it an uncertain proposition for the masses. Thus, television started out as a "tavern" medium. Bar owners would buy a set for their taverns, which became the center for viewing and public conversation. And more often than not, the taverns featured sports programs for their primarily male clientele. Slowly but surely, the technology advanced far enough to produce more reliable and more affordable sets for the average consumer. In 1948, less than 200,000 homes had television sets. By 1950, the number had grown to almost four million. And by the end of the 50s, more than 40 million American households had a television set. Today, the total number of television households

Table 1-2   The Growth of Television Technology

Era	Video Innovations	Audio Innovations	Graphic Innovations
1939	2 cameras; no zoom or replays possible	1 microphone for announcer	No graphics
1944	3 cameras; no zoom or replays possible	1 microphone for announcer	No graphics
1953	4 cameras; no zoom or replays possible	Microphone for crowd noise added	One monochome line of graphics
1957	5 cameras; one added in centerfield	2 microphones; analyst added	Two lines of graphics possible
1961	5 cameras; limited zoom and replay	2 microphones	Two lines of graphics possible
1969	5 cameras; color now standard	2 microphones; improved audio	Electronic graphics introduced
1974	7 cameras; split-screen and chromakey used	Audio still mono	Electronic graphics
1985	8 cameras; super slo-mo introduced	Mono	Computer-generated graphics with multiple colors
1996	10 cameras; digital technology available	Stereo surround; wireless mics	Computer-generated

Source: Fox Sports. Chicago Cubs vs. Los Angeles Dodgers, August 26, 2000

in the U.S. approaches 100 million (see Table 1-3). Television moved out of the taverns and into the living room for good, and the stage was set for more creative programming.

The Era of Creativity: 1960–1975

Just as radio enjoyed its "Golden Age" during the 30s, so too did television have a similar period in the 1950s. Industry leaders seemed to invent television as they went along and during this period produced program formats that still exist today. The situation comedy, soap opera, network news, and quiz show all came from radio and all flourished on television. In many cases, the same stars that performed on radio simply moved their talents to the small screen.

But television also developed creative new formats uniquely suited to the medium. Many of these groundbreaking efforts came in news and documentaries and most of them seemed to come from CBS. Edward R. Murrow helped pioneer the television documentary and his *See It Now* programs

Table 1-3   Number of American Households with Television Sets

Year	Number of Households	Percentage of U.S. Homes
1947	14,000	0.04
1948	172,000	4.0
1949	940,000	2.3
1950	3,875,000	9.0
1951	10,320,000	23.5
1959	43,950,000	85.9
1970	58,500,000	95.3
1980	76,300,000	97.9
2001	102,200,000	98.2

Source: Sterling and Kittross, 1978 (as cited in Sterling, 1984, and Nielsen Media Research, January 2001)

had great influence on American life and culture. Another important development came in September 1951, when a transcontinental cable link was completed, finally joining the entire United States by television transmission. Shortly afterwards, Murrow commented on his program that, "For the first time in history, people can look at live pictures of the Atlantic and Pacific Oceans at the same time."

As television finally moved past the stage of technological possibility, the industry began to look more closely at the type and quality of the programming. Up until this time, programs had been fairly staid and traditional—more in keeping with the old radio formats. But now television could start to experiment and that included sports programs.

One of the major innovations came along in 1961 with the debut of *Wide World of Sports* on ABC. Sports programming up to this point was usually no nonsense—mostly live events with some bread and butter reporting thrown in. "You'd be shocked at what television sports was as of 1960," said NBC executive Dick Ebersol. "You would have a couple of cameras at some event and just sit them down and shoot the action." But Roone Arledge of ABC wanted something different. He began putting microphones and cameras in unusual places, like the bottom of a diving pool. He also began airing sports that American viewers had never seen before, like ski jumping and lumberjacking. And most of all, he focused on the personalities and the stories behind the events. "Many sports on *Wide World* people didn't know much about," he said years later. "We had to get them interested. In almost any field, human stories are what's most important." History has proven Arledge right. *Wide World* is still going strong into the twenty-first century—one of the longest running series in television history.

Arledge used that same philosophy a decade later to create another perennial sports powerhouse—*Monday Night Football*. And again, it was based on the premise that the audience wanted something different. During the 60s, CBS dominated pro football on television by emphasizing the game and the action. But Arledge wanted to turn pro football into a *show,* and what better way than to put it under the bright lights of prime time with an entire nation watching.

The final touch of showbiz was the hiring of three men in the broadcast booth instead of two, the most prominent being Howard Cosell (see Chapter 16). Cosell started out as a lawyer but turned to sports broadcasting and made his reputation as a controversial, egomaniacal figure. Putting him in the booth guaranteed that ABC would have its show, for good or bad. "Arledge wanted to combine football and entertainment," said ABC executive Dennis Lewin. "We wanted to show people that football was more than a game of Xs and Os. If we wanted Xs and Os, we wouldn't have hired Cosell." Once again, Arledge and ABC were right, and *Monday Night Football* joined *Wide World of Sports* as one of the most successful sports formats in television history.

ABC also pushed coverage of the Olympics to new creative levels. CBS actually televised the first Olympics from Squaw Valley, California in 1960. In keeping with CBS's traditional and reserved style, the coverage was fairly short (only 15 hours total) and straightforward. ABC began televising the games in 1964 and immediately began implementing its "personality-oriented" approach. Viewers became much more interested in the events because of performers like Olga Korbut and Nadia Comenic, both of whom became international stars because of the television exposure. ABC also increased the amount of coverage, going from 43 hours in 1968 to 62 hours in 1972. In the 1972 games from Germany, Arab terrorists held several Israeli athletes hostage before finally killing them. The ensuing coverage by ABC won several awards and introduced a new form of sports reporting—the sports tragedy. "If you look at how the Olympics grew," said ABC sports executive Don Ohlmeyer, "much of it is due to Roone Arledge and his direction of storytelling."

The creative period of television also saw incremental gains for blacks and other minorities. In the late 1960s, Diahann Carroll and Bill Cosby became the first blacks to have leading roles in network television shows. Gains for blacks were significant on the field, but somewhat slower in the broadcast booth. Not until the 1970s did they begin to earn positions of notoriety in sports broadcasting, most notably Irv Cross who starred on *The NFL Today* pre-game show on CBS.

The NFL Today earned a distinction for giving blacks and women an opportunity on a national sports stage. Working alongside Cross was Phyllis George, a one-time Miss America winner who became the first woman to host a national sports program (see Chapter 16). ABC had used former athletes Judy Rankin and Donna deVarona in supporting commentary roles, but George became the first to take center stage. Even so, CBS was not completely egalitarian. George mainly handled the lighter pieces on the show, such as interviewing players or their wives. And CBS certainly promoted the sex appeal of the former Miss America, which attracted a large male following and helped *The NFL Today* dominate the pre-game football ratings. George opened the door for women to follow and today women, blacks, and other minorities are commonplace on sports shows all across the country. Diversity has become more common in a business once dominated by white males (see Chapter 13).

The Era of Accountants: 1975–Present

Two technological developments helped push television into a new era of unheard of profits. Satellite transmission became possible in the 1960s and became widely accepted. Satellites made it possible for instantaneous live coverage of any event in the world, something that had direct application to sports. It opened the door to a myriad of sports programming possibilities and soon American audiences had access to events from any corner of the globe.

The other major development was the growth of cable television. Cable (or CATV) originally began in the 1970s as a means of improving signal quality in places where antennas could not reach. But as more of the nation became wired, programmers discovered a new series of profit possibilities. Soon, subscription services like HBO popped up and became huge successes, demonstrating the power of pay television. It appeared consumers wanted more choice, especially in sports, and were willing to pay for it. This included strictly "pay-per-view" events, such as boxing or pro wrestling, delivered from satellite via cable. Such events have shown to be enormously profitable, like the boxing rematch between Evander Holyfield and Mike Tyson in 1997. Close to two million people paid to watch the fight, making it the most-watched pay-per-view event in history.

Boxing and wrestling remain the prime outlets for pay-per-view, but other sports have gotten involved. College football now has a pay-per-view plan, where viewers can see certain regional games not televised in their area. And if pay-per-view becomes as successful as projected, more and more sports now seen for free could eventually cost the consumers money. Baltimore Ravens owner Art Modell says it's too early to start thinking about a pay-per-view Super Bowl, but he admits, "Can you imagine what it would make? It's unthinkable."

Another outgrowth of the satellite and cable revolution is the growth of the superstation. Stations such as WGN in Chicago and WTBS in Atlanta had broadcast a full schedule of major league games for their local teams. For the most part, only local audiences could see these games until the advent of the new technology. Satellite and cable made it possible to beam games from the Cubs and Braves into almost every wired home in America, which opened up new markets for advertisers and, of course, increased profits.

The rise of the superstations points out the changing landscape of sports broadcasting. The key is technology and choice. Now viewers can have satellite signals brought directly into their homes, bypassing cable completely. And digital television (see Chapter 15) promises to deliver even more programming and more viewing options. With all this new technology, it's not really correct to call it "sports broadcasting" anymore, because the term broadcasting implies the limited delivery of over-the-air signals to a mass audience. Sports programming delivery is now highly sophisticated and aimed more at niche audiences than the captive mass audiences of the 50s and 60s.

It's important to remember that this explosion of sports programming took place not just because it was possible, but also because there was and is demand. Sports have always been some of the most highly watched formats in all of television. The highest rated single show in the history of television is the last episode of *M*A*S*H*, which aired in 1982. But ranking number four is the 1982 Super Bowl game between San Francisco and Cincinnati. Five of the top 10 rated shows and 11 of the top 20 are all sports events (see Table 1-4). It's not that demand has suddenly increased; it's just that technology has finally caught up with demand.

Sports programming has become so attractive and so profitable that it can literally make or break a programming provider. Fox television struggled in the early 90s to create a fourth network to compete with ABC, NBC,

Table 1-4   All-time, Top Rated Television Programs

Program	Date	Rating[1]	Number of TV Households
1. *M*A*S*H*	2/28/83	60.2	50,150,000
2. *Dallas*	11/21/80	53.3	41,170,000
3. *Roots*	1/30/77	51.1	36,380,000
4. Super Bowl XVI	1/24/82	49.1	40,020,000
5. Super Bowl XVII	1/30/83	48.6	40,480,000
6. Winter Olympics[2]	2/23/94	48.5	45,690,000
7. Super Bowl XX	1/26/86	48.3	41,190,000
10. Super Bowl XII	1/15/78	47.2	34,410,000
11. Super Bowl XIII	1/21/79	47.1	35,090,000

[1]Rating indicates percentage of all U.S. television sets

[2]Women's figure skating final involving Tonya Harding and Nancy Kerrigan

Source: 1997 ESPN Sports Almanac

and CBS. Fox executives knew they had a problem because the network didn't have a signature programming series around which to build an audience. So when new NFL contract negotiations began in 1993, Fox decided to push all its chips into televising pro football. The network bid hundred of millions of dollars and successfully grabbed the NFC package away from CBS, which had televised pro football since the 50s. The daring move gave Fox stable and attractive programming along with instant credibility, as did hiring CBS announcers Pat Summerall and John Madden. CBS went into a sports programming slump, until it spent even more millions to take the AFC package away from NBC in 1998.

Of course, demand does have its limits and many wonder if we have reached a saturation point. Getting a network contract with NBC saved the fledgling American Football League in the early 1960s, but in the 1980s not even a strong television package with ABC could help the United States Football League. In 1990, CBS gambled with a network baseball television deal that lost around $500 million over the life of the package. So, while the bottom line remains that most television sports make money—lots of money—they also cost a tremendous amount because of the high price of developing technology. And there are signs that the incredible profits reaped from sports television may not last forever.

WHO CONTROLS SPORTS?

The profits may not last because we have seen a shift in the ongoing power struggle between sports provider, televiser, and viewer. For most of the twentieth century, up until the 1970s, the sports themselves controlled the broadcasting dynamics. In 1936, the courts and the FCC ruled that the baseball teams, not the broadcasters, owned the rights to disseminating the product. That is, broadcasters would have to buy rights to air the games from the teams, which could set conditions such as cost and scheduling. In the 1940s and 50s, general manager George Weiss of the Yankees kept strict control on how many cameras he would allow in the stadium, where they would be placed and the type of shots he would allow on the air.

A similar situation existed in other sports. Notre Dame has always exerted considerable control over the televising of its football team. As late as the 1960s, the school did not allow more than two television timeouts per half and only a total of six commercial minutes per game. In addition, Notre Dame got to approve the copy and scheduling of the ads. Even when other schools began to lose control of their product in the 1990s, Notre Dame signed an exclusive football package with NBC worth $7 million a season. One of the reasons that teams enjoyed such control was the fact that they all got to cut their own deals. Major league baseball teams and NFL teams contracted individually for television rights with the networks. But soon a man named Pete Rozelle would change all that, and the balance of power would swing dramatically toward the networks.

The Money Rolls In

As the demand for more programming escalated in the 1950s, the system of teams individually negotiating broadcast rights developed major problems. In 1950, the Los Angeles Rams became the first NFL team to televise all their games—home and away. With the games available on television, attendance dropped by 50 percent. The NFL eventually instituted a policy of blacking out home games, which was upheld by the U.S. District Court. Of greater concern was the likelihood that large, attractive cities like Los Angeles would be able to command more for broadcast rights compared to teams in smaller markets. If the Rams could make substantially more money from television rights, it would make the franchise more profitable and ultimately create a competitive advantage over the television have-nots, like Green Bay, which practically gave its television rights away for nothing.

This is the situation Pete Rozelle inherited when he became NFL commissioner in 1960 and he immediately began work to change it. Rozelle believed that the league needed a single network package that included all the teams and split the revenues equally. Otherwise, the league would self-destruct because of lack of competitive balance. Rozelle had to clear several steps to achieve his goal, including convincing reluctant owners and getting an anti-trust exemption in Congress. The result came to be known as the *Sports Broadcasting Act* (15 USC 1291) and it allowed professional sports leagues to collectively bargain television rights, without fear of anti-trust legislation. The bill became law on September 20, 1961 and by the end of that year, the NFL and CBS had agreed to a four-year deal worth $4.65 million dollars annually.

Actually, the American Football League set the precedent for the league-wide television deal, signing a contract with ABC in 1960. The AFL and NFL deals originally raised eyebrows in the Justice Department, leading Rozelle to lobby for the anti-trust exemption. The result was tremendous profits for everyone involved, especially the NFL. According to Dallas general manager Tex Schramm, "the networks—and more importantly the advertisers—recognized that football and TV went together. TV was ready to explode and we were ready to explode. We just exploded together."

The explosion sent shock waves still felt a generation later. The league-wide television contract remains a staple of the sports broadcasting business and it eventually shifted power away from the sports provider toward the broadcaster, especially the networks. Flushed with success, networks began to spend more and more for rights fees (see Table 1-5 and Table 1-6). And as networks began to spend more to televise the games, they began to make

Table 1-5 Major Television Sports Contracts, 1999

Sport	Network	Rights Fees	Length of Contract
NFL	Fox	$4.4 billion	8 years
	CBS	$4.0 billion	8 years
	ABC	$4.4 billion	8 years
	ESPN	$4.4 billion	8 years
NBA	NBC	$1.75 billion	5 years
	TNT	$890 million	5 years
MLB	Fox	$575 million	4 years
	NBC	$400 million	4 years
	ESPN	$440 million	4 years
NHL	ABC	$600 million	5 years
PGA Tour	Multi	$650 billion	4 years
Nascar	Fox	$3.2 billion	8 years

Source: Foxsports.com, 1999 (www.foxsports.com/business/resources/broadcast/)

Table 1-6 Olympic Broadcast Rights Fees

Olympics	Location	Network	Rights Fees
1996 Summer	Atlantic	NBC	$456 million
1998 Winter	Nagano	CBS	$375 million
2000 Summer	Sydney	NBC	$714 million
2002 Winter	Salt Lake City	NBC	$555 million
2004 Summer	Athens	NBC	$792 million
2006 Winter	TBA	NBC	$613 million
2008 Summer	TBA	NBC	$894 million

Source: 1997 ESPN Sports Almanac

more demands to justify their huge investment. Jim Spence of ABC commented, "Anyone who thinks that television is not going to ensure its economic investment, is being naïve."

The immediate impact was on scheduling. Television wanted to showcase sports during prime time, when the biggest audiences could watch. The first World Series night game took place in 1971, and by 1985 all series games were played under the lights. Just eight years after the first series night game, baseball writer Roger Angell complained, "This year's playing conditions were the worst in World Series history. For years, baseball has been vulnerable to this chronic disaster, because the owners and commissioner . . . are willing captives of the television networks, which want the games played at night and during the week. It clearly doesn't matter to them that their famous showcase now offers a truly inferior version of the pastime." In the mid-1990s, baseball joined other leagues in expanding its playoff format to include more teams and produce longer (and more lucrative) playoff series. In the NBA, the playoffs now last from mid-April until late June. "We are subject to the gods of television," said Miami Heat coach Pat Riley. "But to stretch [the first playoff round] over two weeks is absolutely insane. It's losing its competitive edge."

Sometimes the demands had more far-reaching consequences. In 1960, the NFL had two teams in Chicago, the Bears and the Cardinals. But CBS had problems in televising both teams' games because of a league rule, which forced the network to blackout games within a 75-mile radius. CBS solved the problem by pressuring the Cardinals to move to St. Louis, despite the team's 40-year history in Chicago. Sig Mickelson of CBS said that in audience terms "it was a good trade."

Yet owners did not openly complain because of the enormous sums of money involved. For college football, it meant an increase in television revenue from $1.2 million in 1952, to $78 million in 1984. And just a couple of appearances on national television could provide college football programs with plenty of recruiting money. Bear Bryant, the legendary football coach at Alabama once commented, "You folks [the networks] are paying us a lot of money to put this game on television. If you want us to start at two in the morning, then that's when we'll tee it up."

Vox Populi: Let the Networks Beware

The networks' firm control of television sports began to loosen in the late 1970s. We've already discussed the impact of satellite, cable, and other technological advancements, which gave the networks competition for their sports programming. At first, these other outlets televised the sports scraps and network leftovers, like lacrosse, equestrian events, and made-for-TV sports. This was standard fare for a new all-sports cable venture called ESPN, which started in 1979. But ESPN soon started to produce its own programming, such as televising much of the NFL draft and eventually it built a strong viewer base. As ESPN continued to grow it became a major player in professional and college sports and in the late 1980s became the first non-network organization to win a contract to televise NFL games. Today, ESPN is a multi-million dollar money-maker, complete with its own line of all-sports channels and other media and is owned by Disney.

ESPN is just one competitor the networks have to face for sports programming. Other organizations have staked a claim in the game, thanks in part to an important court decision in 1984. That year, the U.S. Supreme Court settled a lawsuit spearheaded by the University of Oklahoma and the University of Georgia. They represented the so-called "major college" football schools, which claimed they had been unfairly treated by the networks and the NCAA in the latest television contracts. The big-time programs felt that restricting the number of times they could appear on the networks amounted to restraint of trade and cut down on their revenues. The NCAA countered with the logic used by major league baseball teams when radio first came to power: that broadcasting more games would hurt attendance and lead to an unfair advantage for the bigger schools.

The Court disagreed with the NCAA and decided in favor of the schools. The written opinion noted that, "The NCAA television plan constitutes a restraint of trade . . . unresponsive to consumer preference" (468 U.S. 85), which in effect, opened up the televising of college football to anyone who was interested. The reference to "consumer preference" hit the nail right on the head, because viewers wanted a lot more college football on television. And as soon as the dam burst, they got it. The free-for-all included independent companies like Jefferson-Pilot, regional cable outlets like Fox Sports Net and of course, ESPN, which aired games on its regular two networks and also gave viewers the choice of buying access to other games through pay-per-view. Where once consumers could watch at most two games a weekend, now they could see dozens, running from early in the afternoon to late in the night.

The result of all this is a shift in the balance of power away from the networks to the consumer; a shift that will continue to develop as technological developments open up more avenues for programming and give viewers more choice. Anyone with a home computer and Internet access can get sports highlights, scores, and information any time of day or night. Online sports services have become big business, such as mvp.com, which in late 1999 was bought out by athletic superstars Wayne Gretzky, Michael Jordan, and John Elway. Sports sites may not have made much profit yet, but the consumer base is there (see Table 1-7). Jupiter Research predicts that by the year 2003, online sports purchases will reach $3 billion. "What we will do is

Table 1-7   Most Active Internet Sports Sites (Ratings Period: October, 1999)

Site	Audience in Millions
espn.go.com	3.7
sportsline.com	3.5
nfl.com	2.4
sports.yahoo.com	1.5
wwf.com	1.5
cnnsi.com	1.4
nascar.com	1.3

Source: Nielsen/Net Ratings (as cited in the *Chicago Sun-Times*, 1999, December 27)

try to satisfy consumers and move them along in a virtual cycle, anytime of the day in any media," said Dick Glover, executive vice president of Internet Media at GO.com and ABC.

The FCC-mandated switch to digital broadcasting promises even more possibilities. The primary advantage of digital over analog is a much clearer, sharper picture. But because digital compression takes up less spectrum bandwidth, it could create thousands of extra channels. The same bandwidth stations now use to broadcast one analog channel could be used to create four digital channels. In essence, each station could have its own mini-cable system. That means four times as many opportunities for sports programming, although broadcasters have said that at least in the early stages of digital they would prefer not to split the signal for sports, but show the events in the higher-definition format.

Still, the possibilities seem endless. We already have direct importation of satellite signals into homes, including digital satellite transmission. Convergence with the Internet and home computer also opens up different dimensions, such as simulcasting. Time-shifting allows the viewer to tape a program and replay it whenever he or she wants. Technology also exists to improve and personalize time-shifting. Now, the consumer can list a set of preferences and the technology will search for those programs. He or she can also pause a real-time game or event, then come back and pick up the live action from where it left off.

All of this is not lost on the sports providers and organizations. They now realize they must try to meet the consumer's demands or get lost in the programming shuffle. NFL Commissioner Paul Tagliabue wants to make sure the NFL continues at the peak of consumer popularity. He says, "In the future, fans will be able to view live or taped games on demand, much as hotel guests can watch movies in their rooms. As for the actual game, fans will have options they never had before. A choice of camera angle—watching the game from behind the quarterback, from the sideline, or overhead."

Without a doubt, all of this reflects the tremendous impact sports and especially televised sports have had in the American culture.

REFERENCES

"A Quick Word." *Terre Haute, IN Tribune-Star*, April 21, 2000.

Angell, Roger. *Late Innings*. New York: Ballantine, 1982.

Catsis, John R. *Sports Broadcasting*. Chicago: Nelson-Hall, 1993.

Celizic, Mike. *The Biggest Game of Them All*. New York: Simon & Schuster, 1992.

Ditingo, Vincent. *The Remaking of Radio*. Boston: Focal Press, 1995.

Duncan, James H. *Radio Revenue Distribution*. Indianapolis, 1996.

"ESPN Radio Signs 100th Full-time Station." [Online]. Available: http://espn.go.com/liveradiotv/s/00307radiosign.html. May 1, 2000.

Frank, Reuven. *Out of Thin Air*. New York: Simon & Schuster, 1991.

Golenbock, Peter. *Bums*. New York: Pocket Books, 1984.

Halberstam, David. *The Summer of '49*. New York: Avon, 1989.

Hassan, John (Ed.). *ESPN Sports Almanac*. Boston: Information Please LLC, 1997.

Heard, Robert. *Oklahoma vs. Texas: When Football Becomes War*. Austin, TX: Honey Hill Publishing, 1980.

Hilmes, Michelle. *Radio Voices*. Minneapolis: University of Minnesota Press, 1997.

Kane, Margaret. "Study: Sports a $3B Online Biz." *ZDNet News*, March 1, 2000.

Koppett, Leonard. *Sports Illusion, Sports Reality*. Boston: Houghton Mifflin, 1981.

McClellan, Steve. "The Rights of Spring." *Broadcasting & Cable*, March 27, 2000.

Mickelson, Sig. *The Decade that Shaped Television News*. Westport, CT: Praeger, 1998.

Patton, Phil. *Razzle-dazzle*. New York: Dial Press, 1984.

Ritter, Lawrence S. *Lost Ballparks*. New York: Penguin, 1992.

Seventy-five Seasons. Atlanta: Turner Publishing, 1994.

Smith, Curt. *Voices of the Game*. South Bend, IN: Diamond, 1987.

Spence, Jim. *Up Close and Personal*. New York: Atheneum, 1988.

Sportscasters: Behind the Mike. [Television show]. The History Channel, February 7, 2000.

SportsCenter of the Century: The Most Influential People. [Television show]. ESPN, February 20, 2000.

"Sports-talk Radio Host." [Online]. Available: http://espn.go.com/special/s/careers/sptalk.html, September 7, 1999.

Sterling, Christopher H. *Electronic Media: A Guide to Trends in Broadcasting and Newer Technologies, 1920–1983*. New York: Praeger, 1984.

"Web Sports Sites." *Chicago Sun-Times*, December 27, 1999.

2

Impact

Leonard Koppett has built an impressive career as a sports writer, covering national and international events for *The Sporting News* as well as papers in New York and California. In addition to event coverage, Koppett is particularly interested in the impact sports has had on American life. "As mass entertainment," he said, "sports plays a larger role in American culture than in any other society, past or present. All [sports] can supply a sense of common identity, no matter what our particular views. These strands form a web of common interest and every society needs such webs to stay intact."

It's hard to disagree. No culture on earth places as much emphasis on sports. And as America looks back on the twentieth century, it will note the tremendous impact sports had on all aspects of its culture, but most especially its impact socially, emotionally, and financially. And all of it has been influenced by the media and most particularly television.

AN ARMY OF STEAMROLLERS

Sports have become imbedded in the American psyche, taught to children at a very young age and passed down to succeeding generations. Author and sports writer Roger Kahn recalls his childhood and the impact sports, and especially baseball, had on his youth. "I wanted to understand the world around me and to be respected as a person capable of understanding. My father understood everything and I wanted to be like my father. I wanted to enter the world of men. Baseball became my magic portal." In the highly successful motion picture *Field of Dreams,* actor James Earl Jones remarks, "America has rolled by like an army of steamrollers. It's been erased like a blackboard, rebuilt, and then erased again. The only constant is baseball."

Baseball has the longest history and has perhaps influenced more generations than any other sport. As far back as 1903, a New York newspaper ran a help-wanted ad looking for "a boy who had never seen baseball and didn't know the difference between first and third base." In response, the *Washington Post* commented that if such a youngster could be found, he would likely "crawl off somewhere and die . . . worthy of study by some 'bugologist.'" As novelist Zane Grey put it, "Every boy likes baseball and if he doesn't, he's not a boy."

The media played a central role in this process. Thanks to the press, sports reached every corner of the country, no matter how remote. In the early part of the century, that meant newspapers. "I grew up in San Diego and the closest big league baseball was 2,000 miles away," recalled Hall of Famer Ted Williams. "It seemed like the end of the world. But I did read the sports pages, and when I was as impressionable an age as can be, the names of certain big leaguers were always on my mind."

Radio then took center stage and became one of the "webs" that held communities together. Nowhere was this more apparent than in Brooklyn, where people believed in God, family, and the Dodgers, and not necessarily in that order. Author Peter Golenbock wrote, "For some, a whole summer was based on the team, and wherever people gathered in Brooklyn, at game time there would be a radio. At the beach, in homes, in stores, in cars, in baby carriages, there would be a radio. You could walk through the streets of Brooklyn and follow the play-by-play of a Dodger game wherever you were going."

As years went by, television became mass marketers of the American sports dream and baseball began to lose its preeminent place in the nation's culture. Television helped create a boom period for professional football in the 1950s, especially after the Colts–Giants championship game in 1958. At that time, football appealed to the younger generation of fans, as did television. Growing up in 1960s in Dallas, author John Eisenberg remembered, "Just as young fans in New York were raised in the thrall of Jackie Robinson's Dodgers and Mickey Mantle's Yankees, and those in Baltimore fell for Johnny Unitas and the Colts after the Giants game of '58, those of us who grew up in Dallas in the 60s lay claim to the Cowboys as secular religious figures. These were the heroes of my youth."

As youth matures into adulthood, the web grows stronger and tighter, nourished by the ever-present hand of the media. Fans need to get the pregame information, the matchups, and the predictions. The game itself brings an avalanche of numbers, statistics, details, and emotions that need reporting. Then, finally, comes the post-game analysis. What happened and why? Where did things go wrong? Where do they go from here?

As a youth, Brooklyn native Donald Honig remembers waiting out this endless sports cycle on a street corner near his home. "Every night at nine we would stand in front of the candy store waiting for the *Daily News* truck to come up. It was like the docking of a luxury liner. Why was this such an important event? Because the details of the Dodger game were in there. We already knew every pitch that was thrown. We listened to the game on the radio. We discussed it for three hours. Now we were going to read about it." Of course, the electronic media has now considerably shortened the process. Fans have instant access to countless scores of radio and television reports, as well as Internet sources that allow them to pick and choose their own services. The Internet allows personalized service for all kinds of sports information, mainly tailored to fit the needs of the individual. But just as television flourished as a "tavern" medium, sports essentially remains a social phenomenon. It impacts our culture mainly by bringing us together and pointing out similarities that show our dependence upon one another. A game or series of games, amplified and disseminated by the mass media, can bridge all sorts of racial, ethnic, and economic differences.

Baseball writer Roger Angell has spent a lifetime writing about such events. Of all the games he has covered, Angell vividly remembers the deciding game of the 1986 National League Championship Series between the New York Mets and the Houston Astros. To Angell, the game was certainly memorable for its dramatic ending (the game lasted almost five hours, with the Mets finally winning in 16 innings), but also for the way it brought a city together. He called it, "Something along the order of a blackout or armistice: a great public event. Men and women on commuter trains followed the game on Panasonic or Sony, clustering around each radio set for the count and the pitch. There were portables and radios at Lincoln Center, too. On a commuter train a frightful communications disaster—a long tunnel—was averted when it unexpectedly ground to a halt ('signal difficulties' a conductor announced), and stood there until the Mets scored three in the top of the sixteenth and service resumed."

Such moments are possible because of the power of sports broadcasting. Researchers and academicians have also argued the other side, about the negative impact of the electronic age: the widespread growth of violence, the loss of literacy, and the increasing isolation and fragmentation of society. Violence on television remains an unresolved issue, and certainly sports plays a key role in the debate. The very qualities that make sports on TV so attractive to men—contact, aggression, and pain—can be extremely dangerous outside the confines of the broadcasting medium. The larger question is, does sports create social forces or reflect them? The answer will have to wait until Chapter 3.

MADE FOR TV

Beyond a social impact, sports broadcasting has had a very real effect on the sports themselves. Before radio and television, only newspapers reported on sports on a regular basis. And the reporting process of the newspaper business did not really create any unusual problems for sports owners or players. With an overnight deadline, newspapers had plenty of time to file stories and reports, no matter when the games started. Morning papers concentrated mainly on the facts of the game, while afternoon editions focused more on features and related stories. Relatively primitive black-and-white photography made no demands on the sporting business to make the game more "colorful" or attractive for the fans.

We have already discussed how the electronic media changed the sports deadline, necessitating games be played at odd hours and in odd places to coincide with maximum audience exposure. The coming of television also changed sports "visually," in that they had to become more appealing to the home viewer. This obviously affected the "look" that teams presented to the audience, especially when color television became accepted in the 1960s. Up until this time, major league baseball uniforms came in two basic colors—white and gray. But in 1963, the Kansas City Athletics introduced an exotic combination of green, white, and gold uniforms. Soon, other teams followed suit, including the Houston Astros, which during the 70s started wearing a psychedelic rainbow outfit. Baseball historian Mark Okkonen said, "the proliferation of color TV coverage . . . probably did more to invite the use of brighter and nontraditional uniform color schemes of the 1960s."

Not only uniforms changed color with the times. In 1965, the NFL changed the color of its penalty flags to yellow to better catch the viewer's eye. The same thing occurred with tennis balls, which also went from white to yellow. The NFL experimented with a white stripe around the football for night games, so fans (and players) could see it more easily, but as lighting and stadium conditions improved, the league eventually did away with it. As technology developed it allowed for even more visual improvements. Fox Sports tried to attract attention to its pro hockey coverage by putting a computer-generated comet "tail" on the fast-moving puck. The network highly promoted the red streak, which ostensibly helped viewers follow the action better, but it never seemed to catch on and Fox quietly dropped the idea.

NBA coaches and players wish the league would drop its idea of putting a live microphone on coaches and using locker room cameras during nationally televised games. Faced with a television ratings decline of almost 20 percent in 1999–2000, the NBA mandated the changes as a way of attracting more viewers and threatened noncompliant coaches with a fine of $100,000. "I don't want to belittle their [players and coaches] concerns," said NBA deputy commissioner Russ Granik, "but it has been determined this is how we want the business to go." Only after extreme criticism did the league finally back down and rescind the threats, but it is still pushing ahead with plans such as putting live microphones on players during games.

Not only the visual quality of the games changed, but sometimes the games themselves. Owners and leagues made concessions and even rule changes to help their games fit into the fast-paced electronic format. College basketball added television timeouts at predetermined intervals to make sure the networks could get in all their commercials. Even today, several coaches complain that the unnatural timeouts create a different and often difficult game. In the 1980s, the NCAA added a shot clock and a three-point line, in reality because slow-downs and stall tactics had threatened to hurt television ratings.

The most obvious example of television's influence in this area is the use of instant replays, most notably in the NFL. The league approved instant replay in 1986, but immediately discovered the plan had a fatal flaw: going up to the replay booth to confirm or overturn controversial calls slowed the game like molasses. The criticism got so heavy that league owners finally discontinued replay after six seasons, only to vote it back in a different form for the 1999 season. This time, the decision belonged to referees on the field, who had only a minute and a half to view the replay and issue a ruling. Even though the new system didn't work perfectly, league owners voted overwhelmingly (28–3) to retain instant replay for the 2000 season.

Sometimes the influence of television goes beyond simple tinkering with rules and involves an entire sport. Some events—notably professional wrestling, roller derby, indoor soccer, and arena football—exist solely because of their television potential. The derisive term is "made-for-TV sports," which implies that such events have all the quality and production value of a tired movie-of-the-week. In reality, these events can and do make a lot of money, especially pro wrestling (see Chapter 3). Quality is in the mind of the viewer.

Essentially, made-for-TV sports are created because of their potential television appeal. Roller derby certainly has a higher visual and entertainment quality than, say, billiards. Usually, such events are fast-paced, aggressive, and have formats that translate well onto a television screen. The Major Indoor Soccer League shrank the game down and put it on a basketball-sized field, complete with sideboards that produced all kinds of strange bounces. The idea was that compressing the game would speed it up and create more scoring, thus making it more acceptable to television audiences. But the MISL could not overcome America's relative lack of interest in pro soccer and the league eventually folded. Arena Football has enjoyed more limited success with basically the same concept. And in the late 1990s, ESPN introduced the *X-Games*, non-traditional sports like skateboarding and skydiving specifically targeted to younger viewers. In most cases, such events can still be considered legitimate sporting contests. But sometimes, television creates events so convoluted and bizarre that they raise serious questions about credibility. Weekly shows like the *World's Strongest Man* and special events like the *Superstars* serve no athletic purpose other than to make money for the programming provider. The *Strongest Man* features such events as car-pulling, keg tossing, and bending steel bars, while the *Superstars* involved athletic stars from various sports competing against each other in beach volleyball, canoe paddling, obstacle course racing, and the like. In 1975, CBS touted a special tennis match between Jimmy Connors and Rod Laver as "winner take all." But two years later it came out that the network had guaranteed a large sum to the loser as well.

By far, one of the strangest events ever staged for television was in 1974, when Evel Knievel attempted to jump the Snake River in Idaho in a "motorcycle." The motorcycle was actually a rocket-powered capsule, which malfunctioned on lift-off and sent Knievel on a bumpy landing down one side of the riverbank. But not before ABC had created millions of dollars of publicity for the event and televised it live across the country.

At the time, former major league baseball pitcher Jim Bouton was working as a sportscaster for WABC in New York—the flagship station of the ABC network. But Bouton resisted pressure to publicize the event, which he felt was nothing more than a corporate stunt. "As if it weren't enough that television has become partners with sports," Bouton later wrote, "they're now inventing sports—the propriety of which may be as questionable as the events themselves." But Bouton also said he could understand why the network wanted the event hyped, not criticized, because of the millions of dollars involved.

THERE'S NO BUSINESS LIKE SPORTS BUSINESS

"How did baseball develop from the sandlots to the huge stadiums—from a few hundred spectators to the millions in attendance today?" asked Hall of Fame manager Connie Mack. "My answer is: through the gigantic force of publicity. The professional sports world was created and is being kept alive by the services extended the press."

Mack wrote that a half-century ago, but his words are truer now than ever. Of the massive impact media has had, none is bigger or more obvious than its effect on the business of sports. When the twentieth century began, sports leagues were dominated by "gentlemen" sportsmen; the economic elite of the country who got into sports purely as a diversion. Phil Ball made his money in glass, William Wrigley in chewing gum, and Jacob Ruppert in beer, and they owned baseball teams as a side business, not as a bottom-line necessity. Today, several teams in almost every sport are considered conglomerate enterprises, owned as a small piece of a larger financial empire.

Pushed by a growing economy and the influence of television, these franchises have gone from mom-and-pop operations to multi-million dollar enterprises. When George Halas began organizing the NFL in 1920, he and other investors agreed on a $100 entrance fee to get into the league. When the Dallas Cowboys came into the NFL in 1960, the asking price went up to $550,000. In 1993, both Jacksonville and Carolina had to fork over $140 million apiece to become the league's newest members. And when Daniel Snyder bought the Washington Redskins in 1999, he paid $800 million—a record for a pro sports franchise, but one that might not last too long. Established sports franchises have become solid investments and almost guaranteed money-makers (see Table 2-1).

Television, of course, has played a central role in this process. Before the electronic media arrived, teams made most of their money from ticket sales. The live gate was the economic lifeblood of a franchise, which is why owners fought so long to keep games off radio and television. But eventually radio and TV did prevail, and the rights they paid to televise sports skyrocketed into the millions (see Chapter 1). This created a new economic structure for sports, in which most of the operating money and profits came from television and the live gate became almost an afterthought. Consider the 1999 TV contract of the NFL. Split evenly between the league's 32 franchises, the payout comes to more than $68 million per team.

While the owners love all that money rolling in, they could not foresee the way it would empower the individual athlete. For most of the twentieth century, professional athletes served more like indentured servants to teams and owners. Baseball's reserve clause, for example, bound a player to the same team for life. Outfielder Curt Flood issued a legal challenge to the reserve clause in 1970 and his case eventually paved the way for its destruction and the beginning of free agency. Players can now move freely from one team to another and sell themselves to the highest bidder once their contracts have expired.

And with all that television money on hand, the athletes have collected plenty (see Table 2-2). Such figures don't even include the estimated $36 million Michael Jordan made in the last year before his retirement, or his

Table 2-1 1999 NFL Team Values

Team	Value in Millions
Dallas Cowboys	$663
Washington Redskins	$607
Tampa Bay Buccaneers	$502
Carolina Panthers	$488
New England Patriots	$460
NFL average	**$385.3**

Source: Forbes (as cited in http://www.foxsports.com/business/resources/values/nfl/sml)

Table 2-2 Biggest Individual Contracts/Winnings, 1999[1]

Player	Sport	Contract/Winnings[2] per Year
Shaquille O'Neal	Basketball	$17,150,000[3]
Barry Bonds	Baseball	$11,450,000
Jaromir Jagr	Hockey	$10,359,852
Deion Sanders	Football	$7,579,000
Tiger Woods	Golf	$6,616,585
Jeff Gordon	Auto racing	$5,281,361

[1]In December 2000, Alex Rodriguez signed a 10-year, $252 million contract with the Texas Rangers, becoming the highest-paid athlete in the history of professional team sports.

[2]Does not include any outside earnings, such as endorsements

[3]Estimated

$40 million in endorsements. Compare Deion Sanders seven-figure salary to the 1933 NFL average of $8,000, when players routinely had to work second jobs in the off-season. The resulting financial increase has also empowered the players in relation to owners. The reserve clause, or forms of it in other leagues, kept salaries and players in line. Now, players command more power and have a rich cadre of owners willing to pay handsomely for their services.

That shift in power has had serious consequences for sports businesses and especially labor relations. In the first half of the century, sports leagues and owners had the legal and financial advantages to prevent athletes from forming player unions. The first attempt at baseball unionization, the Brotherhood of Professional Base Ball Players, appeared in 1885, but despite strong support, it died at the hands of organized baseball in 1890. Similar attempts in other leagues also failed, mainly because of the owners' absolute power and their fear of unionization. In 1957, one of the best players in the NHL, Ted Lindsay, was traded from Detroit to Chicago simply because of his efforts to start a hockey players union. But the players' union movement finally began to pick up steam during the turbulent 60s and as the players' stature increased, the labor organizations grew more powerful and more militant. This directly led to baseball strikes in 1981 and 1994, football strikes in 1982 and 1987, a hockey strike in 1994, and a walkout among NBA players in 1997–98.

The major league baseball strike of 1994 vividly demonstrates the power television and media wield in labor negotiations. Players walked away from the game in the middle of that season, forcing cancellation of the World Series for the first time since 1904. The players union and negotiating chief Donald Fehr objected to owners' plans to control costs by instituting a salary cap. The reason owners wanted the cap had to do with unequal distribution of cable television rights. Each of the major league teams and owners share network television money equally, but are free to negotiate their own deals with local cable and broadcasting outlets. These deals can add up to millions of dollars, depending on the team and the size of the market. The Yankees, playing in the biggest market in the country, can make significantly more in a deal with the Madison Square Garden network (MSG), than the Milwaukee Brewers can with an outlet in their much-smaller market (see Table 2-3). The owners felt this unequal distribution of money would eventually shift the competitive balance on the field, as the richer teams could afford to buy better players.

The players eventually made the owners back down and the idea of a salary cap was dropped, but the end of the strike did not solve the problem. And commissioner Bud Selig (not coincidentally, once the owner of a small-market team) believes that this basic economic imbalance remains the league's most important problem heading into the new century. Results from play on the field would seem to bear that out, as the Yankees—baseball's richest, most powerful team—won three of the last four World Series to end the 1990s. Since the strike year of 1993, no team without a payroll among the top 10 clubs has qualified for the World Series and only teams with a top-five payroll have actually won it. The economic imbalance has become so pervasive in major league baseball that team owners met in July 2000 to consider elim-

Table 2-3 Major League Baseball Local Broadcasting Revenue, 2000

Team	*Broadcast/Cable/TV Revenue in Millions*
Top revenue clubs	
New York Yankees	$48.8
Texas Rangers	$25.0
Boston Red Sox	$23.6
Baltimore Orioles	$23.5
Los Angeles Dodgers	$22.5
Bottom revenue clubs	
Milwaukee Brewers	$4.6
Minnesota Twins	$5.0
Cincinnati Reds	$7.0
Kansas City Royals	$7.5

Several teams, including the Cubs, Angels, and Braves, have partnership agreements with parent media corporations. In April 2000, the Montreal Expos had no English-language deals for radio or TV.

Source: Broadcasting & Cable, March 27, 2000

inating one or two small-market teams. "I don't want to rule anything out to-day, because there's no question that we do have to solve that problem," said Selig, "because [the disparity] is getting worse by the day."

The idea of economic imbalance impacts other sports as well, including professional football. In 1995, Dallas Cowboys owner Jerry Jones angered other NFL owners by striking merchandising deals on his own with companies like Nike and Pepsi. The deals amounted to an end-run around the NFL's league-wide contracts and figured to give the Cowboys an additional $40 million over ten years. The league sued Jones and the Cowboys for $300 million over what it called "ambush marketing deals," but that did not seem to deter the maverick owner. In 2000, Jones voted against other NFL owners who wanted to bring all team Internet operations under tighter league control. Jones said he wanted to aggressively market the Cowboys Internet site as a way to bring in even more money, via merchandising, advertising, and ticket sales.

THE SPORTS EMPIRES STRIKE BACK

We have already seen how television has made sports franchises so valuable, inflating team values and athlete salaries almost beyond comprehension. But television gets something out of the deal too—programming that is highly rated, highly profitable, and available year-round. It has become a match made in media sports heaven.

The Telecommunications Act of 1996 passed by Congress ushered in a new era of media conglomeration. It relaxed rules on station ownership, and giant media companies were eager to snap up valuable smaller properties. In 1998, for example, Fox owned 24 television stations reaching 35 percent of the national audience—the maximum allowed under the new regulations.

At some point the proverbial light bulb went on in the heads of media executives. They already owned the means of distributing the product. If they could also own the product itself, they could increase profits by controlling both halves of the equation. The avalanche started when Ted Turner bought the Braves as a showcase for his growing media empire, including a 24-hour cable news service. That gave Turner a ready-made outlet to market his product. In the following years, the Tribune Company would buy the Chicago Cubs, Disney would take over the Anaheim Angels and the NHL's Anaheim Mighty Ducks, and most recently, Fox would unload millions to buy the Los Angeles Dodgers (see Table 2-4). Ed Snider of Comcast-Spectacor, which owns the Flyers and 76ers, said, "Sports programming can make a (media) company stronger. Ownership gives the company control of [its] own destiny in terms of broadcasting rights."

In 1999, the New York Yankees upped the ante by announcing a new partnership with the NBA's New Jersey Nets to form "YankeesNets," which

Table 2-4 Media Owned Sports Franchises, 1999

Media Company	*Holdings*
Cablevision	New York Knicks (NBA) New York Rangers (NHL)
Comcast-Spectacor	Philadelphia Flyers (NHL) Philadelphia 76ers (NBA)
Disney	Anaheim Angels (MLB) Anaheim Mighty Ducks (NHL)
News Corp.	Los Angeles Dodgers
Time Warner	Atlanta Braves (MLB) Atlanta Hawks (NBA) Atlanta Thrashers (NHL)
Tribune Co.	Chicago Cubs (MLB)

Source: FoxSportsBiz.com (www.foxsports.com/business/bites/z1028hicks1.sml)

would provide year-round sports programming. Industry analysts estimate the new company will double both its take from local sports rights and its end of the national rights package for major league baseball games, by creating its own broadcast outlet. Recognizing the threat, Madison Square Garden Network sued the Yankees in the summer of 2000, asking for a permanent injunction to keep the Yankees from closing a deal with any other television carrier and to declare that MSG has the right to meet and beat any offer the Yankees get.

There's only one problem in the current environment: television revenues, while still impressive, have started to flatten out and might not be able to keep up with rising salaries (see Chapter 15). Fox reduced its role in the Dodgers and Disney has aggressively looked to unload the Angels and Ducks. And despite great tradition and tremendous fan support, the NHL's Montreal Canadiens went up for sale in June 2000. Brewery giant Molson, which has been associated with the Canadiens for 40 years, said it could no longer make money "given the current economic conditions in the NHL," and was selling so that it could concentrate on its beer business. Serge Savard, former Canadiens general manager and player, said hockey clubs have become too expensive to operate. "Nobody could have predicted this five years ago that all professional teams would lose money," he said.

In the meantime, there is another very real effect of the television age—rising costs for consumers. If television can't continue to pay the bills, sports owners must look elsewhere. Sometimes, this means looking out of town, as owners have successfully moved franchises to improve tax and stadium situations. Even if the team stays, owners can hold fans hostage. In 1995, the Mariners gave fans in Seattle an ultimatum—approve a new sales tax hike or the team would leave. The voters agreed and the Mariners completed their new $410 million dollar stadium in 1999.

Owners have taken advantage of similar situations in Baltimore, Nashville, Oakland, and Cleveland, just to name a few. And even when teams decide to stay, the fans still end up footing most of the bill. This can include such things as the funding of stadium improvements to the selling of personal seat licenses (PSL). PSLs have become a popular way for owners to hit ticket payers with double jeopardy, because they require a deposit for the rights to "hold" a seat or group of seats, then more money to buy the actual tickets. All of this has caused sports agent Leigh Steinberg to comment, "It's like the California gold rush with teams prospecting for the richest stadiums they can find. Kids and working families are not going to be able to buy tickets."

According to Team Marketing Report of Chicago, it already costs a family of four more than $266 to attend *one* NBA game, with football and hockey ranking very close behind. That price includes tickets, parking, food at the game, and souvenirs. Baseball ranks as the best bargain at "only" $121 per game. But if television revenues can't continue to sustain player salaries and provide more profit, that price will continue to go up and the merry-go-round of team relocations will spin even faster. "The middle-income and lower-income fans are being priced out of the game," says Andrew Zimbalist, a professor of economics at Smith College. "It threatens the mass character of sport, and over time there is a gradual loss of interest, which hurts TV ratings and licensing deals."

Congress has made some attempts to get involved, most notably with the *Stadium Financing and Relocation Act of 1999 (S 952)*. Senator Arlen Specter (R-Pennsylvania) sponsored the bill and said, "I have long been concerned with the pressure put upon communities by baseball and football clubs seeking new playing facilities, where, responding to a team's overt or tacit threat to move to another city, government leaders feel compelled to have taxpayers finance the lion's share of ballpark and stadium construction costs." But the bill never gained much traction in the Senate, primarily because it required pro sports leagues to set aside 10 percent of their network television money to pay for up to 50 percent of new ballpark construction. Representatives from several major sports leagues, led by NFL Commissioner Paul Tagliabue, lobbied effectively against the bill. But that may not stop the legislative efforts. In 1998, U.S. Senate Majority Leader Trent Lott said, "This abuse of people, taxpayers, cities—like we have seen with football and with baseball—is wrong, just wrong. And they've got to answer to somebody."

WANT TO BET?

In addition to the consequences discussed previously, television and the electronic media have had a very real impact—both good and bad—on the periphery of the sporting world. Chief among these is the role the media have played in the tremendous upsurge in sports gambling, which has become almost as much a "national pastime" as the events themselves.

Sports gambling had become a serious problem long before the electronic media ever existed. Not only would fans make wagers on games, but the players would bet as well, usually to supplement their income in the days before the big-money contracts. The early history of baseball is filled with shady players who had the reputation of finagling a game to make some side money. According to baseball historian Harold Seymour, this included players like Hal Chase, "who not only threw games himself, but corrupted or tried to corrupt other players."

Obviously, organized sports have always taken a dim view of such tactics. The most famous incident occurred in 1920, when major league baseball suspended for life eight members of the Chicago "Black Sox" for fixing the previous year's World Series. Nearly 70 years later, Pete Rose was kicked out of the game for his alleged involvement in betting on the team he managed. NFL commissioner Pete Rozelle also took a strong stance, suspending stars Alex Karras and Paul Hornung for the entire 1963 season for betting on games. With this long history, you would think no athlete would dare get caught again, but in 1998 federal authorities indicted four former Northwestern University players for fixing college basketball games. A study conducted by the University of Michigan that same year showed the problem of sports gambling has intensified at college campuses across the country.

According to a 1998 University of Michigan study regarding college sports gambling:

- 72 percent of college athletes have gambled in some form since entering college.
- Nearly 35 percent of that group has gambled on sports while in college.
- More than 5 percent of male college athletes have provided inside information for gambling purposes, bet in a game in which they participated, or accepted money for performing poorly in a game.

Television and other electronic media have had very little impact in cases where athletes or managers bet on their own teams. But emerging media and technology have played a critical role in one of the largest industries in the United States—illegal gambling by fans on sporting events.

Sports bettors in Nevada, Oregon, and Delaware can legally bet on college sports, but the bulk of the action takes place in Nevada, where figures from the state's gaming control board put legal sports betting at $2.3 billion. But that's chump change compared to illegal gambling all across the country, which includes things as sinister as phone calls to the local bookie or as innocent as the office pool for the NCAA basketball tournament. *U.S. News and World Report* did a study of gambling in the late 1990s and estimated illegal action in the U.S. at $100 billion dollars a year, more than twice the country's illegal drug trade. The magazine also noted that "both legal and illegal gambling have grown tremendously as the number of athletic events on cable and satellite television have soared."

It's not hard to see why. Primarily, the media have opened up public access to thousands of sports events. Newspaper sports sections and radio talk shows routinely provide betting lines for upcoming college and pro games. In Las Vegas sports books, bettors can watch dozens of screens, each carrying a different game or a different sport. Horse racing commands much of the attention, thanks in part to off-track betting parlors that specialize in simulcasting races from all across the world. Electronic communications has also made it much easier to place a bet any time of day or night. Sports writer Kirk Bohls flatly says, "A complete ban on betting would absolutely kill the NFL. That league thrives on gambling interests, which is why it releases detailed injury reports each week. Television ratings would shrivel if legalized gambling on pro sports in Vegas was banned."

Add to this the growing problem of Internet gambling. Not only can bettors get instant and updated information to place bets, they can actually make their wagers online. Such gambling is illegal in the U.S., but companies get around the problem by basing their services in another country. Experts say such businesses handled $60 million in action in 1996 and ten times that much just two years later. The federal government has shown a willingness to get tough with the problem, and in 1998 authorities arrested 14 people representing 6 offshore Internet gambling sites. "To Internet betting operators everywhere we have a simple message," said former U.S. Attorney General Janet Reno. "You can't hide online and you can't hide offshore."

As of 2000, the U.S. Congress toyed with legislation that would ban all gambling on high school, college, and Olympic sports. The bipartisan bill meant well, but insiders say it has almost a zero chance of even making it to the floor for a vote. There are too many questions of gambling's popularity and the difficulty of enforcing any legislation. The combination of television, radio, cell phones, faxes, and the Internet means that the gambler not only has access to thousands of sporting events around the world, but he can also lay a bet in a matter of seconds. And as new digital and interactive technology hits the market, it promises to make sports gambling easier to do and harder to catch. Says U.S. Congressman Anthony Weiner (D-NY), "Whether it's horses or jai alai or dogs . . . Internet gambling is tough to get our arms around."

THE MEN OF "TEAL"

Sports leagues and franchises obviously don't make any money off of gambling, but they do collect millions of dollars from another outgrowth of the electronic age—sports merchandising and endorsements. During the first half of the twentieth century, sports merchandising was fairly limited. The highly successful and visible players would endorse various products, mainly because of their appeal and name recognition.

Now, the electronic age has opened up a whole new ballgame for advertisers and marketers. The visual appeal of sports coincided with the athletes' new status as "celebrities," to create a high demand for anything associated with the event. Suddenly, fans had to have shirts, caps, jerseys, pennants, or other items associated with their favorite teams and stars. When hockey superstar Wayne Gretzky made his much publicized move from Edmonton to Los Angeles in 1988, sales of Kings merchandise such as caps and t-shirts went from dead last to number one in the league. That kind of star power pushed endorsement deals to staggering figures, much more than an athlete's base salary. Golfer Tiger Woods has deals estimated at $100 million for the next five years. NBA star Alonzo Mourning once said flatly, "I don't work for the Charlotte Hornets, I work for Nike."

Merchandising became a powerful way to make money. The NFL established "NFL Properties" to handle such efforts and soon began raking in millions of dollars. Other sports and leagues followed suit with similar success. Soon, a team's "look" became as important as its play on the field. Expansion teams of the 1990s, including the Jacksonville Jaguars, Anaheim Mighty Ducks, and Florida Marlins had one other thing in common—their uniform scheme included the color teal. Research had shown that teal would help sell more merchandise because of its visual appeal and popularity with the public.

Sports franchises also found ways to make more money simply by changing the names of their stadiums. With more and more electronic media coverage, the stadium name became a visual and aural way to increase awareness for advertisers. Announcers routinely mention the name of the stadium dozens of times during a broadcast and corporations pay good money for this ancillary form of advertising. Thus, Reunion Arena in Dallas became the American Airlines Center at a cost of $195 million dollars for 30 years. In 1999, 51 other arenas in all the major sports had similar deals worth billions of dollars.

The next step may be sponsorship of the teams themselves. Corporate sponsorship has already taken over professional tennis, the PGA Tour, and the college football bowl games. For the moment, the major professional U.S. sports (football, basketball, baseball, and hockey) have rules against mixing corporate and team names. But according to Jeff Knapple, who heads up Envision, which specializes in venue naming rights, corporate ownership is the last step before the dam bursts completely. "It [putting sponsor names on to sports teams] has already started to happen in Europe, even as we speak."

Things like merchandising and stadium rights have taken the focus away from the action on the field and put it in the boardroom. Critics would say it's also a reflection of the growing influence of entertainment that is sweeping through American media at the end of the 1990s.

TEN WITH IMPACT

Sometimes, sporting events transcend the athletic arena and have a greater impact on society, culture, or the media. The following is a list of ten games or events (in no particular order) that because of their exposure on the electronic media have an impact that's still felt today.

1. **Bobby Thomson's "Shot Heard 'Round the World," New York Giants vs. Brooklyn Dodgers, 1951.** Russ Hodges's call of Thomson's dramatic game-winning home run may be the most famous sports call ever on radio, and it demonstrated the power of the medium to create indelible memories. Sportscaster Bob Costas said, "That moment would not live quite the way it has, now a half century later, if not for Russ Hodges."

2. **NFL Championship game, Baltimore Colts vs. New York Giants, 1958.** The overtime game (eventually won by the Colts) mesmerized a national television audience and started the electronic revolution that would eventually see football overtake baseball as America's national pastime. "I still think the biggest game we ever had was the Colts' win over the Giants," said former NFL Commissioner Pete Rozelle. "I think that was the first game that got television coverage across America. It reached fans who had never seen pro football before."

3. *Wide World of Sports,* **ABC.** As the Colts-Giants game introduced a nation to pro football, *Wide World* introduced the country to strange events in distant lands. Most of all, it presented sports in a whole new way, focusing on the personalities behind the events. "I was trained to be a reporter," said long-time host Jim McKay, "and that's the way I was. I tried not to be the story, but the storyteller." McKay and *Wide World* told compelling stories and ushered in a whole new way of looking at televised sports.

4. *Monday Night Football,* **ABC.** When Roone Arledge and ABC began the *Monday Night* series in 1970, it did more than just add another day of the week to the sports calendar. It turned sports into a prime-time entertainment show that could attract more than just hard-core fans. "*Monday Night Football* has been a happening on television and in the stadium," says ABC sports executive Dennis Lewin. "It's a show everyone wants to see. It started what some people called appointment television: people set time aside and make a point to see it." That was especially true in the 1970s, when the show featured the controversial talents of Howard Cosell. Hall of Fame quarterback Roger Staubach once said, "I [was] disappointed if he missed the game. That's the uniqueness of Howard. You love him. You hate him. But you miss him when he's not there."

5. **Army vs. Navy, 1963, CBS.** The importance of the football game is not really in the final score (Navy won 21–15), but what happened dur-

ing the telecast: CBS decided to unveil a new gimmick. Sportscaster Lindsey Nelson introduced the nation to instant replay, which grew to become one of the most important breakthroughs in sports. Today, not only does instant replay analyze an event from every conceivable angle, it also figures prominently in the way games are played and decided. Several leagues and organizations (notably the NFL and NHL) rely on instant replay to settle disputes during the game, vividly demonstrating the impact of technology on sports.

6. **Oakland Raiders vs. New York Jets, 1968, NBC.** With the Jets comfortably ahead in the final minutes, NBC decided to leave the game at 7:00 P.M. in order to air its regularly scheduled program. While a national television audience watched a production of *Heidi*, the Raiders scored two touchdowns in the final minute to win. Most people watching didn't figure out what happened until they read the newspaper the next day, then they besieged NBC with calls and letters. Sportscaster Curt Gowdy worked the game and said the network asked him to "fake" a description of the game's final minutes for the next morning's newscasts. "You can imagine how tough it was to fake surprise and enthusiasm after the fact," he said later. From that point forward, no network would dare cut away from a live sports program, except under the most extreme circumstances.

7. **Super Bowl III, 1969, NBC.** Just two months after the *Heidi* game, Gowdy found himself behind the mike for Super Bowl III between the Baltimore Colts and New York Jets. The Colts were heavily favored to continue NFL dominance over the upstart AFL, but led by brash young Joe Namath, the Jets pulled off one of the biggest upsets in sports history. The game evened the balance of power between the two leagues and solidified football as the premier television sports event of the era. Author Marty Ralbovsky said, "It may have been the most important single professional football game ever played."

8. **1972 Olympic Games, Munich Germany, ABC.** The murder of 11 Israeli athletes by terrorists played out on the biggest television stage in history. ABC sportscaster Jim McKay anchored almost straight through the crisis, climaxing his report with the simple phrase, "They're all gone." ABC and McKay won several awards for their coverage, which demonstrated that sports could report intelligently on serious issues. "It showed people that sportscasters have an interest in things other than sports," said McKay. Added fellow sportscaster Jack Whitaker, "What Jim McKay did in Munich was one of the all-time high points, not just in sportscasting, but in reporting."

9. **U.S. vs. U.S.S.R., 1980 Winter Olympics, ABC.** Almost every sports fan remembers the "Miracle on Ice," as the upstart American hockey team stunned the Russians, 4–3. Part of what made the telecast so memorable was Al Michael's call "Do you believe in miracles?" in

the game's final seconds. "I remember as the seconds ticked down, the word that kept coming to my mind was 'miraculous,'" he later said. The game demonstrated the power of a single sports event to unify a viewing audience, and was voted by several organizations as the number one sports story of the twentieth century. But it also may have negatively influenced future sportscasters. "Now, announcers will go into a game thinking of what they will say, under certain circumstances," says Michaels. "That's terribly wrong, because there needs to be that element of spontaneity." One thing most people probably *don't* remember about the telecast is that it was actually played earlier that day and shown on tape delay by ABC that night in prime time. While tape delay was fairly common at that time (that same year, many of the NBA Final games were shown tape delayed), the "Miracle on Ice" virtually ended the practice. Fans wanted to see the drama live, even if it meant missing some soap operas in the afternoon.

10. **Gator Bowl, Clemson vs. Ohio State, 1978.** This game will not be remembered for any outstanding plays or performances, but rather for its tragic conclusion. Near the end of the game, a Clemson player intercepted a pass, killing an Ohio State rally and ending any hopes the Buckeyes had of winning the game. As the player returned the ball out of bounds on the Ohio State sideline, he was punched and nearly choked by legendary coach Woody Hayes. Hayes had a long history of embarrassing incidents on the field, such as ripping up a sideline marker and knocking over a cameraman. But by the time of this particular incident, television sports had grown too big and the electronic eye had become too omnipresent to ignore. A national television audience witnessed the attack, which prompted Hayes's immediate dismissal as coach. It also put other coaches and players on notice: the cameras don't miss a thing. Television had become the new courtroom of public opinion, with the audience as judge and jury.

REFERENCES

"All Bets Are Off for Offshore Bookmakers." *U.S. News & World Report.* March 16, 1998.

Alm, Richard. "In On the Action." *Dallas Morning News,* April 14, 2000.

Anderson, Porter. "What's in a Name?" *Southwest Airlines Spirit,* January 2000.

Angell, Roger. *Season Ticket.* Boston: Houghton Mifflin, 1988.

"At Least $15 Billion May Be Spent on 75 Stadiums this Decade." *The News and Observer Publishing Company,* September 2, 1995.

Blum, Ronald. "Owners Think of Eliminating Teams." *Associated Press,* July 13, 2000.

Bohls, Kirk. "Kirk Bohls Says: Don't Bet on Proposed Gambling Ban Succeeding." *Austin-American Statesman,* February 19, 2000.

Bouton, Jim. *Ball Four Plus Ball Five.* New York: Stein & Day, 1981.

"Canadiens for Sale: Must Stay in Montreal." *Associated Press.* [Online]. Available: http://www.espn.go.com/nhl/news/2000/0627/606311.html. June 27, 2000.

Catsis, John. *Sports Broadcasting.* Chicago: Nelson-Hall, 1993.

Connor, Anthony J. (1982). *Voices from Cooperstown.* New York: Macmillan, 1982.

Costas, Bob. *Fair Ball.* New York: Broadway Books, 2000.

Eisenberg, John. *Cotton Bowl Days.* New York: Simon & Schuster, 1997.

"Go Figure." *Sports Illustrated,* March 6, 2000.

Golenbock, Peter. *Bums.* New York: Pocket Books, 1984.

Jenkins, Chris. "Mavs' Cuban Puts Right Spin on Web." *USA Today,* December 26, 2000.

Kahn, Roger. *Memories of Summer.* New York: Hyperion, 1997.

"Local TV and Radio Lineup." *Broadcasting & Cable,* March 27, 2000.

Mack, Connie. *My Sixty-six Years in the Big Leagues.* Philadelphia: Winston & Co., 1950.

Maull, Samuel. "MSG Sues Yankees over Cable Contract." *Associated Press.* [Online]. Available: http://live.altavista.com/scripts/editorial.dll?ei=1990165&ern=y. July 14, 2000.

McGraw, Dan. "Big League Troubles." *U.S. News & World Report,* July 13, 1998.

———. "The Boom and Bust in Sports Gambling." *U.S. News & World Report,* April 7, 1997.

Mermigas, Diane. "Buying Stations while the Getting Is Good." *Electronic Media,* May 18, 1998.

"NBA Threatens Coaches with $100,000 Fines." *Associated Press,* March 8, 2000.

"NFL Takes Cowboys to Court over Nike, Pepsi Deals." *Associated Press,* September 18, 1995.

Okkonen, Mark. *Baseball Uniforms of the 20th Century.* New York: Sterling, 1991.

Ralbovsky, Marty. *Super Bowl.* New York: Hawthorn Books, 1971.

Romano, Allison. Second Thoughts. [Online]. Available: www.foxsports.com/business/bites/z1028hicks1.sml, November 15, 1999.

"Senator Specter Calls for NFL and Major League Baseball to Pay 50% of Stadium Construction Costs." [Online]. Available: http://specter.senate.gov/990504.htm, May 4, 1999.

Seventy-five Seasons. Atlanta: Turner Publishing, 1994.

Seymour, Harold. *Baseball, the Golden Age.* New York: Oxford Press, 1971.

"Sold at Last: Nuggets, Avs, and Pepsi Center Sold to Liberty Media." *Fox Sports Biz.* [Online]. Available: www.foxsports.com/business/bites/z000222nuggets1.sml, February 22, 2000.

Staubach, Roger. *Time Enough to Win.* Waco, TX: Word Books, 1980.

Sportscasters: Behind the Mike. [Television show]. The History Channel, February 7, 2000.

Sportscenter of the Decade: The 90s. [Television show]. ESPN, December 14, 1999.

Sports Century: 50 Greatest Athletes. [Television show]. ESPN, December 17, 1999.

"Wal-Mart Heir Kroenke Reaches Agreement." *Associated Press,* April 24, 2000.

"You Wanna Bet?" *Wall Street Journal,* January 28, 2000.

3

Style versus Substance

BLESSING OR CURSE?

As television entered the late 1990s, it had a 50-year track record as one of the most important and influential inventions of the twentieth century. It had revolutionized the way Americans thought, worked, and played. It had brought culture, information, and entertainment to almost every corner of the nation. And it had a profound impact upon America politically, economically, and socially.

But despite all this, more often than not television and the electronic media came under intense criticism. Sociologists said it endangered children because of its preoccupation with violence. Anthropologists said its hold on the nation destroyed literacy and turned people into passive robots. Others said its portrayal of blacks and other minorities painted a false picture of the country.

One criticism in particular became amplified as the 90s came to a close: that the electronic media and especially television had become too entertainment-oriented and that the lines between news and entertainment had begun to blur and blend together. It's a charge critics have also levied against television sports.

"INFOTAINMENT"

In May of 1997, WMAQ-TV in Chicago dropped a bombshell when it hired sensational talk show host Jerry Springer for a series of commentaries on its nightly newscast. Springer's show already had a reputation for violence and tawdriness, and his hiring did not sit well with WMAQ anchors Ron Magers and Carol Marin, both of whom abruptly quit the station in defense of what they called "traditional journalism." Eventually WMAQ backed down from hiring Springer, while Magers and Marin found other jobs with competing stations in the market.

The episode vividly demonstrates how pervasive entertainment has become in the news business. Critics have a derisive name for it—"infotainment." The growing numbers of stations that emphasize infotainment usually use the same formula, including an emphasis on sensational stories mixed with pretty anchors and lots of music and graphics. Even as far back as 1977, Pulitzer prize winning television critic Ron Powers wrote, "TV journalism in this country—local TV journalism, in particular—is drifting into the sphere of entertainment."

It was a charge that could also be made of the early days of radio broadcasting. News broadcasts from the early 30s more closely resembled vaudeville acts than public service, but that was when the medium was still trying to define itself. Led by men such as CBS founder William S. Paley, radio and then television followed a much stricter course. Paley began CBS on the premise that a superior news product would eventually win audience support and to Paley a "superior product" meant truth and objectivity.

Edward R. Murrow moved over from radio and became the first television news star. He shared Paley's commitment to news, but also believed the medium had responsibility to the less fortunate in society. Murrow championed the underdogs and those he felt unjustly attacked, particularly during the "Red Scare" of the early 1950s. Historians believe that his two programs dealing with Joseph McCarthy played the pivotal role in bringing down the demagogue senator. News producer and writer Reuven Frank of rival NBC said, "Some suggested McCarthy was already falling and it made no difference. [But] CBS did it—no one else." It was not long after the *See It Now* broadcast of March 9, 1954 that the U.S. Senate censured McCarthy, thus ending his communist witch hunt.

But even in those early days, entertainment began to make its presence felt. In July of 1955, NBC invested a lot of time and money on a show promoting a political summit in Geneva, Switzerland—the first such conference since the end of World War II. NBC producer Pete Salomon guessed that "all right-thinking people on the planet" would focus their thoughts on Geneva, but he didn't realize the level of competition. Up against ABC's live broadcast of the opening of Disneyland and Ethel Merman singing on the *Ed Sullivan Show* on CBS, NBC's *Meeting at the Summit* drew a rating of 0.7—for years, the smallest audience ever to watch a Sunday night network show.

Has this trend toward entertainment actually increased over the years? Probably not. More likely, the technology to bring televised entertainment into the home finally caught up with the country's desire to see it. According to author Neil Postman, "Entertainment is the supraideology of all discourse on television. The overarching presumption is that it is there for our amusement and pleasure. We are not assembling news to be read or broadcasts to be heard. We must follow where the medium leads."

The message to networks and programmers is clear: news is fine, but entertainment brings in the audiences. And a combination of news and entertainment is the best of both worlds. Thus, in the past generation we have seen the rise of "happy talk," tabloid television, the infomercial, and "trash talk" television. It's become impossible to tell the difference between what's real and what's simply staged for the audience's benefit.

THE PLAY'S THE THING

Certainly, this trend has not escaped televised sports. If anything, sports led the way because of its very nature. Events were not considered hard news, yet they weren't pure entertainment, either. Sports still exists under a television microscope, where what you see depends on who's doing the looking.

Nothing demonstrated this better than boxing and wrestling, which became the sports entertainment of choice in the medium's infancy. Wrote Orrin Dunlap of the *New York Times*, "The roped area is the perfect size for a camera to cover. The scene is packed with action, which is the lifeblood of television. The colorful sounds punch realism in the picture. Carnage has been a dream of television."

Wrestling and boxing became a staple of sports television on Friday and Saturday nights. And when eventually eclipsed by other professional sports, wrestling re-invented itself in the 1980s. Now, the World Wrestling Federation and its contemporaries dominate the cable ratings with high-energy music, laser light shows and soap-opera plots. Wrestling routinely makes millions of dollars in pay-per-view specials.

Such success spawned a host of other similar shows, mixing sport and entertainment. These include a variety of formats, including professional athletes competing in nontraditional events (the *Home Run Derby* shows of the 1960s, *Superstars* of the 1970s, and *The Skins Game* of the 1990s) and amateur athletes engaging against each other in contests of strength or skill (*The World's Strongest Man* and *American Gladiators*). Another interesting format is the "Battle of the Sexes" match, which became quite popular during the women's rights movement of the 1970s. Tennis players Billie Jean King and Bobby Riggs showed the popularity of this kind of event with their match in 1973. Thanks to heavy pre-event promotion and publicity, the match drew a huge crowd inside the Houston Astrodome and attracted millions of viewers on national television. The popularity of such events waned a bit in 1975 after a made-for-television horse race involving Foolish Pleasure and the filly Ruffian. The popular Ruffian broke a leg during the race and had to be destroyed. ABC revived the format in the 1990s, involving golf pros from the PGA, Senior PGA, and LPGA tours. But nothing yet has matched the success and staying power of professional wrestling, perhaps because it makes no pretense of legitimate competition and instead focuses on promotion, entertainment, and marketing.

Sports announcers also started becoming more entertaining. We've already discussed the role of ABC, which introduced two watershed concepts in sports entertainment—*Wide World of Sports* and Howard Cosell. More than any other announcer, Cosell institutionalized the role of an entertaining sports broadcaster on a national level. According to Dave Kindred of *The Sporting News*, Cosell "had no abiding interest in the game itself, but he certainly loved the stage it gave him. And no one entertained more sports fans than Cosell on Monday nights. Not in the sense that people loved him, but entertained in that fans listened to every word he said." Certainly announcers entertained fans long before Cosell. But men like Dizzy Dean, Bob Prince, and even Cosell's partner Don Meredith were more often viewed as clowns and looked down upon by other broadcasters. Cosell and his national stage legitimized the place of sports as entertainment.

What Cosell did on the national stage, baseball broadcaster Harry Caray had done on a more limited scale. Caray started doing St. Louis Cardinals games in 1945 with a style he described as "designed to get noticed." Caray was enthusiastic, colorful, and above all, a born showman. But it wasn't until Caray reached Chicago in the 1970s that the lid came off. As a White Sox broadcaster, he routinely did games from the centerfield bleachers. And when the Cubs and their superstation WGN gave Harry a national stage in 1982, he unofficially became the "Mayor of Rush Street"—the most popular man in Chicago and maybe the country. Not even a stroke could keep him from entertaining fans and leading the crowd in singing during the seventh inning stretch. His philosophy? "Man, baseball can be dull enough without dull announcers. Make it fun, that's what I say. It's not life or death" (see Chapter 16).

Cosell and Caray are both dead, but they set in motion the age of the entertaining sportscaster. According to *Electronic Media*, "Somewhere along the line, sportscasts became less important for substance than style. They became diversions that could be used to entertain viewers and hold on to people who didn't care about the information they heard." ESPN seemed to lead the way with a stable of young, irreverent sportscasters, many of whom had far stronger backgrounds in entertainment than sports. Craig Kilborn always dreamed of a job in television entertainment and went to ESPN because it offered him a national showcase for his talents. After a few years, he left to host a late night interview and comedy show on CBS.

The trend really picked up steam in the mid-1990s with the pairing of Dan Patrick and Keith Olbermann on ESPN (see Figure 3-1). Their humorous interplay created more fans than the sports events they covered and

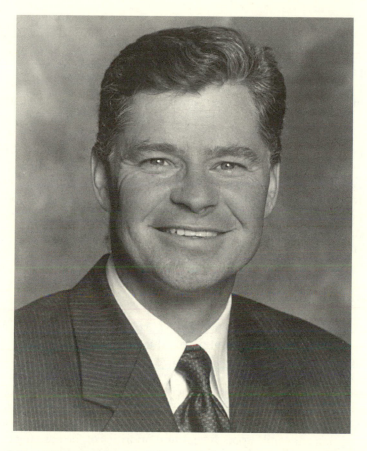

Figure 3-1 ESPN's Dan Patrick, Without His Long-time Partner Keith Olbermann (Courtesy ESPN/John Atashian)

eventually led to a book, *The Big Show.* The party ended for Olbermann and Patrick when the former left ESPN after a contract squabble and eventually resurfaced on Fox Sports Net. But their style and success encouraged a nation of would-be sports funnymen, complete with their own wisecracks, nicknames, and entertaining shtick.

Men like Fred Roggin, George Michael, and Al Leitner would not say they're imitators at all, but pioneers. In places like Los Angeles, San Diego, and Washington, D.C., they have developed a trademark style to fit their personalities. Roggin uses videotape and sound effects, while Leitner prefers creative segments, such a hockey fights with no highlights and a segment called "Deep Thoughts with Charles Barkley." Many sports hosts and reporters on radio have done the same thing. "I have to be interesting more than anything," said sports talk show host Mike Gastineau of KJR-AM in

Seattle. "People ask me, is it journalism or entertainment? Well, it's a hybrid, but it's got to be interesting. For example, how many preset buttons do you have on your car radio? Ten or fifteen? It takes two seconds for you to be driving along and say this is boring and go to another station."

On any stage and in any format, sports as entertainment has a strong foothold in the electronic media. Tim Keown of *ESPN The Magazine* says that became particularly clear to him when ABC fired *Monday Night Football* commentator Boomer Esiason in March 2000. "The network acknowledged one salient fact," wrote Keown. "The game isn't enough anymore. It doesn't matter whether the game features a compelling story line or a storied rivalry or a quarterback every woman in America loves. It doesn't matter because on UPN there's wrestling with all its homoerotic, daytime soap opera permutations. There are shirtless men being handcuffed and hauled out of rusted trailers on Fox. There's a guy up for murder describing his multiple-personality disorder on *Dateline*. That's the new world order."

THE CHICKEN OR THE EGG?

No doubt, entertainment has influenced sports and vice-versa. But how does everything fit in the larger context of American culture? In other words, does sports influence social values or merely reflect them? Leonard Koppett argues strongly for the latter. "Sports have the form they have," he writes, "because they were shaped by the society in which they developed. To argue that sports lead rather than follow public fashion, simply ignores reality." And according to psychologist Dr. Joyce Brothers, the success of organized sport depends upon the cultural priorities of the country in which it is played. This seems especially true when considering the ways the media have covered sports during this century.

The Age of Heroes: 1920–1950

As America entered the 1920s, it did so with a gigantic sigh of relief. The past two years had witnessed the end of a world war that resulted in 350,000 U.S. casualties, an outbreak of influenza that killed some 25 million people worldwide, and a series of labor strikes that threatened to cripple the American economy. The nation was ready to party as the 20s began and forget the problems of the past few years. Historians have called the decade the "Jazz Age" or the "Roaring 20s" for its emphasis on free spirits, good times, and relaxed inhibitions. Prohibition did not stop the party, it just created an opportunity for organized crime, and the gangsters seemed to make the era that much more romantic and dangerous. The optimism of the period created larger-than-life heroes—men like Charles Lindbergh, F. Scott Fitzgerald, and even Al Capone. The media of the day were willing accomplices in the hero-making effort, especially for Lindbergh. His nonstop flight across the Atlantic transformed him from an anonymous flyer into a instant icon. Typical press reports of his feat referred to Lindbergh as a "modern Magellan," and "the greatest of heroes mankind has produced since air became a means of travel."

The sports of the times had their own Lindbergh, in fact several of them. "It was the first real development of the superhuman athlete," noted sports writer Furman Bisher. "[Sports writers like Grantland Rice] were the first to pin the name 'Golden Age' on the times and they did make it a golden age." Newspapers and radio featured the exploits of men like Red Grange, Bobby Jones, and Jack Dempsey, and helped make their feats seem larger than life. Grange became "The Galloping Ghost" at the University of Illinois and despite a rather mediocre professional career, his mere presence is credited with helping solidify the struggling NFL. "The weekly newsreel clips that made the rounds of the movie houses back in those days took the images [of Grange] and enhanced them," wrote sports writer John Underwood. "They stoked the illusion of speed and made even more impressive the other eerie components of his long touchdown runs. Reviewing those reels now, you get the impression that if Red Grange were not, indeed, a Galloping Ghost, he surely must have seen one."

But no one became a bigger American hero than Babe Ruth, who more than anyone typified the decade—strong and powerful, yet seemingly carefree with huge personal appetites. "Everything he did smacked of hyperbole," said sports writer William Nack. "He ate too much. He drank too much. And when he hit another of his titanic shots, the reporters covering his games wrote the prose of excess, as if nothing could do justice to his swats." The press well knew of Ruth's weaknesses, especially his fondness for liquor and prostitutes, but never reported any of it because it would tarnish his heroic image. There is a well-documented story about writers traveling on the team train late one night. First, a naked Ruth ran through the car, followed by a woman wielding a knife. One reporter looked at another and said, "It's a good thing we didn't see that, otherwise we'd have to report it."

This reflected the close relationship reporters enjoyed with players during this simpler era. Sports reporting positions were few and extremely hard to get. Because there were so few, it allowed reporters to develop a special trust with the players and protect them. David Halberstam noted, "The writers and players were friends, but not peers. The writers knew about the personal lives of the players, but that information was never used." Certainly not for Ruth, who became a symbol of his era and a permanent American icon. "Sometimes I still can't believe what I saw," said former teammate Harry Hooper years later. "This crude, poorly educated kid . . . transformed into the idol of American youth and the symbol of baseball the world over. I saw a man transformed from a human being into something pretty close to a god."

The Age of Cynicism: 1950–1980

America went through a significant cultural transformation in the second half of the twentieth century. The 1950s have been described as an age of youth and innocence, but in truth the Cold War gave rise to an atmosphere of fear, intimidation, and suspicion. According to Joe McCarthy, communists were operating at the highest levels of the federal government. The entire world seemed on the brink of nuclear disaster during the Cuban missile crisis in 1962.

The 50s also marked the beginning of the civil rights movement, which seemed to divide the nation along black and white lines. Television brought it all right into America's living rooms—the protest marches, the violence and the hatred. Politically, the issue ended with the Civil Rights Act of 1964, but deep scars remained. Less than four years later, civil rights leader Martin Luther King was killed, touching off rioting and burning in American cities.

Just two months after King's death, a gunman killed presidential candidate Bobby Kennedy. Americans took to the streets not only to protest the violence, but also to voice growing concerns over some place called Vietnam. The conflict there would ultimately cost more than 50,000 U.S. lives and divide America into young and old, hawks and doves. Young people in America became increasingly suspicious and distrustful of the federal government and the way it approached these issues. That mistrust culminated in the early 70s with the Watergate cover-up and the eventual resignation of President Richard Nixon.

The American press and especially television reflected the growing cynicism. Even during the *Leave it to Beaver* era of the 50s, shows such as *See It Now* and *CBS Reports* documented the growing problems in American society. Historians call the Vietnam War the first "living room war," but NBC news producer Reuven Frank says the distinction actually belongs to the Korean conflict. On shows like the *Camel News Caravan*, "those pictures were seen in millions of living rooms night after night. Frozen marines retreating down a mountainside, hollow eyes, and bearded cheeks showing through and rags over their combat boots to keep them warm."

The media had covered World War II as a patriotic duty, cheering on Allied victories and encouraging people to keep up the fight on the home front. But in Korea and Vietnam, the media reported with a much more cynical eye. Correspondents went to the front lines and reported on the dark side of war, including the terrible slaughter of civilians and the underlying political issues involved. CBS anchor Walter Cronkite went to Vietnam and reported not the government line of inevitable victory, but of a bloody stalemate with no end in sight. And according to a story that got back to Cronkite, the reports greatly influenced President Lyndon Johnson's decision not to run for re-election. "When I lost Cronkite, I lost middle America," Johnson reportedly said.

Richard Nixon lost America and his presidency with the Watergate scandal that started in 1972. Many historians believe that if not for the media, Nixon might have survived. But the work of Carl Bernstein and Bob Woodward at the *Washington Post* and the committee hearings on television reflected the growing cynicism of the American public. Ben Bradlee worked as an editor at the *Post* during the scandal and helped Woodward and Bernstein put the story together. "Vietnam, followed by Watergate, changed the rules forever," wrote Bradlee. "After Watergate, [journalists] assumed that government officials generally and instinctively lied. 'Look for the lies' replaced 'look for the women' or 'find the money' as the shibboleth of journalism."

Much of the same transformation took place in sports journalism. ABC executive Jim Spence says, "For so many years, sportscasters had spent their time fawning over athletes, coaches, and managers . . . as though these people were gods. [But] it was a time for people to quit looking at sports merely as amusement. There were social and economic and legal issues involved." Sportscasters and writers began asking serious questions about issues, backgrounds, and personalities. It wasn't enough just to report what happened anymore, sports journalists needed to know why. "The trend of reporting has changed considerably, which I think has to do with TV," said former baseball player and now broadcaster Ralph Kiner. "The media situation has become more of a factor. Back then it was, 'How did the game go?' Today, it's 'What happened to your psyche when you were seven years old?'"

Two athletes in particular received rough treatment from the media. Ted Williams had a stormy 21-year relationship with the Boston press, most notably with Dave Egan of the *Boston Record*. While Williams had Egan to contend with, Roger Maris seemingly had to fight the entire New York media. In 1961, Maris presented the first serious challenge to Babe Ruth's home run record. But far from celebrating the event (as they did with Ruth in 1927), the media turned on Maris for daring to challenge the Babe. Reporters came from all over the world and analyzed his every move. Normally taciturn anyway, Maris became even more moody and tried to fight back. His hair began to fall out in clumps and he told teammates, "It's no wonder I'm going nuts." And when Maris eventually did break the record, it did not change his treatment in the media or his standing with the public. "The community of baseball feels Mickey Mantle is a great player," wrote New York columnist Jimmy Cannon. "They feel Roger Maris is a thrilling freak who hit .269."

A pivotal moment in sports reporting came with the publication of *Ball Four* in 1970. Major league pitcher Jim Bouton wrote the book, which became a controversial sensation for its honest depiction of players, including their sexual adventures and psychological hang-ups. The book horrified baseball executives, who saw it as a "threat to the game," and baseball purists, who did not know how to handle such truthful reporting of sports figures. Bouton later wrote, "I think the overreaction to the book boiled down to this: people were simply not used to reading the truth about professional sports. By establishing new boundaries, *Ball Four* changed sports reporting . . . it was no longer possible to sell the milk and cookies image again."

Growing media competition also played a part in the process. As radio and then television outlets got involved, newspapers no longer had a monopoly on sports coverage. Reporters that used to get intimate interviews with players after a game, now found themselves fighting to get just a few minutes. With so many reporters looking for "scoops," players became distrustful of the media and their relationship became adversarial. Nowhere was this more evident than during the Yankees "Bronx Zoo" era of the mid-1970s, when Reggie Jackson proclaimed himself "the straw that stirs the drink." "Give the [team] a day off and the New York writers will use it to come up with a discontented player," wrote baseball author Bob Marshall. "For the writers it was just a matter of spacing out the complaints so that there would be a fresh story every week."

Up until this point, newspapers, radio, and television pretty much had the sports beat to themselves. But that would soon change, along with another swing in American cultural values.

The Age of Celebrity: 1980–Present

Much as America seemed anxious to enter the decade of the 1920s, so too did the country want to leave behind the problems of the 60s and 70s. When 52 American hostages returned in January 1980 after more than a year imprisonment in Iran, it seemed to signal the end of a long, gloomy period in U.S. history. Moving hand-in-hand with the change in mood were technological advances that would make the media even more omnipresent in people's lives.

The late 1970s saw the rise of cable television, increasing options and signal delivery to millions of new customers. Satellite transmission became commonplace, linking people and places and providing instant access from anywhere in the world. The globe continued to shrink with the development of cell phones, digital technology, and the Internet, all of which gave the consumer thousands of options for sports and entertainment.

The developments also impacted sports reporting and reporting in general. Where once the three major networks dominated coverage, now the industry splintered into hundreds of program providers. Cable outlets, superstations, and even Internet sites now battled ABC, CBS, and NBC for supremacy with the viewers. Newsrooms and operations grew steadily in size to keep up with demand, as viewers began to expect more and more. Technological advances fueled the development of a society of "instant gratification," a fast-paced, helter-skelter lifestyle where people wanted a lot and wanted it all now.

And the media tried to give it to them. CNN pioneered the first 24-hour cable news network; now viewers could get information at any time of day or night, not just at six or eleven o'clock. Personal computers and the Internet shortened the delay even more, allowing instant access to volumes of information in just a few seconds. As a result, the "news cycle" shortened to just a bare few minutes for the Internet. Major stories, once debated and discussed in media boardrooms, got immediate play on the Internet before moving on the traditional media. Sometimes the results were disastrous, such as when the *Dallas Morning News* and *Wall Street Journal* both ran unsubstantiated and factually incorrect Internet stories concerning the affair between President Clinton and Monica Lewinsky. Says Robert Bianco of *USA Today*, ". . . ever-increasing competitive pressures have led electronic journalists to decide what matters most is being first, even if that means being wrong."

Monica Lewinsky, O.J. Simpson, and Princess Diana all fed the consumer demand for more and faster information and reflected a growing culture of the "celebrity," not only in society, but in journalism and sports reporting as well. Celebrities perfectly fit into the new definition of media: they were plentiful, could be recycled continuously, and forgotten instantly. Where once network documentaries investigated the problems of poverty and migrant workers, the airwaves and cable channels became filled with favorite recipes, off-screen romances, and tawdry gossip. *Washington Post* media critic Howard Kurtz writes, "[It's] a news culture that runs through celebrities like Kleenex and nothing is more important than being wealthy or famous. The media play a crucial role in marketing these larger-than-life personalities." According to historian David Boorstin, "Two centuries ago, when a great man appeared, people looked for God's purpose in him; today, we look for his press agent."

Sports reporting had no trouble with the shifting culture, where the events became less important than the athletes themselves. The NHL was stagnant until the arrival of Wayne Gretzky, who according to Mike Lupica of the *New York Daily News*, saved the entire league. "He turned it into a West Coast, sunbelt sport for the entire public. Wayne Gretzky saved the NHL." The NBA couldn't even get its championship series on live television until the arrival of Larry Bird and Magic Johnson. And thanks to Tiger Woods, the new PGA television deal signed in 1999 allowed the tour to almost double the money it pays at tournaments. "Tiger has changed the ratings in golf," said Rob Correa, CBS Sports programming senior vice president. "He's worth, on a Sunday, 50 to 60 percent higher ratings than that same tournament without Tiger Woods." Says sports writer Mitch Albom, "The biggest currency athletes have today is celebrity. It's not important what you've done on the field anymore."

Nowhere is that more true than at ESPN, which has institutionalized the star power of the professional athlete with its nightly display of dunks, spikes, fights, and other sensational behavior. And don't forget the network's clever series of promos for its own *SportsCenter* show. "In its ascent, ESPN increasingly bowed to the lowest populist denominator by aligning itself with the worst acts," wrote Phil Mushnick of *TV Guide*. "ESPN, it seems, exists to reward showoffs."

The biggest collision of sports and entertainment in recent years happened during the Olympic ice skating trials in 1994. Nancy Kerrigan was attacked by an unknown assailant and immediately the attention focused on competitor Tonya Harding, who denied any part in the incident. But just days later, her bodyguard was arrested as the prime suspect. Kerrigan recovered enough to skate in the Olympics, which set up a soap opera showdown with Harding and fueled an unheard of media frenzy. "We basically ignored every other athlete in the Olympics," says Albom. "We were too busy covering Tonya and Nancy's practice sessions." Jim Nantz helped anchor the CBS Olympic coverage and noted, "This is a tabloid-crazy society. We love nothing more than a good scandal."

Harding skated poorly in the finals and eventually confessed to "obstructing the investigation," although she never admitted any knowledge about the attack. That fueled another round of intense media scrutiny, as did her suspension from sanctioned skating events. Kerrigan skated very well and just narrowly missed a gold medal. The medal ceremony should have ended the media's fascination with Kerrigan, but they just couldn't get enough. In the days that followed, they reported on Kerrigan's complaints about the judging and her subsequent critical comments at a Disney parade. "The media used me for months," she said later. "And then they just threw me away."

Media critic Tom Shales now says preoccupation with entertainment and hype makes today's sports coverage look more like a production of *The Young and the Restless*. "The Olympics may simply have become a victim of television's incredible sports glut," he says, "something that has grown exponentially and geometrically in the years since ESPN first signed on." Such is life in the high-tech, high demand world of sports reporting heading into the twenty-first century.

REFERENCES

Bianco, Robert. "Instant Gratification Results in New Journalistic Standard." *USA Today*, December 26, 2000.

Bradlee, Ben. *A Good Life*. New York: Touchstone, 1995.

Bouton, Jim. *Ball Four Plus Ball Five*. New York: Stein & Day, 1981.

Connor, Anthony J. *Voices from Cooperstown*. New York: Macmillan, 1982.

Curran, William. *Big Sticks*. New York: William Morrow & Co., 1990.

Fendrich, Howard. "Tuned in to Tiger: Woods TV Watchers Keep Multiplying." [Online]. Available: http://www.foxsports.com/business/bites/z000629tiger_tv.sml, June 29, 2000.

Frank, Reuven. *Out of Thin Air*. New York: Simon & Schuster, 1991.

Friendly, Fred W. *Due to Circumstances Beyond Our Control*. New York: Random House, 1967.

Iyer, Pico. "The Unknown Rebel." *Time*, April 13, 1998.

Johnson, Steve. "How Low Can TV News Go?" *Columbia Journalism Review*, July–August 1997.

Keown, Tim. "It's More Than a Game—It's a TV Show." ESPN. [Online]. Available: http://www.espn.go.com/gen/s/keown/0310.html, March 10, 2000.

Kindred, Dave. "Top 5 Ornery Charmers: Number One, Howard Cosell." *The Sporting News*, July 7, 1999.

Koppett, Leonard. *Sports Illusion, Sports Reality*. Boston: Houghton Mifflin, 1981.

Kurtz, Howard. *Media Circus*. New York: Times Books, 1993.

Laurence, Robert P. "Leitner's Light Touch." *Electronic Media*, March 22, 1999.

"Lindbergh's Own Story." *Associated Press*, May 22, 1927.

Mickleson, Sig. *The Decade that Shaped Television News*. Westport, CT: Praeger, 1998.

Mushnick, Phil. "Sports View." *TV Guide,* January 1, 2000.

Nack, William. "20th Century Sports Awards Nominees." *Sports Illustrated*, August 24, 1998.

Not-so-great Moments in Sports. [Home video]. HBO Video: New York, 1985.

Patton, Phil. *Razzle-dazzle*. New York: Dial Press, 1984.

Postman, Neil. *Amusing Ourselves to Death*. New York: Penguin, 1985.

Ralbovsky, Marty. *Super Bowl*. New York: Hawthorne, 1971.

Rosenthal, Phil. "Everybody's a Comedian." *Electronic Media*, March 22, 1999.

Shales, Tom. X, "Oh, the Tragedy: Olympics Coverage Is Just Too Sad." *Electronic Media*, 4. June 29, 2000.

Smith, Curt. *Voices of the Game*. South Bend, IN: Diamond Press, 1987.

Spence, Jim. *Up Close and Personal*. New York: Atheneum, 1988.

SportsCenter of the Century: The Most Influential People. [Television show]. ESPN, February 20, 2000.

SportsCenter of the Decade: The 90s. [Television show]. ESPN, December 23, 1999.

Sports Century: 50 Greatest Athletes. [Television show]. ESPN, December 17, 1999.

Sports Century: 50 Greatest Athletes. [Television show]. ESPN, December 26, 1999.

"Sports-talk Radio Host." *ESPN*. [Online]. Available: http://espn.go.com/special/s/careers/sptalk.html, September 7, 1999.

Underwood, John. "20th Century Sports Awards Nominees." *Sports Illustrated*, August 24, 1998.

4

Writing

OVERVIEW

News directors around the country don't pull punches when it comes to the quality of writing in broadcast journalism. Back in 1995, Marselis Parsons of WCAX-TV in Burlington, Vermont said, "Absolutely it's a problem. We have to constantly review the writing of our staff." Television producer Warren Cereghino added, "Many reporters and anchors are just sloppy and others don't seem to care." Some long-time newsmen say the problem actually starts at the top with management. "Too many news directors pay lip service to good writing," says Merv Block, a news writing coach and former CBS writer. "They may say writing is important, but when it comes right down to it, writing is not foremost in their calculations."

While such comments apply to the broadcasting industry as a whole, they certainly include writing for sports broadcasting, which has been a much maligned and often ignored part of the process. Today's emphasis on entertainment (see Chapter 3) has prompted sportscasters to focus more on appearance and presentation. As a result, much modern writing has become redundant, recycled, and riddled with clichés. Sportscasters don't take the time to come up with original writing and instead settle for cheap imitations of the successful names in the business. News director David·Jensch of KBJR-TV in Duluth, Minnesota says, "I'm looking for somebody who knows sports without falling into the use of hackneyed sports clichés. [If I hear] one 'double dip' or 'bada bing, bada bang,' I eject the resume tape. I'm looking for, above all else, a good writer and inquisitive reporter."

Many of those clichés come right from ESPN, which has taken its share of heat for "dumbing down" sports broadcast writing. In a series of clever and popular promos run in the late 1990s, the network portrayed its anchors as obsessed with coming up with a new "catch phrase." When the anchors were shown writing at their desks, other co-workers would pelt them with fruits and vegetables.

Certainly, there are good writers at ESPN and at other sports departments around the country. But as mentioned, the quality of broadcast writing as a whole has fallen to depressing levels. There's no secret how to fix the problem: return to the good fundamentals of writing and broadcast journalism that have often been ignored in today's present environment (see Figure 4-1).

BACK TO BASICS—10 RULES FOR SPORTS WRITING

In many respects, writing for sports broadcasting is the same as writing for news, because most of the same basics apply. There are some differences that apply only to sports, but for the most part, good writing is good writing.

1. **Use active voice.** This is one of the basic commandments of broadcast writing, but one of the most ignored. Basically, beware of the verb "to be," which indicates the passive voice. You should always try to write that the

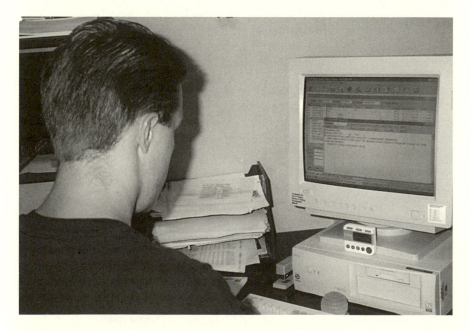

Figure 4-1   Modern Technology Has Made Sports Writing Easier—But Not Necessarily Better

"player caught the ball," rather than "the ball *was* caught by the player." Active voice is shorter, more conversational, and more ideally suited to writing about sports action (think of the impact of such words as "slammed," "knocked," or "flattened"). Writing in active voice is easy, but often ignored because it takes a little more time and creativity. The easiest way to convert to active voice is simply to turn around the sentence:

> Passive: The game was over by halftime.
>
> Active: The Lakers ended the game by halftime.

In situations where you can't turn the sentence around, you can change the verb:

> Passive: Michael Jordan was in Chicago today.
>
> Active: Michael Jordan visited Chicago today.

In such situations, remember that changing the verb should not change the meaning of the sentence. It's also permissible in broadcast writing to simply drop the verb:

> Passive: The Cowboys were busy in the draft today.
>
> Active: The Cowboys busy in the draft today.

In some rare situations, it's simpler and easier to leave the passive alone, especially when trying to change it to active convolutes and confuses the meaning. But in most situations, using active voice makes for better, more memorable, and more conversational writing.

2. **Use proper grammar.** With a few minor exceptions, such as the one noted in Rule 1, writing for sports broadcasting should follow the rules of basic grammar. That means proper sentence structure, style, and word usage. Some of the more common mistakes made by sports broadcasters include:

- **Pronoun agreement.** The pronoun must agree with the subject, which can cause a lot of confusion.

  > Wrong: Pittsburgh has the ball on their 20-yard line.
  >
  > Right: Pittsburgh has the ball on *its* 20-yard line.

  Always remember that a team, group, or city referred to as a singular is an "it." More than one player, team, or group is a "their or they" ("The Steelers have the ball on *their* 20-yard line").

- **Attribution.** Attribution always goes first in broadcast writing, while newspaper writing puts it second. Since the listener or viewer only gets one chance to hear the information, it's important to know who's saying it.

    Wrong: The Rangers need a complete overhaul in the off-season, according to general manager Glen Sather.

    Right: General manager Glen Sather says the Rangers need a complete overhaul in the off-season.

    In the first sentence, the listener can't immediately tell who has the opinion, and might attribute it to the sports anchor.

3. **Use simple words and numbers.** Keep in mind that you're trying to communicate a story or idea. Using words the audience doesn't know or understand slows down and impedes the communication process. This isn't a call for simplistic or monosyllabic words, but merely a reminder that your writing will really hit home when the audience knows exactly what you're trying to say.

    Wrong: Experts say Ravens linebacker Ray Lewis prevaricated to police.

    Right: Experts say Ravens linebacker Ray Lewis lied to police.

    Wrong: Greg Maddux will make $11,555,432 this season.

    Right: Greg Maddux will make more than eleven and a half million dollars this season.

    Is it really important to know exactly how much money Greg Maddux makes, or is it more likely that too many numbers and figures will simply confuse the audience? Is it better to say that Howard Cosell was erudite or that he was well educated and well spoken? Ironically, Cosell's use of big, complicated words may have been a factor in why so many viewers disliked him. And while it may have been part of Cosell's act, in general, talking down to an audience is disrespectful and ineffective.

4. **Keep your writing clean and simple.** It's not just a matter of simple words, but using them in the right way. Too many writers try to get too complicated, with the result that the viewer suffers from information overload. Baseball author Bob Marshall points out the difference between fellow baseball writers Roger Angell and Roger Kahn. "Angell's stock-in-trade is the five-comma sentence. There is usually a clause of explanation and a clause of history that is more important than the verb. Where Angell's sentence's are languid and lazy, Kahn's are short, choppy, and dripping with drama."

    Angell: "The umpires, who were on strike for higher wages last spring, worked the spring games as usual this year, but some of them appeared to be feeling a mite irritable for the preseason, when games are conducted in a lighthearted, almost offhand fashion."

Kahn: "On a warm August night, in a southern Ontario town called Guelph, a dozen Americans are playing hockey. There are no commercial interruptions. There is no crowd. We begin, George and I, to define sport."

While Roger Angell is a delight to read, his style does not translate well to broadcasting because it would overwhelm the audience. Instead, sports broadcasters should strive for Roger Kahn's sense of economy and simplicity.

5. **Use solid reporting skills.** Good writing starts with good reporting, and often a poor final product is simply a lack of basic reporting skills. "[You need] to have an idea of how to write, how to write quickly, and how to write succinctly on deadline," says ESPN anchor Rich Eisen. "[Good writing] also promotes attention to detail and gives you a basic repertoire and background—how to seek out sources, checking sources."

In 1993, the University of Miami (Florida) conducted a survey of daily newspaper sports editors. While the survey did not specifically include sports broadcasters, its findings certainly apply to the overall sports reporting industry. Respondents strongly encouraged the importance of the "five W's" associated with basic news writing: who, what, when, where, and why. "Kids are coming out of school who don't learn the language," said Paul Anger, executive sports editor of the *Miami Herald*. "I think that journalism schools need to emphasize that [we] need people who are willing to get news no matter what."

6. **Learn about more than just sports.** A typical college student interested in sports broadcasting probably has a tremendous knowledge of sports. He or she probably became a fan at a very young age and perhaps played sports as well. But too many students make the mistake of thinking that a tremendous knowledge of sports will translate into good sports broadcasting. Without a doubt, sports broadcasters have to know about the sports they cover. But sports broadcasting now encompasses a wide variety of topics, including drugs, crime, race, politics, law, and religion. Simply put, sports broadcasters can't write effectively if they don't know anything about these other areas. "Every year, sports reporters become more diversified," says Anger. "They have to be more well rounded than any other journalist. They must be critics, reporters and feature writers."

Men such as Cosell, Jack Whitaker, and Jim McKay (see Chapter 16) succeeded as sports journalists because of their interest and background in other areas. Such interests add an important depth and knowledge to your sports writing.

7. **Don't forget creativity and originality.** Many of today's problems with writing are due to a lack of effort on the part of the writer. It's much

simpler and faster (especially when facing a deadline) to recycle old material than to come up with something new. That's why the audience hears so many sports clichés (see Table 4-1).

Creativity does not necessarily mean going over the top. Some simple creative ideas include doing a story in rhyme, using more alliteration, or remembering the "rule of threes." Which of the following sounds more appealing?

"The Cougars showed a lot of poise in their win over Central."

"The calm and collected Cougars showed a lot of poise."

There are literally hundreds of ways to make your writing more exciting and interesting. Just make sure that whatever you do fits in with the general mood and tone of the story. Certain types of writing are inappropriate for certain types of stories, such as taking a light-hearted approach to a very serious story. But in general, don't be afraid to experiment. Creative writing isn't limited to feature stories.

Table 4-1 Sports Clichés to Avoid

Cliché	Comments
"He . . . could go . . . all . . . the . . . way!"	Hear this one and you automatically think of ESPN's Chris Berman. Ironically, Berman began using it as a composite parody of other football announcers. But today it's virtually his trademark.
"Back . . . back . . . back"	Another Berman trademark, which he borrowed from someone else. Berman credits the line to legendary Dodgers announcer Red Barber, who used it in the 1947 World Series. Still used by sportscasters to describe a potential home run.
"You're the man!"	For some reason, spectators on the golf course like to shout this at players after they hit their shots. Much like a poor golf shot, its use has slowly started to fade.
"Whoa Nellie!"	Football announcer Keith Jackson swears he never actually used this line. But even if he didn't, it's so connected to his name that it loses any sense of originality (see Chapter 16).
"Show me the money!"	Not quite as overused as some others, but still identified with the movie *Jerry Maguire*.

Table 4-1 *(continued)*

Cliché	*Comments*
"The thrill of victory and the agony of defeat"	The famous opening lines from *ABC's Wide World of Sports*. Actually, it's so old it's become somewhat fresh again.
"Beaten like a rented mule"	Hockey announcers made this popular to describe a goalie beaten on a shot. It's been so overused, it's the only thing some fans know about the entire sport.
"Dead red," "High cheese," "Chin music," etc.	Any number of baseball terms commonly used by players that have worked their way into the media. The audience can always tell when a sportscaster borrows a term he doesn't know anything about.
"Be the ball."	Hardcore *Caddyshack* aficionados recognize this line, which some sportscasters still use 20 years after the movie came out.
"Goooaaaaallllllllllll!"	Soccer announcer Andres Cantor first made this popular during the 1994 World Cup. He still makes it sound so fresh and interesting, that any imitation pales in comparison.
"from downtown . . ."	Despite the fact that NBA announcer Marv Albert has made this his trademark (see Chapter 16), sportscasters insist on using it to describe any long shots. What's worse, they try to imitate Albert's voice while doing it.
"Gentlemen . . . start your engines"	Made famous at the Indianapolis 500, this line still gets a lot of play, and not just for auto racing.
"The fat lady is singing"	Or any variation such as "it's not over until the fat lady sings." It's hard to trace this one back to the source, but most credit baseball great Yogi Berra. But what was once a cute saying has become a hackneyed phrase.
anything ever said by Dick Vitale	"Diaper dandy," "Windex," "PTPer" were all introduced by Vitale (see Chapter 16). They seem to work for him, but not for anyone else.

8. **Humanize your writing.** We will make the point throughout this book that all stories are essentially about people. Sports stories are not so much about games, championships, or records as they are about people involved. Your writing should not only focus on the people involved, but it should connect to the people in the audience. Why should the people sitting at home care about this story? What does it mean to them? Write *about* the people behind the events and write *for* the people watching at home.

9. **Sometimes less is more.** One of the most common mistakes young sports broadcasters make is to write too much. They feel like they have to analyze every play, describe every piece of video, and explain every sound bite. Remember, in television and radio the words are only one component of the overall presentation. Think of your story as a recipe, with the words as one of the ingredients, along with sound, pictures, and graphics. Sometimes, you need to use more words and other times, hardly any at all.

   In general, pictures and sounds have more impact than words. So, when you have very strong video and audio, keep your writing to a minimum and let the other elements tell the story. When your sound and pictures are poor, you'll have to write more to compensate. Consider a story on a local high school soccer game. If there is an especially dramatic game-winning goal followed by a celebration, you really don't need to write a lot of description; let the video tell the story. But if the game is more mundane and the video unexciting, the story may need more help from your writing.

   Ideally, all of the ingredients should come together to make an enticing final product. But if you don't use them in the right way, the end result can leave a bad taste in the viewer's mouth.

10. **Carefully consider outside elements.** Things such as music, graphics, and standups can really help your writing, but should be used with caution. Any of these outside elements should only be considered if they add something to the story. For example, many sportscasters have gotten in the habit of putting a music track under highlights or in feature stories. Many times, music can add a lot to the story, but more often than not, it becomes a distraction. But by far the biggest offender is the standup.

    Too many sports reporters fall into the trap of putting a standup into every story. There can be a variety of reasons for this—it could be a matter of station policy, the reporter is too lazy to do the extra writing, or he or she simply wants more television "face time." Standups should be used sparingly and *only* when they add something to the story. There are valid reasons for using a standup in a story, such as when it's important to place the reporter at the scene, there's an extremely tight deadline, or there's a lack of quality video. When a standup is used, it presents extra challenges for the writer, who must have the story planned out in his or her mind at the time the standup is shot. Too many times, the reporter doesn't have a plan in mind and later tries to fit an inappropriate standup into the story.

Never let a standup, or any other outside element, take the place of good writing. It may require more work, but doing the extra writing usually makes for a better final product.

LEADS AND TERMINOLOGY

Writing for sports broadcasting can come in various forms. But before we go on, some explanation of terminology is important (the abbreviations are common producing shorthand that appear on the rundown):

Reader (RDR)—A written story with no video, audio, or graphic elements.

Voice over (VO)—A story in which the anchor reads a portion of the copy over video, usually in the form of highlights.

Voice over/Sound on tape (VO/SOT)—A voice over with the added element of a short interview on tape (sound bite).

Package (PKG)—A self-contained, taped story that includes some combination of video, audio, graphics, and natural sound. Usually done by a reporter and introduced by the anchor.

Full screen graphics (FSCG)—Full-page graphic information that the anchor talks over during a story. It usually involves complicated numerical or statistical information that requires more explanation. The CG stands for "character generator," and refers to any written or printed material that appears on the screen. It's also commonly referred to as "chyron" or "supers."

Natural sound (NATS)—The sound that occurs "naturally" at the scene of a story, such as crowd reaction, coaches yelling, or the sounds of the game.

No matter whether the broadcasters use a reader, VO, VO/SOT, or package, all written stories start with a lead. The lead is the first few lines of the copy that set up the rest of the story. Most print journalists were taught to put some form of the "5 W's" in the lead and that form still works for newspaper writing. But in broadcasting, such writing would overwhelm the listener with too much information. Therefore, the main job of writing a sports broadcasting lead is to create interest and attention that compels the listener to stick with the story.

There are several different types of broadcast leads, each of which depends on the tone or style of the story involved. The hard lead is basically a summary of the story in a no-nonsense delivery and is usually reserved for the most serious or important stories.

Hard sports lead: "A jury in Atlanta today acquitted Ravens linebacker Ray Lewis of first degree murder charges."

By contrast, the soft lead is as its name implies and is used primarily for softer, more feature-oriented stories.

Soft sports lead: "Compared to his recent battles with cancer, Lance Armstrong must look at the Tour de France like a ride through the park."

You can see how foolish it would be to use a soft lead for the Lewis story or a hard lead for the Armstrong story. Similarly, you would not want to use a humorous lead for a serious sports story.

Humorous lead: "Who could have guessed before the tournament started that Tiger Woods could shoot a 15 on the final hole and still win the U.S. Open?"

Some leads lend themselves to different types of stories, such as the throwaway lead or umbrella lead. In the throwaway lead, an innocuous line is used before the real story begins. An umbrella lead combines several different points of the same story.

Throwaway lead: "More trouble tonight for Yankees second baseman Chuck Knoblauch. He made three more errors to raise his league-leading total to 16."

Umbrella lead: "While the Lakers worry about Kobe Bryant's injured foot, they also have concerns about Shaq's continuing problems from the free throw line."

There is one type of lead that should be used only in rare situations, if at all. The question lead is dangerous, because it could ask a question that turns off or disinterests the audience.

Question lead: "Could anyone have played a better game tonight than Eric Lindros?"

In this case, the audience could think, "Yes," or even worse, not have any interest in the answer. It's much better to rephrase the question as a statement.

New lead: "It seems impossible that anyone could have played a better game tonight than Eric Lindros."

No matter what type of story, the lead should involve the hook of the story. The hook is simply the main or most interesting part of the story.

Each story has several angles, but usually one sticks out as the central theme. This is the one that should be emphasized in the lead, if possible.

> Poor lead: "More than 15 thousand people watched the Rangers beat Ottawa tonight."

> Better lead: "A hat trick from Adam Graves keyed the Rangers big win tonight over Ottawa."

Unless the attendance figure is the central issue of the game, it doesn't belong up top. In some cases, extremely high or low attendance figures are important, but even then they are rarely used in the lead.

As mentioned, the type of lead used should correspond to the tone and style of the story. Young sportscasters often fall into the trap of cramming too much information in a lead, which either overwhelms the listener or gives away too much of the story. Always remember that the lead exists mainly to compel attention and keep the audience tuned in. Save the details for the rest of the story.

> Poor lead: "Randy Johnson won his biggest ballgame of the season tonight, as he allowed only 1 run and struck out 13 in a 5-1 win over San Francisco."

> Better lead: "Randy Johnson may have won his biggest ballgame of the season tonight."

In the second example, the lead indicates that Johnson pitched well and won, but saves the details for the rest of the story.

Another pitfall for young sportscasters is the plain, or boring lead. The facts and information may be correct, but the lead fails to generate any interest or excitement. Consider our Randy Johnson example:

> Poor lead: "Randy Johnson won his biggest ballgame of the season tonight, as he allowed only 1 run and struck out 13 in a 5-1 win over San Francisco."

> Better lead: "Randy Johnson may have won his biggest ballgame of the season tonight."

> Even better lead: "Randy Johnson's smoke could have started a brushfire in the desert tonight as he won perhaps his biggest game of the season." or "That smoke in the desert tonight didn't come from any Arizona brushfire, but rather from the strong pitching of Randy Johnson."

The vivid images of "smoke," "brushfire," and "desert" all tie in with the theme (good pitching, game involving Arizona Diamondbacks, etc.) and compel much more attention than the vanilla version. The body of the story should be written in traditional broadcast style—short, choppy, and conversational. Think more Roger Kahn than Roger Angell.

PACKAGES, VOs, AND VO/SOTs

All forms of broadcast sports writing should have the same basic elements: beginning (lead), middle, and end. But writing stories that include taped elements requires a little more effort and imagination than writing for a reader.

> **Voice over:** The main focus of writing a VO is to make sure the script matches closely with the video. Ideally, the writer should find a middle ground between writing too specifically for video (the script exactly matches the pictures), and writing too generally (the words and pictures have no relationship at all). Remember, when the viewer can see exactly what's happening, too much description is overkill.

> Poor writing: "Here Smith takes the handoff from Aikman . . . dodges a tackle at the 15, stumbles for a bit . . . then regains his balance and goes into the end zone for a touchdown" (too specific).

> Poor writing: "The Cowboys offense has looked great so far this year and they lead the league in scoring" (too general).

> Better writing: "The Cowboys lead the league in scoring this year and added to that total when Emmitt Smith broke this nice run to make it 14-0."

The first example is more like play-by-play and gives us too much detail. The second example is a little better, but doesn't relate the information to what's happening in the video. It would be much better if it mentioned something about Smith or the score. The third example is the best of both worlds: not too specific and not too general, with some added information for more depth.

> **Voice over-sound on tape:** The VO/SOT requires the same writing to video as the VO and adds the element of a sound bite (taped interview). The main trick of writing for sound bites is the lead-in, or the words that come right before the sound bite. In radio, sound bites (or actualities) have to be preceded by the name of the speaker for identification purposes.

> Radio: "The Lady Volunteers have a tough road ahead, according to coach Pat Summitt." (Actuality) or "According to coach Pat Summitt, the Lady Volunteers have a rough road ahead." (Actuality)

In such situations, it's important to identify the speaker, because the audience has no way of knowing who it is. No such restrictions apply in television, where the speaker is clearly identified by chyron or CG.

Thus, television sports writers can be much more general in introducing a sound bite, and can even omit reference to the name.

Television: "And the Lady Volunteers know they have a tough road ahead."
(Sound bite—Pat Summitt)

In the rare cases where the chyron malfunctions and no name appears on the screen, the sportscaster can simply tell the audience once the sound bite ends.

Television: "And the Lady Volunteers know they have a tough road ahead."
(Soundbite) "By the way, that was head coach Pat Summitt."

In either television or radio, it's important not to introduce the sound bite by repeating what's in the interview.

Poor writing: "The Lady Volunteers say they're fired up and ready for the NCAA tournament." (Soundbite: "We're fired up and ready for the NCAA tournament. We think we can go a long way—even to the national title.")

In this case, the introduction to the sound bite simply duplicates what's on tape. Try to introduce the sound bite in a more general way, by leading into the interview or by adding new information.

Better writing: "The Lady Volunteers seem excited as they head to their 16th straight post-season appearance." (Sound bite: "We're fired up and ready for the NCAA tournament. We think we can go a long way—even to the national title.")

Packages: Because the package combines all the other elements of video, audio, and sound, it's the most difficult and time-consuming format to write. There are no hard-and-fast rules for writing packages, but it's good to keep in mind some of the things we've already mentioned:

Remember your leads

Write to video

Emphasize your best elements (video, interviews, natural sound, etc.)

Take time for natural sound breaks

Keep your writing short, choppy, and conversational

Young writers also worry about the length of a package, figuring that they better make it nice and long to impress their boss and the audience. As a result, they often put in way too much information and over-load the audience. Most often, less is more—and better.

SCRIPTING

No matter what form of story you use, it has to be properly scripted. That is, it must be written in a way that the director can understand. Any story, no matter how brilliantly written, is useless if the technical director can't figure out how to get it on the air.

Each station has its own specific way of scripting, but as a whole, the in-dustry follows a general standard. Take a blank piece of paper and draw an imaginary vertical line down the center. Everything on the right side of the sheet is the copy written for broadcast. It's what will appear in the tele-prompter and what the anchors will say on the air. Everything on the left side is technical information for the director. Each story comes with its own directions, but they usually include most of the following information (see Table 4-2 and Table 4-3):

Talent/Camera: This is indicated in the upper left-hand corner of the script and indicates what anchor is reading the story and on what camera. The name of the anchor is usually indicated by initials.

When to roll tape: If there is a tape in the story, the director must know when to roll it. This can be indicated by the abbreviation VO (for a voice over) or PKG (for a package).

How long the tape runs: This is indicated by a block of time, such as [1:23] or [:14]. For a VO/SOT, the time indication tells how long the sound bite runs. In a package, it shows how long before the report ends and the an-chor resumes talking.

Table 4-2   Example of Scripted Television Package

BES	
Cam-1	A tremendous effort today by the Central High track team led to a surprising—and emotional—win at the state track meet. Joe Jones has the story.
PKG	
[1:31]	
outq: STD	
CG: Springfield	
CG: Jim Smith/Wins Pole Vault	
CG: John Johnson/Central Coach	

Table 4-3   Example of VO/SOT Scripted for Television

BES Cam-1	When Jim Smith soared more than 15 feet in the pole vault today, it wiped away more than 75 years of frustration for Central High at the state track meet.
VO CG: Springfield	Smith's vault not only won him the gold medal in the event . . . but it clinched the overall track title for Central—the first state track title in school history.
SOT [:20] outq: "it's unbelievable" CG: Jim Smith/Wins Pole Vault	
VO	Smith was Central's only gold medal winner, but his win helped the Cougars edge Little Springs for the overall title . . . 121 points to 119.

How the tape ends: The outcue (or outq) tells the director the last few words of the report, so he knows when it ends. For a package, the outcue is often standard (or STD), which is the station's usual sign-off language ("For Channel 13 Sports, I'm Joe Jones)." For a VO/SOT, the outcue is simply the final few words of the sound bite.

Proper CGs: The director must also know what chyrons are needed in the story and where they must appear. Chyrons can be locators (where the story is taking place), proper names, or full-screen graphics. Most newsrooms now have computer software that automatically formats the script in the proper format. But care must be taken to load the correct information into the computer to avoid embarrassing technical errors. Nothing is more frustrating than working all day on an important story, only to see the report fouled up in the control room. And in probably 90 percent of such situations, the reporter is more at fault than the director.

THE BOTTOM LINE

Writing for sports broadcasts isn't that much different than writing for other broadcasts, simply because so many of the same rules apply. Depending on your point of view, that may be bad news or good news. Given the current state of electronic media writing, sports broadcasters have nowhere to go but up.

REFERENCES

"Careers in Sports: TV Sports Anchor." ESPN. [Online]. Available: www.espn.go.com/special/s/careers/anchor.html, September 7, 1999.

Marshall, Bob. *Diary of a Yankee-hater.* New York: Franklin Watts, 1981.

Prato, Lou. "The Business of Broadcasting." *American Journalism Review,* November 1995.

Salwen, Michael and Garrison, Bruce. Survey Examines Extent of Professionalism in Sports Journalism. *Editor & Publisher, 27 (3),* January 15, 1994.

5

Reporting

THE STATUS OF SPORTS REPORTING

We have already discussed how sports, and to an extent sports coverage, is defined by social and cultural values (see Chapters 2 and 3). Thus, when we discuss sports reporting we must always consider the context of a social dynamic. But there are other factors that also affect and influence sports reporting, especially technological developments.

Most obviously, the introduction and growth of electronic media changed the nature of sports reporting. When newspapers had a monopoly on sports, reporting was fairly simple. Sports reporters would concentrate on the basic facts of the game, knowing that fans who hadn't heard or seen the game wanted as much detail as possible. And with deadlines usually hours away, reporters had plenty of time to think about and polish their stories. But things changed dramatically when radio and television came along. Many fans by now had heard the game or at least knew the basic details. "In the era of television and radio," said veteran baseball writer Roger Kahn, "you don't say, 'The Dodgers beat the Giants, 6 to 2,' you say, 'Yesterday, in the Dodgers 6-2 win over the Giants, the most interesting thing that happened was . . .' That's the best definition of what a morning story of a ballgame ought to be. [Baseball writer Dick Young] worked that out by himself and that was the 'New Journalism.'"

According to Kahn, the "New Journalism" included a frankness and critical eye that had never been seen in journalism before. Instead of the "gee-whiz" approach, which dominated sports reporting in the first half of the twentieth century, reporters now criticized, analyzed, debated, and put sports under the microscope for public inspection. All because the developing forms of new media forced sports reporters to think differently about the way they did their jobs. In short, the new media forced sports reporters to actually report.

The leading proponent of this change was Dick Young, who had as many admiring readers as he had indignant managers, players, and baseball executives. Certainly, Young did not invent sports criticism, but rather sharpened and refined it into a new way of reporting. Young covered the Brooklyn Dodgers for the *New York Daily News* and according to Kahn, "If a player had a weakness, Young would write about it, explain it, describe it, analyze it . . . and certain players began to distrust him." Michael Shapiro, who has written sports for the *New York Times* and *Sports Illustrated*, said, "It's hard to imagine today's [sports talk] callers—let alone the mercifully silent listeners—being satisfied with the sort of sports writing of the era before 1950, before Dick Young made his way from the comfort of the press box down to the clubhouse, shoved his mug in a ballplayer's face and asked, 'What were you doing trying to steal third with two men out?'"

Others followed Young's lead, men such as Maury Allen, Leonard Shecter, and most notably Jim Murray of the *Los Angeles Times*. Television and radio seemed to geometrically multiply the number of sports reporters, many of whom now carried cameras and microphones instead of notebooks. Where athletes could once enjoy a nice talk after a game with two or three newspaper reporters, suddenly there were a dozen or more people jostling for position, all trying to position a microphone as close as possible. Locker rooms became war zones as players and coaches increasingly clashed with a growing number of reporters. Bill Plaschke covered the Dodgers for more than a decade in Los Angeles and said, "We're everywhere; we surround them as they are preparing for a game; we barely give them room to dress afterwards; and we're not looking to make friends, but front pages."

The once close relationship between players and media has deteriorated into a cold, distant atmosphere which sometimes breaks into open hostility. "We feel like targets," said major league pitcher David Cone. "A lot of times [the media are] looking for a reason to get on you. Negativity sells." Plaschke noted that former Dodger outfielder Raul Mondesi threatened to beat him up after a critical column. Other players and coaches, notably men like Kirk Gibson, Bobby Knight, Albert Belle, and Bobby Bonilla have cultivated hostile relationships with the media. Reporters recognize and understand the relationship: ask these people a question only at your own risk.

Another important factor to consider is the shrinking deadline. When newspaper reporters had hours to file a story, it gave them the opportunity to carefully consider their comments. Television and radio not only changed the way reporters did their business, they changed the deadline. In many cases, reporters had minutes instead of hours, eliminating the possibility of any circumspection. And now the Internet has shrunk the deadline in some cases to only seconds. The growth of technology has created a sports fan that demands access to instant information. While fans of the 20s and 30s had to wait for the next day's newspaper, today's fan can get information on almost any sports subject from the Internet in a matter of seconds.

As a result, sports coverage now often drifts from reporting into rumor and innuendo. Shrinking deadlines, more media outlets, and demanding fans make it impossible to simply report sports. There isn't enough sports information to go around, either for the media or the fans. Combined with the general trend toward entertainment reporting so prevalent in the media (see Chapter 3), sports reporting more and more lapses into tabloid reports of scandal, celebrity, and crime. Many sports reporters and outlets say it's simply a matter of giving the public what it wants. Linda Verigan, letters manager at *Sports Illustrated*, says the core of the magazine's 3.3 million readers take exception to space devoted to stories about anything less than "honorable."

The magazine received letters for months about the NBC interview between reporter Jim Gray and Pete Rose. During ceremonies at the 1999 World Series to honor baseball's "All-Century" team, Gray managed to get a live, on-field interview with Rose, who was still officially banned from baseball for allegedly betting on games. Gray repeatedly asked Rose about his involvement and whether it was an appropriate time to admit his guilt, a line of questioning that offended Rose. Letters to *Sports Illustrated,* and much of the reaction across the country, criticized Gray for his timing and his persistence. Rob Neyer of ESPN wrote that the incident "sickened, repulsed, and disgusted" him. But Shapiro took a different approach. "What if Gray had not pushed Rose?" he asked. "What if he had reduced himself, as so many of his colleagues have, to the role of asking, 'So, big fella, heckuva night, huh?' Reporting is neither about deference nor is it always about asking nicely. It is about finding out. We need, we want to know, be it profane or sacred." Gray later apologized for perhaps "spoiling the moment," but not for his line of questioning. The following is a partial transcript of the interview:

JIM GRAY: Pete, the overwhelming evidence that's in that report . . . why not make that step tonight?

PETE ROSE: This is too festive a night to worry about that, because I don't know what evidence you're talking about. I mean, show it to me.

GRAY: We don't want to debate that Pete.

ROSE: Well, why not? Why do we want to believe everything he says?

GRAY: You signed a paper acknowledging the ban. Why did you sign it if you didn't agree?

ROSE: But it also says I can apply for reinstatement after one year. If you remember correctly in the press conference . . . as a matter of fact, my statement was 'I can't wait for my little girl to be a year old so I can apply for reinstatement.' So you forgot to add that in there.

GRAY: You applied for reinstatement in 1997. Have you heard back from commissioner Selig?

ROSE: No. That kind of surprised me. It's only been two years. He has a lot on his mind. I hope to someday.

GRAY: Pete, it's been ten years since you've been allowed on the field. Obviously, the approach you've taken has not worked. Why not take a different approach?

ROSE: You say it hasn't worked . . . what do you exactly mean?

GRAY: You're not allowed in baseball, not allowed to earn a living in the game you love, and you're not allowed to be in the Hall of Fame.

ROSE: That's why I applied for reinstatement and I hope Bud Selig considers that and gives me an opportunity. I won't need a third chance; all I need is a second chance.

GRAY: Pete, those who will hear this tonight will say you've been your own worst enemy and continue to be. How do you respond to that?

ROSE: In what way are you talking about?

GRAY: By not acknowledging what seems to be overwhelming evidence.

ROSE: You know, I'm surprised you're bombarding me like this. I mean, I'm doing the interview with you on a great night, a great occasion, a great ovation, everybody seems to be in a great mood, and you're bringing up something that happened ten years ago.

GRAY: I'm bringing it up because I think people would like to see . . . Pete, we've got to go; we've got a game.

ROSE: This is a prosecutor's brief, it isn't an interview and I'm very surprised at you. I am, really.

GRAY: Some would be surprised you didn't take the opportunity. Let's go upstairs to Hannah. Congratulations, Pete.

(*Source:* Courtesy NBC/MLB)

Shapiro's point is that we have sacrificed serious sports journalism to consumer demand, prurient interests, and most especially the bottom line. Simply put, serious sports reporting does not sell as well as the fluff. It's a lesson Howard Cosell discovered during his career, much of which he spent trying to report on serious sports issues. In 1981, Cosell and ABC launched *Sports Beat,* a show dedicated to serious sports journalism. The show focused on issues such as drugs, gender equity, and the relationship between sports and politics. But while Cosell and the show won several awards, it never became a ratings success. "[The show] will never make money or attract ratings," Cosell later wrote. "It has neither. You do it because it's right and it's a public responsibility. The obligation exists to throw a searchlight [on sports]. Anybody who would call himself a journalist has the duty to act as a watchdog, protecting the public interest."

To be sure, many reporters today produce outstanding programs dedicated to serious sports journalism. ESPN's *Outside the Lines*, has investigated several important issues and even the network's regular reporting often exposes abuses in the sports world, such as its exclusive report in 1999 regarding the University of Tennessee athletic department and the tutoring of players. But for the most part, these are the exceptions rather than the rule. Cosell said that reporters would always cater to the fans, the money, and the games themselves. The situation between Gray and Rose, according to Shapiro, was "a metaphor for the inescapable and enduring tension between what we want sports to be and what we want sports stories to tell us. Sports [journalism] has tossed a quilt over genuine concerns and allowed [us] to consider issues that have absolutely no bearing on our lives."

THE CONCEPTS OF SPORTS REPORTING

No matter which side of the fence you sit on, sports reporting for the electronic media involves the same variety of technical and journalistic practices. These are duties required to get the story on the air—photography, editing, interviewing, and the actual process of reporting. Later in this book we will discuss photography and editing at some length (see Chapter 7). But even if the sports reporter has no concept of photography and doesn't know one end of the camera from another, he or she can still make the job a lot easier by establishing rapport and communication with the photographer.

Planning Ahead

Many reporting problems are simply a lack of communicating what shot or angle to get for a story and can be eliminated by talking with the photographer beforehand. Make sure the shooter knows exactly what you want from the story—the story angle, what shots you have in mind, and any specific shots that would require extra effort to get. Certainly, some photographers will balk at being "told what to do." But ideally the reporter and photographer should work together to report as a team and most photographers will not object to anything that makes them and the final product look better. This involves more than just bossing around the photographer; it means having an idea for your story before you get to the scene. Plan the story out in your mind, including pictures, natural sound, and interviews. Often, this process doesn't occur until you get to the scene and get a feel for the story.

And many times the final product won't look anything like what you had mapped out. But preparation is one of the key elements in sports reporting. You would never go to a story without knowing something about the facts beforehand; you should take the same approach with the video and audio elements. Once you get into the edit bay and don't have the material you need, it's too late.

Assume you have been assigned to do a feature story for the evening newscast on a local gymnast training for the Olympic games. You have most of the facts and information you need for the story, but what other information should you consider before you and the photographer begin working? It's helpful to sketch out what elements you'll need to put the story together (see Table 5-1).

Keep in mind all of this could change, depending on what you find when you get to the story. You might not have any access to file video of her performances, or technical problems could ruin some of your audio elements. A lot of reporting has to be done "on the fly," once the reporter and photographer assess what's available to them at the scene. But it's never appropriate to go into a story blind, and many times stories will work out just as you planned them out ahead of time.

Given this situation, how should the reporter put the story together? Always remember to emphasize your best elements. Do you have better video or interviews? It may seem strange not to have a lot of comments from the principal subject of the story, but kids are notorious for giving short, two-second answers. If the video and sound are fairly strong, it's also advisable to forego the music and a standup. Those are elements better used when you don't have strong video or audio. If the sound and pictures are especially good, you might consider a natural sound piece and eliminate the narration. It proves very effective to let the subjects tell the story in their own words.

The same principle applies to natural sound—the sound that occurs "naturally" at the scene of any story. For a football game, it could be the roaring crowds or marching bands. At a golf match, it's the long periods of silence followed by cheers or groans. Natural sound (or "nat sound") has

Table 5-1   Planning Ahead

Possible Video Elements	*Possible Interviews*	*Possible Natural Sound*	*Possible Outside Elements*
Gymnast practicing	Gymnast	Coach during practice	Music
Shots of ribbons medals, etc.	Coach	Gymnast during practice	Video of famous gymnasts competing
Olympic video file	Parents	Previous competitions	
Video of gymnast competing locally	Other gymnasts		

become much more important over the years in electronic sports reporting. Up until a few years ago, most sports reporters ignored nat sound and instead used canned music or just plain silence. But later generations of reporters and news directors realized that natural sound could make or break a story. The cheers of a crowd, the smash of a hockey player hitting the boards, or the sound of the water splashing when a diver hits a perfect dive all contribute to the scene and the mood of the story. Modern-day reporting involves taking occasional pauses to let the nat sound come up to full volume. Just as good play-by-play broadcasters pause after a dramatic moment so listeners can hear the crowd, so too can the sports reporter use nat sound in putting together the daily story.

Occasionally, the reporter finds that he or she has such dramatic video and natural sound that he decides to use them exclusively without any narration. Such pieces can be more effective than the run-of-the-mill story, but the reporter should take caution in such situations. If you have good video and good nat sound, there's no harm in emphasizing them. But such stories are very difficult and shouldn't be done often without a lot of experience in the basics of reporting and editing. There's nothing better than a dramatic "sound and pictures" piece when it's done right, but there's also nothing worse when it's done wrong. As with any reporting or editing technique, nat sound should usually be used in moderation or it distracts from the message the reporter wants to communicate. Never forget you're trying to communicate a story or idea to the audience and shouldn't use any technique that takes away from that.

Usually stories include some combination of narration, video, natural sound, and interviews. The interview has become one of the main elements of sports reporting, much to the disdain of some journalists. During the 60s, the new style of reporting focused on how the athletes and coaches "reacted" to the games, which involved lots of quotes and interviews, but little analysis. Dick Young derisively called this new generation "chipmunks." The chipmunks didn't really take time to figure out why something happened, as long as they had plenty of interviews with all the parties involved.

Preparing to Interview

The proliferation of media in modern society has turned sports reporting more toward analysis and critical thinking, but a majority of the industry still relies on the chipmunk style of reporting. If a batter strikes out in a key situation in the ninth inning, you interview the batter, the pitcher, and the managers after the game. Given the demands of the public and the shortening of deadlines, there's probably no better alternative for most of the sports media. And that's why it's even more important to know the key elements involved in interviewing. Some interviews you can't do anything about, like trying to wedge a microphone in a pack of two dozen reporters surrounding a player after the game. In those situations you take what you get and move on. But much sports reporting involves interviewing where you have time to plan a strategy beforehand to get the best possible responses.

You should never go into an interview without planning a strategy. At the very least, this means getting all the pertinent background and information on the subject. But it also improves the interview to consider elements such as objective and audience. For example, consider how a reporter might handle the following situations:

Situation #1. The reporter is assigned to interview a person who has just been named head coach of a popular and highly successful college basketball program. The interview will appear in the sports segment of the noon news.

Objective: Entertainment/informational

Audience: Expects positive, "feel-good" story

Tone: Light-hearted; non-confrontational

In this situation, the audience probably has high hopes for the new coach and only wants to hear good things about him (especially given the time of day). The danger for the reporter is falling into a trap of "hero-worship" and losing a sense of journalistic integrity.

Situation #2. The reporter is assigned to interview a person who has just been fired as head coach of a popular and highly successful college basketball program. The interview will appear in the 6:00 P.M. news.

Objective: Informational/possibly confrontational

Audience: Expects anger, conflict, possible confrontation

Tone: Deadly serious

Here's the complete opposite of the first situation. In this example, if the reporter does manage to get an interview, he can expect a completely different tone and atmosphere. The coach may feel he was fired unjustly and have an "axe to grind" with his former employers. Even if there's nothing sinister at work, the occasion is very tense and serious, and that's what the audience expects. The concerns for the reporter here are remaining objective and not taking sides in the dispute.

The first element in a strategy is determining the objective of the interview. Most sports interviews are designed to inform, such as "What happened in the first quarter?" or "Who's your backup goaltender this year?"

There's another segment of interviews that are purely for entertainment. When Charles Barkley goes on a late-night talk show, the host does not ask about his groin injury or his rebounding average. He asks about something interesting or funny Barkley has done lately that will entertain the audience. Another type of objective is the confrontational interview. Not many sports reporters want to intentionally provoke an athlete or coach, although sports talk show host Jim Rome might be an exception. Rome has built a national reputation on his willingness to prod and push interview subjects until they respond. (In the case of former NFL quarterback Jim Everett, the response was to physically attack Rome during the show.) Provoking an athlete is physically risky and doesn't do much to help you get further interviews. But in some situations, the reporter must be aware of the potential for a confrontational interview. If a horde of reporters is waiting outside a courthouse to get a comment from an athlete who has just testified about his own drug use, they should expect that the athlete will be reluctant and be prepared for a possible confrontation.

Much of the problems today involving interviews occur when athletes and reporters have different understandings of the objectives involved. Most likely, Pete Rose thought that when Jim Gray wanted to interview him the conversation would center on his inclusion in the "All-Century" team. Gray's objective was seemingly much different, in that he wanted to question Rose about the latter's involvement with gambling and his attempts to have his baseball suspension lifted. It's not known if Gray made his objectives clear to Rose when he asked for the interview, but it's always a good idea to let subjects know exactly what you want from the interview and not to "ambush" them, if possible.

It was also obvious during the interview that Gray had done his homework. He knew the specific details about Rose's situation, the agreement Rose signed when he was banned from baseball, and about his application for reinstatement. Rose could not argue with the facts, only Gray's assessment of them and the forum in which he chose to debate them. There is no substitute for preparation before conducting an interview. Athletes, coaches, and especially the audience can tell if a reporter doesn't have his facts and doesn't know what he's talking about. Such cases are not only embarrassing for the reporter, but also lessen his credibility; a critical mistake that could cause considerable problems in getting future interviews. ESPN's Roy Firestone was reminded of this lesson when he interviewed Indiana basketball coach Bobby Knight in the spring of 2000. Knight had come under tremendous pressure amidst allegations that he once choked a former player during practice. A videotape of the incident had circulated in the general media for quite some time, but Firestone never bothered to view the tape and could not question Knight about it. As a result, Firestone came under criticism for not approaching the subject and being too "soft" on the coach (see Figure 5-1).

Figure 5-1 Roy Firestone (Courtesy ESPN)

Another important aspect of interviewing is considering the audience for the interview. In other words, the reporter should always keep audience expectation in mind when conducting the interview. In what forum will the interview appear? Going back to the late-night talk show, the audience does not expect to hear "exclusives" or "serious journalism" when a sports guest appears on the show and it would be foolish for the host to ask such questions. But the audience for a radio sports talk show or for ESPN expects something quite different. Again, this may have played a role in the problems between Rose and Gray. The World Series attracts a national audience, not entirely comprised of "hard core" sports fans. Many in the audience were people with just a cursory knowledge of Rose or even baseball in general. Given the setting, people did not tune in to see verbal combat, which may account for the negative reaction to Gray's questioning. Did that mean Gray should not have asked what he did? There's nothing wrong with asking tough questions, but in this particular situation the audience may have felt as ambushed as Rose. Certainly, a sit-down, one-on-one interview would have been more appropriate, but perhaps Gray felt this might be his only shot with Rose and he had to take it.

Much of the negative reaction from viewers came from people who admired Rose as a ballplayer. To them, Gray had crossed the line because he had tried to bring down a man who had once been a public hero. Many of the interviewing problems sports reporters face come from the fact that most of their subjects are considered heroes and somehow above ordinary people. It's difficult to report on the playing brilliance of Michael Jordan the mega-superstar basketball player, then turn around and report on his alleged gambling problems.

In many cases, reporters spend most of their time building up a player then later having to tear him or her down. Former sports writer Gene Collier writes, "Sports journalism biblicizes Michael Jordan . . . while simultaneously building databases on the anecdotal idiocies of Dennis Rodman and Lawrence Taylor, then sells it to a sports-addled public eager for violence or competitive validation or some definitive moral scorecard." The challenge for the sports reporter is to cut through the hero-worship and resist the temptation to deify the modern athlete. This is especially difficult for professional athletes, who make millions of dollars and have become larger-than-life celebrities. But to treat them as such prevents the sports reporter from asking serious questions. And according to Collier, it also "produces a creature that expects its strengths will be celebrated and even embellished while its weaknesses will be tolerated, and that the culture exists merely to extend privileges and ignore flaring evidence of arrested development."

Between hero-worship on one end and open antagonism on the other, exists a middle ground where the sports reporter should strive to respect his interview subject. Sometimes this means nothing more than respecting the athlete's right not to talk. Some athletes and coaches, notably people like Albert Belle and Steve Carlton, simply cut off relations with the media and refuse to talk except on their own terms. One of the most successful high school football coaches in Ohio would not let the media talk to his players during the season. In these situations, discretion is the better part of valor. Respect the right not to talk and work around it. Trying to circumvent this situation only leads to more problems and further antagonizes everyone involved.

It also is important to develop respect for the subject, which means to create a relationship of trust between the reporter and the athlete. Athletes and coaches will often feel more comfortable and open up when they believe they can trust the reporter. Sports reporter Tim Cowlishaw covered the Dallas Cowboys in 1986 and 1987 and remembers the first time he had a private interview with then-coach Tom Landry. "The man whose answers seemed so predictable in the daily group interviews—although probably no more predictable than our questions—suddenly became expansive as he relaxed on his sofa." This does not necessarily mean the reporter and athlete have to develop a friendship; in fact, a friendship can be detrimental to the process if the reporter finds out some damaging information about a close friend. Athletes and reporters rarely become "friends" in the current atmosphere of sports reporting, but the reporter can still cultivate a trustful relationship. This is usually accomplished over time, as the athlete gradually understands that the reporter treats him fairly and isn't out to "get him." As part of this process, it's important for the reporter to adhere to some reasonable limits imposed by the athlete. Reporters should try to honor an athlete's requests concerning when or where the interview takes place, such as if the athlete doesn't want to be contacted at home or wants to wait a reasonable amount of time after a game to grant an interview.

A much thornier issue is when an athlete or coach requests that certain information be "kept off the record." In keeping with journalistic tradition, most reporters respect a request to keep information off the record. They attribute the story to "anonymous sources" or file it away for future use. This approach has always come under fire from journalistic purists who insist that any information worth printing or broadcasting should have a name attached to it. The situation can also cause problems as to exactly who's respecting the request to withhold information and who's not. If one station obeys a request and another does not, it creates an embarrassing situation in which the competing stations appear either naïve or unethical. In a typical situation involving former University of Texas football coach Darrell Royal, reporters noticed during practice that several players had switched positions. Royal said, "I don't want that in the newspaper" and the student newspaper complied. But the bigger *Austin American-Statesman* reported on the situation, which in the words of author Robert Heard made the student paper look "foolish." The student paper later apologized to its readers and Royal solved the problem by closing practices to reporters.

As with most journalistic situations, the individual reporter must make a decision he or she thinks works best given the circumstances. It certainly seemed to make sense to report the Royal information, but other reporters will comply with requests to withhold something if they feel it's to their bigger advantage to build trust with the interview subject. As with most ethical situations involving journalists, there seem to be no hard and fast rules covering every situation (see Chapter 11).

Reporters can use such tactics if they have time to develop a trustful relationship with a subject. But much of sports reporting is "hit and run." Sports reporters often interview subjects they have never met and don't know that much about. And while it's impossible to establish a long-lasting trust in such situations, there are some things the reporter can do to put the subject at ease. One thing is to engage the athlete in idle conversation before the cameras or tape recorders start rolling. Such "pre-interviews" involve topics like family, common interests, the weather—anything to put the subject a little more at ease. Sometimes, athletes get so caught up in these harmless conversations that they don't even realize the camera has started rolling (and yes, it's imperative that you always make sure the subject knows the interview has begun).

Another way of putting someone at ease in a hit and run interview is to save the tough questions for the end. Starting with harmless and innocuous questions automatically puts the subject at ease and lessens his fears that you're out to get him. When you eventually get to the tough question, you're chances of getting a willing and thoughtful response increase. Plaschke recalls the game he covered in which a player hit a home run, but later committed an error that cost the game. In the locker room afterwards, Plaschke asked first about the home run and says that the player was then "relaxed (enough) to be revealing and insightful when answering my next question about the error." There's also a very practical reason for this tactic: starting with a difficult or embarrassing question opens the possibility that the subject will terminate the interview and leave you with nothing. If the same thing happens when the question comes at the end of the interview, at least you've got something on tape you can use. In some cases, a reporter who has only one question to ask will start with a series of softball questions anyway to improve his chances of getting a good answer to the only question he really wants to ask.

There are all kinds of theories about what kinds of questions to ask in an interview. Obviously, no one wants a player or coach to glare at him or her after a game and ask, "Where did you come up with that?" But that simply comes with the territory of being a sports reporter and it will happen to anyone who does enough interviews. We're really not talking about dumb questions but rather "obvious" questions. Athletes get most upset at having to hear questions they feel the reporters should be able to answer themselves. Former major league pitcher Jim Bouton once described a situation in which a teammate made a crucial error that lost a ballgame. As writers converged on the player after the game for an interview, other teammates came to his defense. "What the hell do they need quotes for?" asked Tommy Harper. "They all saw the play."

Interview Approaches

The essence of good interviewing is to find the things that aren't so obvious. There are few things as redundant, as boring, and unfortunately as commonplace as the quick on-field interview after a game in which the reporter asks the hero to describe the technical points of a dramatic moment; the same moment just witnessed or heard by millions of people. Interviewers should strive to get responses that tell us something we don't know or something that adds a level of depth to the scene. Instead of asking the player what kind of pitch he hit for the game-winning homer, ask him about what it was like to play after he sprained his knee in the third inning.

Make no mistake, sometimes you have to ask the obvious question anyway. "How does it feel?" "What were you thinking?" "What was it like?" Remember that it's not the question that counts anyway. Sports reporters don't win awards for asking the most penetrating questions. All reporters are trying to do is elicit the best possible response from the subject and if it takes a dumb question to do it, so be it (see Table 5-2).

No player likes to get bombarded right out of the box about the big error he made or how he lost the game. Let players warm up to an interview before you ask the tough questions (assuming you have time).

Too often, reporters get bogged down in the strategy and technical details of a game. Print reporters especially love this, because they have so much space to fill and their readers have time to carefully analyze complicated ideas. But broadcast viewers or listeners have no such luxury, and most of them probably don't care anyway. Don't lose the forest for the trees; most people want to see the big picture. Strategy and detail do have a place, but only in limited situations such as an expanded specialty show, when the audience has the time and desire for it.

Again, don't get too caught up in analyzing plays. Remember, a television audience can see what happened, and except in extraordinary circumstances, the pictures don't need further embellishment. Concentrate more on the motivations and explanations behind the action that provide the viewer or listener with an emotional connection. With some notable exceptions, most details about a game are soon forgotten.

One of the best techniques in interviewing is called the "Golden Moment." That's where the interviewer simply stops talking or asking questions and gives the subject time to respond. It may seem awkward to have

Table 5-2 Interviewing Approaches

Poor Approach	*Better Approach*
(First question) "What about that key mistake you made that lost the game?"	"You really seemed to play well in the early going. Talk a little about that."
"On that 3rd-and-10 play in the 2nd quarter, you seemed to be in the wrong defense."	"That 3rd-and-10 play in the 2nd quarter really seemed like a big play . . . how important was it?"
"What happened here . . . describe this play . . . etc."	"How does it feel . . . what does it mean . . . what happens now?"

long moments of silence after a response, but it indicates to the subject that you expect him to keep going. Often times, responses become better and more thoughtful after such pauses.

ON THE BEAT

While the components of sports reporting are essentially the same, not all sports reporters use them in the same way. Much depends on what kind of sports reporting is being done: beat reporting, event reporting, or feature reporting.

Beat sports reporting is very common in the print media, but somewhat rare for radio and television. Reporting a "beat" essentially means the sports reporter covers the same story or team every day, such as a reporter who would constantly follow a professional sports team. Beat reporting is rare for the electronic media because the beat system requires a large staff capable of confining reporters to a single subject. With the exception of the larger markets, most radio and television stations don't have enough sports reporters to assign them to beats. In addition to financial and staff considerations, most electronic media outlets want their reporters to be "generalists"—people capable of covering a wide variety of sports stories. Even reporters in the larger markets generally can't limit themselves exclusively to a single topic.

Covering the sports beat requires a lot of research, legwork, and old-fashioned reporting. As opposed to the more carefully crafted and thoughtful pieces, beat stories are cranked out daily with an emphasis on information instead of inspiration. The most important consideration in covering a sports beat is to develop and maintain effective working relationships with the subjects you're covering. Working the beat means seeing the same players, coaches, and administrators day after day. Reporters must use this time to create an atmosphere of trust, without which the task of uncovering and reporting information becomes impossible. No one will willingly share or volunteer information with a reporter who can't be trusted.

Athletes measure trust in two basic ways: familiarity and fairness. The familiarity comes from seeing the reporter at work on the beat and becoming familiar with his or her style. Simply put, athletes trust the reporters they know and work with on a daily basis more than they do unknown reporters. Plaschke says, "That's 90 percent of sports reporting—standing around batting cages and end zones and practice courts, just talking. The best sports reporters are the people who are the best at hanging out." Not only does this hard work pay off in better player relations, it also keeps the reporter informed and prevents him from missing a big story.

Players also want to know that they're being treated fairly. They want to make sure they're quoted accurately and the story does not take their feelings or intentions out of context. This does not mean that players or athletes don't expect criticism, which has become an occupational hazard in modern sports reporting. But is the criticism warranted or simply a personal attack? During the 40s and 50s, sports writer Dave Egan of the *Boston Record* carried out a vendetta against Red Sox star Ted Williams. According to author David Halberstam, Egan attacked Williams at every opportunity simply to boost his own career and stand out among the competition. "I get a barrelful of mail every week," Egan once said, "most of them telling me what a bastard I am. Maybe they're right—but I'm the bastard they're writing to." Given the incendiary nature of present-day relations between players and the media, confrontations are bound to occur. In such situations, Plaschke says it's vital that the beat reporter stands his ground. "Once a player thinks he can run you out of the clubhouse," he said, "you'll never feel safe there again."

GAME DAY

Beat reporting certainly has its place in the electronic media, but event reporting is by far much more common. Despite the growing number of side attractions and the rise of celebrity athletes, the games themselves still demand the bulk of the audience's attention. And whether it's the "Game of the Century" between the nation's best teams or just a high school game around the block, sports reporters must first and foremost learn to report on athletic events.

Each event is obviously unique and brings its own set of reporting challenges. A sports reporter would be foolish to cover the city basketball tournament the same way he would cover a weekend golf tournament. Part of a reporter's job is to understand the scene and the mood of an event and communicate that in the proper context to the audience. But aside from such differences, event reporting does carry with it some general practices that hold forth no matter what the situation.

The first element is speed. The electronic deadline is probably the most important consideration that affects every aspect of event coverage. Modern technology has reduced deadlines down to almost nothing and it's not uncommon for a reporter to have an edited story ready to air just minutes after the game has ended. Even when reporters have more generous deadlines, every decision they make about shooting, writing, interviewing, and editing must be made with the clock in mind. In many markets, sports reporters or photographers are expected to cover two or more high school games per night, an effort that requires thorough planning and preparation.

Sometimes, quality must be sacrificed for speed. Deadline sports reporting is usually not award-winning material, simply because reporters don't have time to fuss over their scripts or fine-tune the editing. Many times, poor edits or even factual errors occur. This is not to condone sloppy or haphazard journalism, but the fact remains that event coverage has one rule that supersedes all others: get it on the air and on time. The best writing, most dramatic photography, and most incisive interviewing does no one any good if it's still in the edit bay when the sports deadline hits.

This "need for speed" leads to another important point: event coverage should be played straight. That is, keep the action fairly simple, chronological, and straightforward. When the audience tunes in to see a game story, it wants simple, basic information: "Who won," "By how many," and "How did it happen?" This is best accomplished by presenting the game in an easy-to-follow pattern, taking events chronologically and highlighting the interesting events. At this point, viewers or listeners are not necessarily interested in the deeper, complicated analysis of the game and trying to include this most likely will only add confusion and waste valuable time (yours and theirs). Save all that for the follow-up story. If you absolutely have to include it that night, get another reporter and add a sidebar story (see Figure 5-2).

Chronology is important to the game story because it helps build drama and set the mood of the event. A newspaper writer doing an event story might put the game-winning basket in the lead, but doing that for a television story would ruin the report; it would have nowhere to go but downhill. A good reporter not only reports the events, but also gives them context and meaning to help build the drama. The casual or disinterested viewer wants a reason to keep watching. Setting the proper mood can turn a game into a story and whether the story has a happy ending or a sad one, people usually

Figure 5-2   The Game Day Story: Best to Play It Straight

like to stick around to see how things turn out. Good use of natural sound, video, and editing can all help give a report texture and mood.

Another way to set the mood is to get on-field reactions. Often times, reporters will rush onto the field right after a game has ended in an effort to conduct interviews. The reasoning is that players are much more honest, open, and interesting when approached so soon after the heat of the moment. By contrast, locker room interviews are usually much more canned and contrived after the athlete has had time to cool down. Of course, coaches and administrators discourage on-field interviews for the exact same reasons. They don't want the athlete saying anything in the heat of the moment that might be taken out of context or later regretted. In the early 1990s, the University of Iowa football team had a long winning streak against rival Iowa State. On the field right after another Iowa win, cameras picked up one of the Iowa players telling the Iowa State coach that he enjoyed "kicking his a—" again. The comment received extensive play in the media and the player was later forced to apologize. Because of episodes like that, several organizations have simply banned on-field interviews and made arrangements for players and coaches to get a "cooling off" period. Reporters should not view on-field comments as a chance to create controversy, but rather as a legitimate attempt to capture the spontaneity of the moment and maybe catch a player in the act of being himself. And again, the reporter should try to get the player to move beyond a simple recitation of what happened in the game.

It's also important to remember that not all the action takes place in the arena and a good reporter should always be aware of what's going on around the event. Reactions from players on the bench, coaches, and especially fans can sometimes be stories in themselves. In some rare cases, what's going on in the stands actually is more important than what's taking place on the field. If the fans of two bitter rivals have a history of causing trouble and getting into fights during the game, there's a good chance that's where the action is going to be. Maybe one of the players has a relative watching a game for the first time. The possibilities are endless and not always scripted out in advance. More than once, an angry fan or coach has stormed the court to protest a decision. When Bobby Knight throws a chair or when Miami and Notre Dame football players brawl before the game even starts, then the game itself is no longer as important.

As a final thought on event coverage, keep in mind that the preparation doesn't end when the game does. You should always try to get more than you need, because chances are you'll get the opportunity to use it. Event coverage is usually short and sweet with lots of leftover video and interviews. Hang on to all of it for use down the line, whether it's tomorrow, six weeks, or six months. A look back at a particular game can make for an interesting story when the sports calendar slows down.

FEATURE REPORTING

While event reporting remains the staple of daily sports coverage, feature reporting has become much more popular in recent years. The proliferation of media and the changing demographics of the viewing audience have combined to create a demand for more feature-oriented stories. More media outlets means a greater need for sports programming, which cannot be satisfied simply with traditional game coverage. The traditional male-oriented news and sports audience has also evolved into primarily a female audience, with its own set of preferences on how sports should be presented (see Chapter 15). As a result, more news and sports outlets are demanding that their journalists become proficient in feature reporting.

It's important to realize that feature reporting requires a much different approach than traditional event coverage. In fact, the two situations are almost polar opposites, because the very things that event coverage utilizes do not work for feature reporting and vice-versa. While the former focuses mainly on a sequence of events, feature reporting needs to concentrate more on personalities and people. In other words, it should emphasize the "who" and the "why" instead of the "what" and the "how." A feature report would not look so much at the game-winning shot itself, but more on the strategy and the people who worked together to make the shot possible. It is certainly more in-depth reporting and an attempt to find out the interesting stories behind the facts. Always keep in mind that good stories are about people. The casual fan doesn't care so much about records, awards, and games, but he or she will watch a story about an interesting person, even a person he or she knows nothing about.

As more media outlets have learned this lesson, sports reporting has veered into the realm of the unknown or anonymous athlete. Stories about a weightlifting mother, a physically disabled skydiver, or a precocious gymnastics talent have become extremely popular and quite common. There will always be a place for traditional reporting on games and athletes. But feature stories succeed in a different way because they touch a nerve with the viewer, who can identify with the personal qualities they see portrayed on the screen. Personal stories of endurance, perseverance, courage, determination, and loyalty are not only compelling and interesting, but elicit feelings of admiration and sympathy. The stories become even more attractive when done on the local level and viewers can identify with the people, places, and events.

All of these elements suggest that feature stories should play more to emotion than facts. It's a mildly interesting fact than an 80-year-old man broke the world record in the marathon for his age group. But it becomes even more interesting when you dig into the motivations behind the achievement. Why did this man do it? What did it feel like? What obstacles did he have to overcome? What even made him attempt it in the first place? A good feature reporter can turn a small line or notice in the newspaper into an engaging piece of sports journalism.

The nature of feature stories gives the reporter more freedom to experiment with writing, video, and editing. The feature reporter usually has a deadline of a few hours or even days instead of just a few minutes, which means he or she has time to attempt novel and creative storytelling techniques. There are about as many different techniques as there are stories and much of it depends on the situation and the reporter's personality. Popular ideas include putting a microphone on a coach, player, or fan and doing a story from that single perspective. Some stories exclusively emphasize the natural sound, compelling video, and music or unusual editing. And other reporters feel comfortable experimenting with their writing, such as delivering a story entirely in rhyme. Obviously, not all of these techniques work in every situation. But don't be afraid to experiment and fail. Much of creative reporting is simply trial and error, seeing what works and what doesn't. The only real failure is not attempting anything new and presenting a potentially interesting story in a tired old format.

Writing, shooting, and editing differently also means the reporter should think differently. Don't go into a feature story with the same old approach you would use when covering a game. Breaking out of the highlight/sound bite/standup mold is obviously risky, but also rewarding. Look for not only different ways to communicate the story, but also different stories. Notice things at a game or event that could eventually turn into a feature story. At a high school wrestling meet, one reporter noticed how dramatic and interesting the coaches were. Many times, their actions were far more compelling than the action on the mat. The reporter got his event coverage, but also shot enough footage to create a separate story about what a coach goes through during a match.

Out of the Box

Sports reporters who have worked several years in the same city often complain that they cover the same old stories, year after year. While this complaint often has an element of truth to it, it's up to the reporter to come up with new ideas to cover "old" stories. Feature reporting allows for all kinds of experimentation that can help reporters break out of their rut. Consider the situation of a reporter assigned to cover opening day for the local minor league baseball team; a story he or she has covered several times in years past (Table 5-3).

Table 5-3 Example of Out of the Box Sports Reporting

Conventional Reporting	*Unconventional Reporting*
Interview manager and players	"First person perspective" (put microphone on manager, player, or fan to see game through their eyes)
Interview fans	
Shoot video of opening day festivities	
Possible standup or natural sound	Music piece (something appropriate to tone and occasion)
	Interesting sidebar story (fan who hasn't missed a game in 30 years, etc.)
	Changes from last year (stadium, uniforms, etc.)
	Unusual or interesting video perspective (birds-eye view, bullpen, etc.)

REFERENCES

Bouton, Jim. *Ball Four Plus Ball Five*. New York: Stein & Day, 1981.

Collier, Gene. "The Ex-sportswriter: 'I Was Looking for Heroes in All the Wrong Places.'" *Columbia Journalism Review*, January–February 2000.

Cosell, Howard and Boventre, Peter. *I Never Played the Game*. New York: Morrow, 1985.

Cowlishaw, Tim. "Writers Remember." *Dallas Morning News*, February 13, 2000.

Golenbock, Peter. *Bums*. New York: Pocket Books, 1984.

Halberstam, David. *Summer of '49*. New York: Avon Books, 1989.

Heard, Robert. *Oklahoma vs. Texas: When Football Becomes War.* Austin, TX: Honey Hill Publishing, 1980.

Plaschke, Bill. "The Reporter: 'That's Twice You Get Me. I'm Gonna Hit You Right Now, Right Now!'" *Columbia Journalism Review*, January–February 2000.

Shapiro, Michael. "The Fan: 'Sports Journalism Is about Myths and Transcendent Moments.'" *Columbia Journalism Review*, January–February 2000.

Sportscasters: Behind the Mike. [Television show]. The History Channel, February 7, 2000.

SportsCenter of the Century: The Most Influential People. [Television show]. ESPN, February 20, 2000.

"Us vs. Them: Athletes and the Media." *USA Today,* January 1994.

6

Anchoring and Play-by-Play

ANCHORING

Chronologically, anchoring is the very last thing a sports broadcaster does with his show. It comes after the research and legwork, after the planning and preparation, and after all the shooting, producing, and writing. But anchoring is probably the single most important element of the entire process. Certainly, the other elements are important, but it takes good anchoring and good delivery to bring out the best in the writing and photography. A good sports anchor ties all the other elements together and communicates them in an interesting and entertaining way. It is five or so minutes that will make or break your entire sportscast and in some cases, an entire career.

Tricks of the Trade

From a technical standpoint, sports anchoring is not difficult. Thanks to modern conveniences like the teleprompter, it involves nothing more than sitting in front of a camera and reading material you've already written. The real trick comes in the delivery, style, and presentation of the anchor. Most stations generally have the same stories, the same interviews, and the same highlights. The challenge is to present that material in a way that engages the audience and sets you apart from your competition.

Ask a hundred different people in the industry how to do this, and you'll probably get a hundred different answers. But most news directors, sports professionals, and television consultants agree that good sports anchoring includes some very basic elements.

Control

Perhaps the most important element is that the sports anchor be in control. Control includes several things, including look, knowledge, and voice. Basically, it means that the audience respects the sports anchor as someone who knows what he's talking about and can communicate that information with confidence. That means the ability not only to communicate, but also to handle anything that comes up, including technical problems, disruptions, and other almost daily occurrences.

Look and voice are a big part of control. Most news directors want a mature, established presence on the anchor desk, which is especially difficult for sports broadcasters just starting out. News director Joel Bernell of WGBA-TV in Green Bay, Wisconsin says flatly, "I want someone who would fit in with the makeup of our anchor team, not somebody who looks like the news anchor's son." Obviously, there is very little you can do about how old you look, but you can certainly convey a more mature attitude in other things that you do as an anchor.

One thing is to act relaxed. This is often difficult for young sports broadcasters, who are bound to be nervous. It's also difficult to get relaxed after a long day of producing, writing, and editing, especially if you have to work as a one-man band. But in one sense, relaxation is simply a matter of avoiding extremes. You're looking for the middle ground between hyperactive anchoring (a trap easy to fall into in sports) and low energy anchoring. By definition, most sports anchoring requires a higher level of energy and enthusiasm than news or weather. But it's impossible (and irritating) to maintain a Dick Vitale-style of anchoring for every show and every story. And it would put the audience to sleep to deliver the show in a boring monotone.

Relaxation and control come mainly from confidence that you've done your homework and now feel comfortable in front of the camera. Viewers can tell when an anchor is confident and in control, just as they can sense when he or she is scared or nervous. So far, the only known cure for nerves is practice. You have to get in front of the camera and keep working on your delivery and style until you feel comfortable with it. This is why it's so important to get as much experience as you can, either with internships or at school. Establishing your comfort level as soon as possible puts you that much farther ahead when you go to get that first meaningful job.

Knowledge about the subject also gives the anchor confidence. This is generally not a problem for most people getting into the business, who grew up as sports fans. But the job also demands knowledge of the local sports scene. Viewers can immediately tell if someone mispronounces the name of a school or team, which can create a credibility problem. The athletic teams at Wichita Falls, Texas High School are the "Co-yotes," not the "Co-yotees" and it's important to know the difference. News director Paul Conti of WNYT-TV in Albany, New York says, "Know your material. It's horrible when someone tries to fake it and gets it wrong. Sports viewers are the most unforgiving viewers in TV."

Be Yourself

Without a doubt, the one thing most professionals say is be yourself and develop your own style. Too many people starting out try to imitate a successful broadcaster. Just as viewers can tell when a sportscaster doesn't know what he's talking about, they can also spot a phony. News director Joel Streed of KTTC-TV in Rochester, Minnesota says, "If you're going to do sports, be yourself and don't copy anyone else's style. There's enough Chris Bermans out there." For some reason, Berman has touched a nerve with local news directors (see Figure 6-1). "Don't try to imitate Chris Berman," says Paul Conti. "The student has to have his own style and go with what

Figure 6-1 ESPN's Chris Berman Has Thousands of Imitators (Courtesy ESPN/ John Atashian)

comes naturally. If you have a sense of humor, that's fine. But don't manufacture one."

On the subject of Berman, ESPN's Rich Eisen says his act is completely sincere. According to Eisen, Berman has the same personality when he's off-camera as when he's on-camera. "I think that's the key to succeeding or failing," says Eisen. "Be yourself. Anybody can smell a fake and they won't care, they won't watch, and they won't trust you."

We've already talked about how sports anchoring has leaned more toward style over substance in recent years (see Chapter 3). Because of people like Chris Berman and Stuart Scott at ESPN, and Keith Olbermann at Fox Sports, young sports broadcasters now think they have to have some sort of comedy act to get noticed. But those people make it work because it suits their personality. The key is to find what suits your personality and develop it into a unique and distinctive style.

Be Creative

"Too many sportscasters look and sound alike or try to mimic national sportscasters," says news director Ron Lombard of WIXT-TV in Syracuse, New York. "We like to see people who are natural communicators and can do it with their own style."

There are several ways sports anchors can make themselves unique and set themselves apart from the competition without going overboard on the personality. You can develop and emphasize a particular aspect of your presentation, such as the photography, storytelling, or interviewing. Most sports interviews consist of sticking a microphone in an athlete's face and asking him to talk about a certain play. Very few sportscasters, such as Roy Firestone of ESPN, have developed a more sophisticated approach and turned in-depth interviewing into a career.

Many sportscasters develop their own style by doing nothing more than speaking their minds. The trend has really taken off in radio, where opinionated sports talk hosts like Pete Franklin and Peter Brown have one goal in mind—to provoke the listeners to react. People who listen to these shows may not agree with the host, but they're still listening and driving up ratings.

Anchors on television usually don't act quite as opinionated or brash on the air, but they have the same purpose in mind. "I hear from people who say, 'I don't care about sports, but I tune in to you all the time,'" says Ted Leitner of KFMB-TV in San Diego. "That's exactly what I'm trying to do. People will tune in because they just want to hear what this jerk has to say . . . or because they think it's interesting or funny or whatever."

Obviously, what works for Ted Leitner probably wouldn't work for Bob Costas, and vice-versa. The important point is to find what works for you. Experiment with different styles until you find the one that suits your unique personality, then stick with it.

Entertain

While sports broadcasting is often a difficult and demanding job, you should never forget that it's not life or death. Certainly, sports include some very serious issues involving topics such as money, drugs, and crime. But to most people who watch it on television, sports are a form of escapism. Former U.S. Supreme Court Justice Warren Burger once said, "I read the front page of the newspaper to learn about man's failures. I read the sports section to learn about his successes."

People watch sports to feel good about themselves, share a cultural experience or see something they've never seen before. In many cases, the actual event itself takes a back seat to the televised experience. Howard Cosell was one of the first to realize this when he worked on *Monday Night Football*. "I bridge the gap between entertainment and journalism," said Cosell. "I'm a communicator with the human perspective." When Cosell decided to leave *Monday Night Football* in 1984, he did not want a well-known sports broadcaster to take his place, but instead suggested television star Bill Cosby. "He's a brilliant communicator and his performing skills are beyond reproach," said Cosell. "First and foremost, *Monday Night Football* is prime-time entertainment." While ABC decided to pass on Cosby, it broke new ground in June 2000, announcing that stand-up comedian Dennis Miller would join the *Monday Night* broadcast team starting that fall. "We want to make the game relevant to the hard-core fan, accessible to the occasional fan, and unpredictable to both," said *Monday Night* producer Don Ohlmeyer.

This does not mean that there's no place for serious sports journalists on the anchor desk. But you don't have to look any farther than the success of pro wrestling or similar events to realize that sports today has become major prime-time entertainment. Of course, that also doesn't mean you have to forgo the serious sports journalism. But more and more news directors want someone who can present serious information in an entertaining way. Paul Conti says, "I consider sports to be an entertainment product that happens to air in my newscast. Therefore, I want the sports anchor to be entertaining without looking foolish" (see Figure 6-2).

Sitting down at the anchor desk to deliver a show is probably the most nerve-wracking experience for young sportscasters. The only sure-fire cure is practice, because very few people are born with the proper control, confidence, and personality to deliver a quality product. Practice as often as you can, keeping in mind the points in Table 6-1.

PLAY-BY-PLAY

At the other end of the spectrum from anchoring is play-by-play. While both skills require lots of preparation and research, play-by-play is more

Figure 6-2 Good Sportscasters Communicate a Story Rather Than Read It

Table 6-1 Getting Started

Practice under "game" conditions	If possible, practice with all the elements of a professional sportscast in place, including lights, cameras, dress, and make-up. There's something to be said for practicing at home in front of the mirror, but nothing substitutes for the real thing. Ask your university or college to use their studio during non-peak hours. Get used to sitting in the chair, adjusting your eyes to the lights and looking on- and off-camera.
Try to avoid getting locked into the teleprompter	The teleprompter is a great device that scrolls your script across the camera while you're reading. But too many young sportscasters use it as a crutch and become hooked on it. The result is a "deer-in-the-headlights" look that appears stiff and unnatural. In many cases, the viewers at home can actually see the sportscaster's eyes moving back and forth

Table 6-1 *(continued)*

	during the show. Practice breaking your eyes away from the teleprompter to look down, even if you don't actually read off the copy. These breaks make you seem more relaxed and comfortable.
Work on relaxed body positioning	One of the symptoms of nervousness is stiff body language, so it's important for the sportscaster to work on relaxing. Many times, a sportscaster is so tight, he or she is physically tired after a three-minute show. Sit in a relaxed, comfortable position where you're back isn't ramrod straight. Be in a position that allows your head to move easily in any direction. Young sportscasters often seem concerned with what to do with their hands. Avoid keeping them in a locked, fixed position and instead use them naturally, such as emphasizing a certain point. The hands should comfortably be used to move through pages of your written copy. Much of body language is related to comfort level, and more relaxation comes with more practice and experience.
Work on tosses and ad-libs	Have an idea ahead of time what you're going to say when the anchors introduce you or when you close your show. This "cross talk" doesn't have to be scripted out, but both news anchor and sportscaster should have some idea of what direction to take. Nothing looks worse than long, uncomfortable conversation before a sportscast begins.
Expect the unexpected	Too many sportscasters believe they have to have a perfect show with no mistakes. As a result, they put so much pressure on themselves that their tension and nervousness increase to the point that they make even more mistakes. An experienced sportscaster knows that mistakes are simply a part of the business, especially because so many things are

(continued)

Table 6-1 *(continued)*

out of his or her control on the set (such as problems in master control, engineering, etc.). The important thing is to roll with the mistakes and keep going. Many sportscasters like to poke fun at themselves during these times, which really helps take the edge off. News directors don't expect you to have a perfect show every time, but they are interested in how you handle the mistakes. Learn to find a way to deal with mistakes (yours and everyone else's) that comes across positively on the air.

spontaneous and less rehearsed. It's sports television by the seat of your pants, in that anything can happen and sometimes does. And that very quality of unpredictability is what makes it so attractive to many broadcasters. "I love the spontaneity of it," says ESPN's Charley Steiner, who does most of his play-by-play work on radio. "It unfolds right before your eyes, the complete opposite of the studio experience, which is very scripted and controlled" (see Figure 6-3).

However, don't let the spontaneity of play-by-play fool you. Announcers don't simply walk into a broadcast booth and do a game without lots of preparation, which in most cases takes much more work than a traditional studio broadcast. "I would say that for something like baseball, the game preparation is generally between four and eight hours for each game," said Steiner. "Hopefully, you're prepared for any and all eventualities when you're on the air."

This preparation usually includes reading newspaper and Internet stories about the event and the athletes, going through game notes supplied by the teams involved, and talking to athletes and coaches before game time. The broadcaster can then use all this information during the game, in the form of statistics, information, or simply interesting stories. John Madden is generally recognized as the most accomplished and successful football broadcaster in the game today, and much of his material comes from the preparation he does before the game starts. "In preparing to do a game," he says, "I always come across stories I can use on the air." Steiner says, "The thing I like most is talking with the players in the dugout three hours before the game. You get a sense of who they are and it helps to tell better stories on the air."

Much preparation goes into doing a play-by-play broadcast. Often times, announcers spend several hours getting ready for a single game. Consider a

Figure 6-3   Charley Steiner (Courtesy ESPN/John Atashian)

radio broadcast of a game between two local high school basketball teams, where the preparation might include the items in Table 6-2.

There's also another kind of preparation, in which the play-by-play broadcaster uses aids to help him or her with names, numbers, and statistics. This is usually done with a "spotting board," a visual representation of players, numbers, names, and positions that are arranged for easy access. In a football game, for example, the broadcaster might arrange the spotting board to correspond to the players' location on the field and their position on the team's depth chart. Each broadcaster has his or her way of putting together a spotting board and no single way is better than another. The key is to come up with a board that can be accessed easily and quickly and with as little disruption as possible. Most, but not all, boards include things such as a current depth chart, the stat and play-by-play sheets from the previous game,

Table 6-2 Before the Booth

Pre-game conversations	The broadcaster would probably want to talk to both coaches, both athletic directors, and some players, if possible. The broadcaster is looking for any scoops, new information, or interesting stories he or she can relate during the game.
Taped interviews	Interviews with players, coaches, parents, or fans can be used during the game. This would include information on strategy, how the team is doing, comments about how it's playing, etc. The broadcaster also might want an extended interview to use at halftime. Such interviews should be as interesting as possible, and focus on feature-type material.
Printed information	The broadcaster needs to go over game notes and all information related to the game. This would include rosters, player numbers, and statistical information, all arranged for easy access. During the game, the broadcaster needs to instantly connect numbers to names. Such information also helps in providing background, such as player histories and past performances.
Technical work	Most big stations have engineers working out all the technical details. But in many places, the on-air talent is responsible for setting up the equipment and making sure it all works properly, with a strong signal going back to the station. This is obviously a much longer and more complicated procedure for television than radio (see Chapter 9).
Broadcast responsibilities	The broadcaster must also make sure the call of the game conforms to station standards and policy. Primarily, this means getting the commercials on at the right time and in the right place. The game wouldn't even go on the air if not for the advertisers, and it's extremely important to make sure they're satisfied. Sometimes, the broadcaster will even have to do live commercials or promos during breaks in the game.

the latest media guides and releases, and a "speed card" for quick, instant information (see Figure 6-4).

Whether you're doing a game on radio or television, the preparation is much the same. But after that, the similarities end. Doing games on radio and television are entirely different experiences.

Raised on Radio

Most play-by-play announcers get their start in radio, mainly because the opportunities are so much greater. Almost every local radio station in the country covers some type of sports event, either high school sports, local college sports, or minor league baseball. Because many of these stations don't have large budgets, they rely on young talent seeking to break into the business. Television play-by-play requires years of experience and the field is virtually closed to entry-level applicants.

But there's another distinct advantage to starting in radio. Many current professionals believe radio provides the best training ground for play-by-play because of the unique qualities of the medium. Gary Bender has spent more than 20 years as a play-by-play announcer for CBS television and radio, and he believes young broadcasters must get their play-by-play start in radio. "Until you have learned the nuances of describing an event on radio, of

Figure 6-4 Play-by-Play Requires Instant Access to All Kinds of Information

painting vivid pictures in the listener's mind, you can't do the same for television," writes Bender. "Radio is the cornerstone of a play-by-play career."

Bender and other professionals realize that radio is much different and in many ways much more demanding than television. Because the listener can't see what you're seeing, it's important to create an image of the event in the listener's imagination. "Radio is where you are painting the picture," says Steiner. "You are watching the game for millions of people. It's your eyes, your experience, your use of voice, and the ability to paint that picture and tell the story." A phrase like "painting a picture" can mean several different things, but mainly it involves a tremendous amount of description. Radio announcers should describe as much as possible about what's happening. In a typical baseball game on radio, for example, the announcer would go into great detail about things like how the pitcher looks on the mound, how the batter steps in and out of the box, the size of the crowd, and weather conditions. Such information paints a visual picture of the event for the listener. Longtime baseball announcer Jon Miller says, "You're the conduit from the ballpark to [the listener], and the challenge is to put them in the ballpark."

Most of the description will focus on the action and what's actually going on in the game. But radio announcers must convey detailed information about who's doing what and at what moment. This is called "setting the scene," or putting the action into context. Oftentimes, listeners will simply come across a game while tuning in the radio and want to know why this game is important or why they shouldn't change stations. An announcer that does a good job of setting the scene and providing context can keep someone listening, even if that person has no particular interest in the event or the teams that are playing. "TV is right there—you see it, it's easy to believe," says Mark Gastineau of KJR-AM in Seattle. "To me there's more art in radio, you really have to paint a picture for people. It's the most fun of the media because there really are no rules." Says Milo Hamilton, who has broadcast Houston Astros games for nearly two decades, "I don't think it's an accident that the Ernie Harwells, the Jack Bucks, the Bob Murphys, and myself have chosen in recent years to do radio only. Maybe it's because we're storytellers."

Despite the importance of storytelling, a radio broadcaster should not forget the role of score updates. Above all else, sports emphasize winning and losing. An announcer can be as descriptive as possible and paint beautiful pictures of the game, but it doesn't mean anything if the listener doesn't know the score. Radio pioneer Red Barber learned this lesson early on and used an egg timer to remind himself to update the score at least every three minutes. If that seems silly or old fashioned, think about the last time you listened to a game on the radio and how long you had to wait to find out the score.

Many young broadcasters get into radio play-by-play thinking it's easier than television because the broadcaster has to deal with less equipment. Often, a radio broadcast can be done with nothing more than a microphone and a telephone line. But in many ways, not having a televised picture to fall back on puts more pressure on the broadcaster. "There is no script," says Steiner. "It's uncontrolled. What you do when you go on the air is buckle up your seat belt and go for a ride."

The Electronic Eye

In 1951, New York Giants radio announcer Russ Hodges won broadcasting immortality with his call of Bobby Thomson's dramatic home run to win the National League pennant. "The Giants win the pennant! The Giants win the pennant!" has become a part of not only baseball history, but American history as well. Less well known is Ernie Harwell's call of the same event. Harwell is best known for his long career as a radio baseball announcer (see Chapter 16), but on that particular day he did the game on television. "After Thomson hit the home run," he said years later, "I simply said 'It's gone.' And after that, I didn't say anything for a long time."

One event, two announcers, and two different mediums. The Thomson home run points out the difference between play-by-play on radio and television, a difference not all announcers understood as well as Harwell. Many professional broadcasters had a difficult time making the transition from radio to television, because they thought of television as simply radio with pictures. "In the early days of television, most sports announcers were radio guys and did radio on TV," said veteran sportscaster Jack Whitaker. "The director would always say, 'Don't say he swung and missed—we can see that!'"

Eventually, sportscasters learned the nuances of calling a game on television as a completely different kind of art form that required a different play-by-play approach. One of the men who helped define the emerging form was NFL play-by-play announcer Ray Scott (see Chapter 16). Scott covered the Green Bay Packers during their glory years of the 1960s and developed a "short hand" game description that has become almost the standard today. Instead of saying, "Bart Starr drops back, avoids the rush, throws to Boyd Dowler who catches it on the 20 and avoids two tacklers for the touchdown," Scott would make the description brutally simple: "Starr . . . Dowler . . . touchdown" and let the pictures fill in the details. Over the years, sportscasters embellished Scott's bare-bones style, but the theory remains the same. "On TV, people are seeing the same things you are," says Steiner. "So you have to find a way—through facts, research, knowledge, and insight—to add to what they're seeing."

Calling a game on radio is completely different than doing the same event on television. A good example of the difference can be found in Table 6-3, in a short series of plays from the 1999 NFL game between the St. Louis

Table 6-3 Radio vs. Television

Radio Announcers	Television Announcers
Play by play: "And now with 59 seconds left in the first half, they've got the ball 1st and 10, 33 yard line . . . Isaac Bruce in motion . . . Warner takes the snap and falls down, tackled at the 40 yard line."	Play by play: "Isaac Bruce in motion left . . . and Warner falls down. He gets tripped up by one of his own players."
Analyst: "When things go like that, it's not going your way. He was backpedaling and just trips and falls. I think he got caught up with one of his linemen."	Analyst: "They have played as bad in this first half as they have all year, including the preseason. Everything that could go wrong, has gone wrong."
Play by play: "I want to bring this up, and we talked about it before the game . . . this is the Rams first game this year on grass."	Play by play: "A 7-yard loss."
Analyst: "He got his leg caught up with either the left guard or center."	Analyst: "You can see Newton's right foot gets caught up with Warner's left foot."
Play by play: "2nd down and 16 at the 39 yard line . . . Warner in the shotgun, takes the snap . . . under pressure, steps up and throws to the left sideline, caught by Roland Williams. He can't even get back to the original line of scrimmage, tackled there by Steve Jackson. Rams in the hurry up, 32 seconds to go . . . they'll have 3rd down here at the 45. Warner shotgun formation, 3-receiver set, back to throw . . . has some time . . . throws to the right side and it's nearly intercepted by Dennard Walker, intended for Torry Holt. And the Rams will have to punt."	Play by play: "45 seconds to go. Warner steps up . . . slings it out and the pass goes to tight end Roland Williams; he had a career game last week against the Browns, including a touchdown pass. The Rams now in the hurry up after the 4-yard pickup with less than half a minute left in the first half. 3rd and 13. There's the pass . . . tipped away by Dennard Walker, intended downfield for Torry Holt. So on 4th down, Jeff Wilkins will come in for a field goal."
Analyst: "He had Torry Holt. Tennessee rotated a corner up, or had him go way deep and played a man underneath. If he throws that ball a little earlier, it's a completed pass."	Analyst: "We've seen some excellent play in this first half from the Tennessee defensive backfield . . . they have taken away all the Rams big weapons."

Source: Courtesy KSD-FM/St. Louis Rams, Fox/NFL

Rams and the Tennessee Titans. Notice how the radio announcers added much more information, while the television announcers tried to keep their observations to a minimum.

This is another way of saying that the television announcer should rely less on description and statistics and more on setting the scene. While detailed description may keep the radio listener connected to the game, in television it becomes annoying overkill. Why describe at length what the viewers can already see? Thus, one of the main jobs of the television announcer is to fill in the details and provide context for what the viewer can't see or doesn't know. Marty Bass works as a morning news anchor at WJZ-TV in Baltimore, but he also does work with the Baltimore Ravens radio broadcasts. "Nothing is bigger than the game," he says, "but the game itself can be dull. A good announcer with style can build the drama and build the story around the statistics." John Madden agrees, up to a point. "There's no such thing as a dull game. The person talking about it might be dull."

Just as a good announcer knows what to say, he or she also knows what not to say. One of the cardinal rules of television announcing is "let the pictures tell the story." That is, let the action speak for itself, especially if the action is compelling or dramatic. It's during these times that the television announcer should keep his or her words at a minimum, as Harwell did after Thomson's home run or like Al Michaels after the U.S. Olympic hockey win over the Soviet Union in 1980. One of the main problems television announcers must overcome is the temptation to talk too much and kill the pictures. This is especially problematic in baseball, where there are so many natural lulls and pauses in the game. According to Bob Marshall, ABC ruined coverage of the 1980 baseball playoffs because the network's announcers were competing with each other to dominate the broadcast. "They talked incessantly," said Marshall, "no matter what was going on in the game. And when they ran out of things to say or there was a pause in the action, they talked some more."

This brings up another essential point: the game should not be a showcase for the broadcasters. Many professionals have fallen into the trap of trying to become bigger than the event. Howard Cosell would tell anyone who would listen that most people tuned in to *Monday Night Football* to watch him, not the game. There may be an element of truth in that, but when a broadcaster puts the focus on him- or herself instead of the event, he or she can't do the job as effectively. Even John Madden, arguably the most popular announcer on television today admits, "The game is the thing, not me or Pat [Summerall] or the camera angles. The game is what everybody is interested in."

The Role of the Analyst

Announcing teams usually work in pairs (or sometimes in threes), with an analyst or "color" man broadcasting with the play-by-play person. The analyst position usually goes to someone with an in-depth knowledge of the sport or event, which more than likely means a former athlete. While not many professionally trained broadcasters qualify for this role, it's still important to know what the analyst does, because the two must work together as a team within their roles in order to produce the best possible on-air performance.

Primarily, the analyst provides the "how and why" of the game, while the play-by-play person handles the "who and what." Of course, this is an oversimplification, but it helps explain why the analyst must have such a strong background. He or she is expected to fill in details and explanation that give the audience a deeper understanding. "I tell my analyst to take us beyond what we're seeing," says veteran announcer Marv Albert. "Take us someplace new—someplace we haven't gone before." Adds baseball analyst Tim McCarver, "What can I add to the picture that explains what happened or how it happened?" But while the analyst is primarily concerned with explanation, Albert adds that there's a fine line between being interesting and being redundant. "You want some replays, but not too many. Otherwise, the guy just sits and talks over highlights all night."

That's why so many modern analysts have developed distinct and entertaining personalities. John Madden was one of the first analysts to move the boundaries of the job beyond simple description. Madden diagrams football Xs and Os like any former coach, but it's his presentation that fans remember. "The cornerstone of broadcasting to me, is passion," he says. "I don't really think of myself as a broadcaster." The same could probably be said for basketball analyst Dick Vitale (see Chapter 16 for more on both men).

In some cases, analysts like Madden and Vitale have become even more popular than their play-by-play partners, which is why a good working relationship in the booth is so important. It's very easy for big egos to get bruised and ruin the on-air product. Frank Gifford admits that during the 1980s, Howard Cosell was virtually impossible to work with on *Monday Night Football* because he insisted on dominating the telecast and tried to drown out his broadcast partners. The partnership works best when all the members understand their roles and their place in the broadcast. "Don't just keep talking," says golf analyst Ken Venturi. "It has to have meaning. On television, it's not what you say but what you don't say."

The "Homer"

Sportscasters have long debated the role of the "homer"—the announcer who openly roots for the home team, no matter what the circumstance. The very notion of partial or biased reporting contradicts what many see as the basic principles of sports journalism. "Red Barber was almost contemptuous of the way Russ Hodges called Bobby Thomson's home run," says Bob Costas. "Red said he felt Hodges lost his professionalism and perspective." But others see it simply as a matter of personal choice. "I wouldn't want to do that, because I'm better off giving the whole picture than a biased, one-sided picture," said Dodgers announcer Vin Scully. "Now, there are other fellas who do it totally differently—they are highly partisan and they are rooters, and their communities obviously love them for it, and that's fine, so I'm not holding myself up as the only way to do it." Some of the men Scully referred to, like Bob Prince with the Pirates, Johnny Most with the Celtics, and of course, Harry Caray with the Cubs made a good living as homers and became legends in their respective cities.

Caray was the leader of what baseball author Curt Smith calls "the Midwest cheering school." In the post-World War II era, baseball announcers in the Midwest developed huge followings by promoting the fortunes of the home team. This tactic succeeded in places like St. Louis and Pittsburgh, where there was no other major league competition and regional audiences could adopt a faraway team as their own. Contrast that to the situation in New York, where audiences had three major league teams to choose from, not including competition from Boston and Philadelphia. In those areas, a more impartial style developed, typified by men like Red Barber and Mel Allen.

The number of homer announcers seems to have dwindled in recent years. For one thing, technology has eliminated the regional boundaries that created the "us against them" mentality. Superstations like WGN in Chicago and WTBS in Atlanta promote their teams to a national audience, and it hardly makes sense to alienate potential viewers. In fact, much of these audiences watch to root for their home teams against the Cubs and Braves. This same technology has also opened up doors for sportscasters, which didn't exist generations ago. There are many play-by-play opportunities today on cable and satellite, but a national stage demands an unbiased announcer. Networks and other outlets can't take a chance on a homer who doesn't have national appeal. Someone like Jon Miller does play-by-play for the San Francisco Giants, but he also does weekly baseball games for ESPN because of his impartial style.

Miller went to San Francisco after a long career in Baltimore because of pressure from Orioles management to get him to tow the company line on the air. The incident serves as a reminder that new media conglomerates can and do exert certain pressures on sportscasters. In June 2000, radio station WIP in Philadelphia suspended host Mike Missanelli for two days after critical comments he made against Flyers management and specifically, general manager Bobby Clarke. WIP is owned by Infinity Broadcasting and owns the rights to the Flyers and 76ers basketball games. "We have a deal with WIP," said Flyers executive Ron Ryan. "We don't have a problem with them criticizing how we run the team. It's the personal attacks we don't want." In the new media environment, some broadcast outlets have a vested interest in making sure the home team plays well, which is something of a disturbing trend for those sportscasters who practice objectivity and criticism.

FINAL ADVICE

Some final thoughts about the play-by-play booth, whether it's for radio or television:

- **Style.** Just as in anchoring, it's important to be yourself and not copy anyone else. "Imitation is flattering," says Gary Bender, "but you can't build a career on it. The key is to develop a distinct style of your own, based on your own strengths and weaknesses. Style is a product of being yourself." Curt Gowdy agrees, "I loved the voices of guys like Ted Husing and Bill Stern, but I never tried to copy them. That's the worst thing you can do. You have to be yourself."
- **Practice.** Many play-by-play broadcasters started out with a tape recorder, a game program, and a secluded spot in the high school gym. Trying to describe the action seems awkward at first, but that's the point. Smooth out the rough spots at an early age, then you can work on the finer points of style and technique. It also helps to share your work with a trained professional who can offer advice and suggestions. In many situations, the local radio broadcaster will be more than happy to help out. With enough practice, whether it actually makes the air or not, the fundamentals of good play-by-play become second nature. "What I do has to be instinct and reaction," says Madden. "If you start questioning your instincts, you'll be afraid to make a mistake or say the wrong thing."
- **People, not statistics.** Always remember that games are played and watched by people. Young broadcasters often fall into a trap of trying to fill the game with too many numbers and statistics, especially if there's time to fill or the action seems to drag. Marty Bass says that Jim Hunter of CBS radio is one of the best play-by-play men in the business. "But during a baseball rain delay, he fills the extra time with stats. I don't know how many people have driven their cars off a bridge listening to endless talk about somebody's ERA. Contrast that to ESPN's Jon Miller, who is likely to break into his Vin Scully impersonation if things get too slow."

Bass says firmly "stats killed sports." That may be an overstatement, but it's certainly easy for a play-by-play announcer to kill a game by concentrating too much on the numbers and ignoring all the interesting stories. Author Curt Smith adds, "The play-by-play men of today are not as interesting or distinctive as those of two or three decades ago. But thank God, there are exceptions." (See Figure 6-5.)

Figure 6-5   Play-by-Play Broadcasters

REFERENCES

Bender, Gary and Johnson, Michael L. *Call of the Game: What Really Goes on in the Broadcast Booth*. Chicago: Bonus Books, 1994.

"Careers in Sports Journalism: Play-by-play Announcer." ESPN. [Online]. Available: www.espn.go.com./special/s/careers/anno.html, September 7, 1999.

"Careers in Sports Journalism: TV Sports Anchor." ESPN. [Online]. Available: www.espn.go.com/special/s/careers/anchor.html, September 7, 1999.

Cosell, Howard and Boventre, Peter. *I Never Played the Game*. New York: Morrow, 1985.

de Turenne, Veronica. "Dodgers and Scully Still Moving On." *Scripps Howard News Service*, October 1, 1996.

Greppi, Michelle. "'MNF' Runs Rant Pattern, Brings Miller to Booth." *Hollywood Reporter*, June 23, 2000.

Houck, Jeff. "Philadelphia Story: Philadelphia Radio Host Suspended for Criticizing Flyers GM." [Online]. Available: www.foxsports.com/business/bites/z000623 flyers_critic1.sml, June 23, 2000.

Laurence, Robert P. "Leitner's Light Touch." *Electronic Media*, March 22, 1999.

Madden, John and Anderson, Dave. *All Madden*. New York: HarperCollins, 1996.

Marshall, Bob. *Diary of a Yankee Hater*. New York: Franklin Watts, 1981.

Martzke, Rudy. "Albert's NBA Schedule Filled with Traveling Calls." *USA Today*, April 28, 2000.

National Sports Report. [Television show]. Fox Sports, August 25, 2000.

Sportscasters: Behind the Mike. [Television show]. The History Channel, February 7, 2000.

"Sports-talk Radio Host." ESPN. [Online]. Available: http://espn.go.com/special/s/careers/sptalk.html, September 7, 1999.

7

Photography

Think of the most memorable moment in sports broadcasting history and you'll probably think of an unforgettable visual image. Some events stick in our memories because of the power of the pictures, like Dwight Clark's catch in the 1982 NFC Championship game, the 1967 Ice Bowl in Green Bay, or Carlton Fisk madly waving his arms to help his home run stay fair in the 1975 World Series.

All of these images came from the cameras of sports photographers. Granted, they usually had the help of highly sophisticated equipment, which is not readily available in smaller markets. But whether you're shooting the Super Bowl for the networks or simply covering the local high school basketball game, the basics of sports photography remain pretty much the same.

EVENT PHOTOGRAPHY

Much of sports photography (or "videography") includes covering events or games for the local high school or college. Basketball, football, baseball, and all the other sports each have their own unique challenges, but there are some general rules of sports photography that apply to them all.

Always keep the action in front of you. This is common sense—you want the viewer to see the action coming at him or her, rather than going the other way. There are always exceptions because of the unpredictable nature of the event. You may be in perfect position to get the game-winning touchdown, only to have someone make an interception and run 99 yards in the opposite direction. But for the most part, position yourself so you can see the action unfold in front of you (see Figure 7-1).

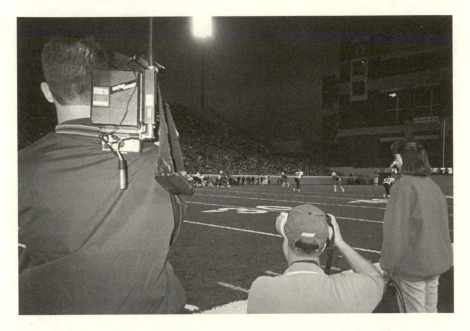

Figure 7-1 A Sports Photographer Should Always Have the Action Coming in His or Her Direction (Courtesy Mary Lou Sheffer)

Just like real estate, in sports photography it's location, location, location. Positioning yourself in the right place is more than half the battle in getting good pictures. And every event demands that you be in the right place at the right time. We'll talk more about positioning in a minute.

Anticipate what's coming next. If you're covering a football game and it's 3rd and 10, what's likely to happen next? Probably a pass, which means you want to stay a little looser in your shooting and get ready for the ball to come downfield. If it's the last few seconds of a quarter in a basketball game, be ready for that long shot at the buzzer. Be aware of special situations like these and where you need to be.

Be prepared for anything. That includes the ball coming right at you, and more importantly, large players coming right at you. A photographer getting run over looks hilarious on the sports bloopers, but in reality it's painful and often dangerous for you and the equipment. Sports photographers often joke that news directors are less concerned about them than the equipment. While something of an overstatement, it does have some basis in fact. Today's equipment is extremely sensitive and easily broken, often at a cost of thousands of dollars. Some of the damage is unavoidable, but much of it is due to just plain carelessness. Don't set your camera on the ground and leave it unattended, even for just a few minutes, and the same goes for the tripod. Almost every station in the country has a story involving a wrecked camera that slipped off an unattended tripod. As a side note, the tripod is used infrequently in sports photography. It's a necessity for shooting up top in a pressbox, but completely unworkable on a sideline or field level situation. Since most of the compelling sports photography involves good close-ups, most photographers prefer to shoot "off the shoulder" on field level.

Make sure you have the proper framing. Most sports photography involves a happy medium between too loose and too tight. If shot too loose, viewers can't identify the action or the players involved. Coaches love this wide angle when studying game footage, but for the people at home it's almost useless. There's also a recent trend to shoot everything ultra tight, zooming in on faces, hands, or the ball. But this also frustrates the viewer because it doesn't give any depth or background, which adds important information to the picture. A close-up of a running back plowing into an unidentifiable pile of bodies ruins the drama of a game-winning touchdown. Better to pull back to catch other players and even fan reaction. It's fine to start tight, but then pull out so the viewer can see what's going on. For example, you can start extremely tight on the quarterback calling plays at the line of scrimmage, then quickly pull out as the ball is snapped to catch the action. It's also acceptable to go the other way—start loose and zoom in. This works particularly well for events like swimming and track meets, where you can start wide on the entire field then slowly zoom in to focus on the leader.

Don't cross the axis. The axis is an imaginary 180-degree line that runs in front of your shooting position (see Figure 7-2). Crossing the axis would mean shooting from the other side of the field, looking back toward your original position. By doing this, you would see action going in both directions at the same time. Cutaways wouldn't make any sense because everyone would be looking in different directions. For continuity and easier editing, stay behind the axis, which simply means stay on the same side of the field and shoot in a consistent direction. Don't forget to factor the sun in the equation—you always want it behind you. Veteran photographers know this lesson well because shooting an old tube camera into the sun (or any bright light) burns an image into the lens. While this doesn't present a problem for today's sophisticated chip cameras, shooting into the sun does darken the action and can turn the players into silhouettes.

Get cutaways at appropriate times. Cutaways are the short, non-action shots used to add meaning and fill time between edited plays. A coach shouting at players, fans standing and cheering, and the scoreboard clock are all cutaways. Good cutaways can add some sense of drama and heighten the impact of the story. But make sure you get cutaways during the lulls in the

Draw an imaginary horizontal axis across the event you're shooting. You can shoot on one side
of the axis (anywhere in the white area) or on the other side (anywhere in the shaded area).
But it's important not to cross the axis and shoot in both areas during the same event.

Figure 7-2   Don't Cross the Axis

action. Don't try to get a shot of the crowd when a golfer has a putt to win the
tournament. Get reaction shots before and after the big play. Viewers are
still more interested in the action on the field.

Save the experiments for later. In a game report, viewers want to see the
nuts and bolts of the event. Fancy shots and strange camera angles don't answer their basic question—what happened? If you feel you have enough
solid shots to tell the story, feel free to try something different. But keep the
viewer and the game in mind.

SHOOTING ON LOCATION
Football

No sport, with the exception of golf, requires you to cover more ground than
football. Unless you're shooting up top in the pressbox, you simply can't stay
in one place and hope to get good pictures. You constantly have to move and
readjust your position, usually between plays with only a few seconds to get
to the next location.

There are three basic positions for shooting football (see Figure 7-3).
Position A is one of the most common at almost every level of football.
With pressbox space at a premium, most photographers will have to shoot
from the sidelines. Most shooters try to position themselves about 10–15
yards in front of the line of scrimmage with the play coming toward them.
This allows them to follow a runner or receiver into the end zone. Shooting from the sideline also makes for more close-up action and better natural

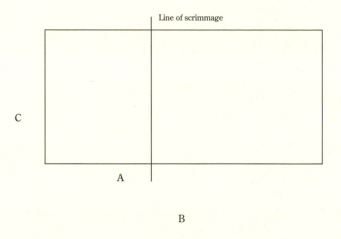

Figure 7-3 Photographer Positioning for Football

sound, which helps place the viewer in the game and gives him or her a better sense of the action.

The shifting depth of field makes this a difficult shooting position, as the photographer must constantly change focus as the action moves downfield. The changing focus is the most challenging aspect for young photographers, who find it difficult to keep one hand on the focus ring, while the other hand steadies the camera and operates the zoom knob. Be sure to know which way to turn the focus ring to keep the action in focus as it moves toward or away from you. In some cases, you can also get your focus during breaks in the action. For example, in a football game, photographers will quickly zoom in and focus on the quarterback. That way they can be assured that the upcoming action will be in focus.

There is also the possibility of players and coaches moving off the bench and getting in the way. Sometimes, the shooter may actually have to step out onto the field to follow the action. The NFL and most colleges have a 5-yard buffer zone around the sideline, which makes this very difficult, and sometimes photographers will lose the action for a few seconds or more.

Position B is the recommended position for inexperienced shooters. Staying up top and as close as possible to the 50-yard line affords many advantages. The shooter can actually put the camera on a tripod (one of the few instances in sports photography where this is possible) to ensure a solid shot. Depending on the position, the shooter will not have to adjust the focus much, if at all. Most of the action will take place in the same depth of field and since the action is somewhat easy to follow, very seldom does the photographer get faked out or lose sight of the play. One of the drawbacks of this position is that it doesn't allow for many good close-ups. In many college and pro stadiums, the pressboxes are hundreds of feet above the playing field. From this position, it's extremely difficult to capture the flavor or excitement of the event, so most of the footage shot from this location is used primarily for highlights (see Figure 7-4).

Most large sports organizations routinely send two (or more) cameras to cover bigger games: one camera up top and another on the sideline. This certainly makes it easy to edit and helps avoid the problem of missing certain plays. If you've only got one camera, placement depends on the skill and experience of the photographer. It's advisable to shoot every play in a game until the outcome has been decided. Even then, if you put the camera down for just one play, you could miss something you'll never see again.

Position C is often used by photographers when the action gets close to the goal line. Standing at the back of the end zone ensures that the action has to come right at you, as opposed to the sideline where the action often goes far to the other side of the field. Remember to stand on the side of the end zone closest to your sideline position to avoid crossing the axis. Again, this position is not recommended for beginning shooters, as it is often hard

Figure 7-4   Pressbox Photographers (Courtesy Mary Lou Sheffer)

Figure 7-5 Photographers Crowd Along the End Line (Courtesy Mary Lou Sheffer)

to follow the action and tell exactly where the ball is going. And you still run the risk of missing the play if there's a turnover and the ball heads downfield in the opposite direction (see Figure 7-5).

Basketball

Shooting basketball is much like football, except on a smaller scale. And because of the continuous action, you won't have time to move around, but will have to find one spot and stay there. There are basically two positions from which to shoot (see Figure 7-6).

Position A is on the floor, in one of the corners. Which corner depends on your axis and what side you start on, but generally the home team or the team of interest will move toward you. Depending on local rules, you may have to sit or kneel in this position the entire game. In light of that, many experienced photographers will wear kneepads or some sort of brace, so they won't get too uncomfortable.

You want to use the corner instead of the center of the baseline for several reasons. Most obvious, the basket support makes it almost impossible to get any game action from a dead-center position. Since most of the action

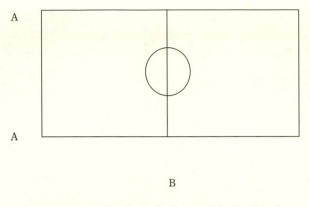

Figure 7-6 Basketball Photography Positioning

takes place inside the lane, the referees will also get in the way. Shooting from the corner also allows you better proximity to cutaways of the crowd and the bench.

Like football, shooting from the floor affords the viewer a more intimate view of the game and brings him or her more into the action. The size and skill of the players become even more apparent when shooting from floor level. But the same dangers apply as in football concerning the possibility of contact with players. In fact, there are probably more camera–player collisions in basketball because the area is so much smaller and there isn't any room to escape. The changes in the depth of field are even more drastic than football, and keeping good focus is a constant problem. One solution is a quick focus on the basket where the action is headed. Zoom in for a focus, then pull back out to the action.

Position B is probably the more desirable location and shooting from this position gives all the advantages mentioned for football, including steadiness and control. But again, availability may be a problem. Every high school and college gym is configured differently and space becomes a premium, especially when the place is packed. Be prepared to shoot anywhere—on staircases, from balconies, or even a catwalk above the playing court.

Shooting basketball is not difficult once you get used to it. It's fairly easy to follow the action by simply following the player with the ball. It's customary for the shooter to follow the player who has scored for a few seconds after the basket, then return to the action. Some shooters like a quick cutaway of the scoreboard after every basket for later help in identifying game situations during editing. Other times, the photographer will grab a quick cutaway after an important basket.

Shooting an entire game is impractical and seldom done. Usually, photographers will have to cover several games in one night, never spending more than a few minutes at each location. For the shooter, this means getting a few quick shots of each team making some baskets, and some cutaways. Obviously, you're looking for the spectacular—the breakaway dunks, the long heaves at the buzzer, or something else out of the ordinary. But for the most part, the action will look the same.

Baseball

Without a doubt, baseball is the hardest sport to shoot with one camera. The ball moves too fast to follow—sometimes close to a hundred miles an hour. There are long periods of inactivity, then when the ball is in play, several things happen all at once and it's hard to figure out where to point the camera. And no matter what your position, you're in danger of getting clocked with a line drive or foul ball. But you can minimize your danger and improve your photography by shooting from the following locations (see Figure 7-7).

Position A affords the safest location and is the easiest place from which to shoot. By positioning yourself above the action (the higher, the better, within reason), you can more easily follow the ball. The phrase "within rea-

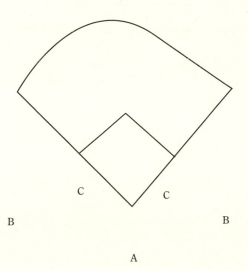

Figure 7-7 Baseball Photography Positioning

son" means you shouldn't be too high above the action. If you've ever sat on the top row of a big baseball stadium, you know how poor depth perception can make it difficult to follow the action. Ideally, you want to look up to see a high fly ball, not down. At a higher elevation, you should start shooting loose and slowly zoom in. If you stay too wide, it makes it much harder to tell what's going on, especially considering the size and speed of the ball.

Position B is also on a higher elevation, but on one of the baselines. This position often creates certain problems. From dead center, it's much easier to follow the flight of the ball, but from the sides, the ball will quickly travel out of your viewing frame, which means you have to guess or anticipate where it's going. One way is to pull out wider until you locate the ball. But you can also use your open eye (the eye not in the viewfinder) to peek at the position of the fielders. Using the open eye seems strange at first and takes lots of practice, but it can help in a variety of sports other than baseball.

In baseball, it's much easier to follow the fielders than the ball because they move so much slower. And fielders will always take you right where you need to be. Many shooters will find the correct fielder, then wait for the ball to arrive—especially if it's a long drive that appears headed out of the park. The photographer can stay focused on the fielder, then pull back to see the ball. It is extremely difficult to try and follow the ball with the camera and only the most experienced photographers should try it. Even when it can be done, it's probably still advisable to follow the fielders, because they create all the action in the game.

Position C is the most difficult and dangerous place in the park—field level adjacent to the dugouts. If you ever get the chance, look at some old baseball action photos from the 30s and 40s. Sometimes you can see photographers on the field of play, just a few feet from the batter's box—during the game! Shooting from this position is slowly becoming extinct, but it's still possible to shoot from several other areas at field level.

Following the action is very difficult from these positions, which should only be used by the most experienced photographers. The danger of getting hit by a stray ball increases, which requires maximum anticipation and awareness. This position also requires superior reflexes, as it's much more difficult to follow the action.

From whatever position, it's important to establish the position of the ball, then pull back to the batter or runner. If a batter singles to left with a man on second, follow the action until it's apparent what happened to the ball, then return to pick up the runner crossing the plate. As in basketball, stay with the runner for a few seconds after he's scored, then return to the batter standing on base. There are an infinite number of possible outcomes associated with each pitch, and more than any other sport, baseball photography requires anticipation, quick thinking, and knowledge of game strategy. In a first-and-third situation, the photographer has to be aware of a possible double steal and a runner trying to steal home. The same can be said for the sacrifice, suicide squeeze, or a pickoff move.

It's also advisable to shoot everything possible as time and resources allow. The two-out solo home run in the first inning could be the only run of the game. Because baseball has such long periods of inaction, cutaways become important. Tight shots of the pitcher delivering the ball, the batter swinging or the managers in the dugout can make the final product more memorable. Just be sure to pick the right spots for these cutaways. More than once, photographers have focused on a close-up of the pitcher, only to have the batter hit a home run. Those are the ones you can't get back.

Other Sports

There are no hard and fast rules for shooting other sports, but the following suggestions might help you in the different situations you encounter (see Table 7-1).

Table 7-1 Shooting Various Sports

Sport	*Shooting Suggestions*
Soccer	Follow the ball; it moves slowly and nothing important happens without it.
Golf	Focus on the putts—that's what wins a tournament. Everything else is just a cutaway.
Hockey	Like basketball, only much faster. Follow the players and keep the shots fairly wide.
Boxing	Fairly easy because the action takes place in a small, enclosed area.
Volleyball	Follow the ball.
Swimming	Start wide, then focus on the leader.
Track	Same as swimming.
Tennis	Easier to shoot from above, because the action can fit in the frame. From ground level, position yourself in the corner to see both players. If you have to shoot from the sides, shoot long sequences of each player that you can later match edit together.
Auto racing	Put yourself somewhere where you won't get killed. There's no experience in the world like holding a camera in the front straightaway at Indy with cars coming at you at 200 miles an hour with only a 3-foot concrete wall between you. I'll never forget shooting a drag race from a certain position, then moving to a new location. Less than two minutes after I moved, a dragster went out of control and crashed right over the spot where I had been standing. I hope that the tape would have survived.

FEATURE PHOTOGRAPHY

As sports reporting becomes more viewer-friendly and personality-oriented, feature reporting has become more essential. Sports departments now depend on these features to help attract newer and younger audiences, and feature photography can play a key role.

Shooting for features is entirely different than covering an event. In this situation, you're not trying to report hard, statistical information, but rather create a mood and draw the viewer into the story. You have to make the viewer care, and photography can go a long way in accomplishing that.

There are some general rules for feature photography:

Emphasize close-ups. Close-ups can tell a story that other shots can't, such as players crying after a tough loss, the sweat and strain of a weight-lifter, or the joy of a new state champion. In some cases, good close-ups can tell almost the entire story with no narration. Some of the best sports reporting pieces are all photography and natural sound. Viewers care about stories because of good characters, and close-ups reveal character.

Don't be afraid to experiment. This is a chance to do all those experiments you had to put off at the game. Play with the camera and try different angles or different shots based on the mood you're trying to create. Lighting can be effective, especially sunlight, and things shot at dawn or dusk automatically have a different look and feel. One of the most famous football shots of all time is the shot of former Dallas Cowboys coach Tom Landry. The photographer shot into the sun at Texas Stadium with Landry in the foreground, and the result was a classic silhouette of the coach in his trademark Fedora. Angles also can change perspective, such as lowering the camera to ground level and shooting up at an athlete, which gives him or her a bigger and more intimidating presence. A popular angle now used in the NBA is the camera mounted on top of the backboard looking down on the players. Wayne Gretzky once said that he missed 100 percent of the shots he didn't take. The same can be said for feature photography—you don't know what you miss unless you shoot it.

Try first-person action. Ultimately, all sports are about people. What's it like to score the winning touchdown, hit a home run, or sink the winning putt? Use the camera to put the viewer in the place of the subject and give him or her a feel for what it's like down on the field. More and more sports leagues are emphasizing this as a dramatic way to attract new viewers. Some of the experiments include a helmet cam for football players, a catcher cam in baseball, and the goal cam in hockey. Once a station ran a feature on a local athlete trying to make the U.S. Olympic bobsled team. He trained all summer by pushing a cart loaded with cinder blocks across the high school parking lot. It was one thing to show him pushing the cart, but something else to put the camera on the cart and let the viewers feel him push it.

Above all, still tell the story. No matter how fancy you get, how many great shots you take, or how much you experiment, it means nothing if you don't convey the basics of the story. Sometimes photographers get so wrapped up in the technical aspects of their work that they forget the big picture. The raw tape may have some quality shots on it, but nothing that can be put together in a cohesive story. Good reporting and good photography are about communicating and telling stories, and if your shooting doesn't do that, you've failed your job.

PRACTICING

As with anchoring, the only way to get better as a sports photographer is to practice. Take the camera to live sports events as often as possible, keeping the following points in mind:

1. **Respect and take care of the equipment.** The best photographers treat their cameras like members of their family, and not just because of the tremendous expense involved. Photographers know they can't produce good video without good equipment, and at most stations photographers are responsible for taking care of their cameras on a daily basis. Nothing will get you in trouble at a station faster than abusing the equipment, so take care to use the proper techniques in removing, using, and storing the camera. This also means using protective gear when the situation warrants.
2. **Know what the camera can do.** It's important to know about all the functions of the camera. First and foremost, this means being able to turn on the camera and prepare it for use. Learn about the power switches, iris, gain, filter, zoom control, and white balancing, because each camera is different. Other photographers can help, or you can simply read the manual. Getting the most out of the camera can save you in a difficult shooting situation, such as poor lighting. Countless tapes have been ruined because someone forgot to white balance or shot on the wrong filter.
3. **Concentrate on framing and focus.** There are a million things for young photographers to worry about at a game, and many times they will not come back with perfect video. But there's a difference between good video and usable video, and as long as you have the proper focus and framing, the video is usable. Framing means keeping the action the proper distance away, which is most easily accomplished from an up-top

position. The same goes for focus, which is why it's so advisable for inexperienced photographers to shoot from a higher position, where focus and framing remain fairly constant. With more practice you can go down to field level and develop stronger instincts (see Figure 7-8).

4. **Practice keeping your other eye open.** Cameras are built so the user puts his right eye in the viewfinder and keeps his other eye free. Work on using the left eye to expand your field of vision and keep you abreast of what's going on. This requires extreme concentration, but can alert you to situations that need your attention.

5. **Work on anticipation.** Try to guess where the next play will occur and react accordingly. Each new play is a completely different situation, but with practice you can prepare yourself for what will likely happen. Then it's simply a matter of putting yourself in the best position for the shot.

6. **Be prepared.** Shooting is hard work and involves heavy equipment. Dress accordingly for the camera and the weather. Plan ahead where you need to be and at what time, and give yourself enough time to get there.

Figure 7-8 Sports Photographers Concentrate on Location, Anticipation, and Good Positioning

THE PHOTOGRAPHY OF NFL FILMS

The people at NFL Films have the reputation as some of the finest sports photographers in the industry, and over the past 40 years they have built one of the best sports libraries in the world. NFL Films now has 250 employees processing 800 miles of film into 2,000 hours of original programming a year. A few years ago, several NFL Films photographers sat down in a roundtable discussion and talked about how they approach their jobs. NFL Films edited the discussion for its television series, *NFL Films Presents*, and the suggestions apply to anyone who wants to learn more about sports photography.

- Strive for perfection. Try to make every play the best it can possibly be.
- Look for emotion and reaction. Many times a frustration shot is more compelling than a celebration shot.
- Simple close-ups can tell you what the athletes are feeling.
- Respect the subject.
- Capture the moment. The best way to do this is to be in the right place at the right time.
- Try something different. Steve Sabol, who now runs NFL Films, gives a $1,000 bonus to anyone who makes a really big mistake. "You wouldn't make that mistake unless you were trying to do something interesting," he said.

EDITING

Editing is a very unappreciated part of the sports reporting process. You can have all the great shots in the world on your raw tape, but if you can't edit them together in the right way, you can't tell an effective story.

Not too long ago, all shooting and editing was done on film. The tape had to be physically cut and spliced together, which was an extremely time-consuming and difficult process that often made it impractical to get same-day highlights of events. The advent of videotape in the 1970s was a tremendous leap forward and helped speed up and simplify the editing process. Now, new digital technology promises to streamline the process even further. As stations begin the switch to digital equipment, the editing process will become more like home computing, with an emphasis on cutting and pasting. The final product will not even exist on tape, but rather will be sent in digital form to a central computer for playback (see Figure 7-9).

In most large markets, editing (and photography) is a union job. That means you can't touch a camera or any editing equipment unless you join the union. But just about everywhere else, you'll be doing your own editing. And whether you're working with videotape or digital equipment, there are some essentials to good editing for any sports story.

Figure 7-9 One Version of a Digital Editing System Used in Television Sports Departments

Don't let the highlights go too long or too short. So many times, because of time constraints, video is cut off just before the conclusion of a play. Nothing is more frustrating to the viewer than to hear, "Trust me folks . . . he eventually gets into the end zone." The average length for a single highlight play is between 10–15 seconds, so make sure you give yourself enough time. At the same time, don't give too much time to highlights. Remember, viewers can see the exact same thing on ESPN, CNN, and countless other outlets. Nothing is more boring than watching two minutes of highlights from a game you may have just watched on TV. Let the viewer see what's important, but save your real time for things that matter to the audience.

Don't be afraid of natural sound. The cheering crowd, the excited announcer, and the coach yelling instructions to his or her players, all add something to the final presentation. Not too long ago, most sportscasters used either silence or canned music behind their stories. But natural sound adds something to the story that interests the viewer. Witness the popularity of "behind the scenes" sports films and putting a microphone on players during the game.

Cutaways can help, but don't overuse them. Some sportscasters (and especially news directors) fall in love with cutaways. Such shots always will have a special place in sports stories, but remember what viewers want to see. Too many side shots lead to clutter and the story loses its momentum. In some cases, it's almost like the commercials between news stories.

Let the pictures tell the story. Truer words were never spoken. Good pictures can make or break a story much more so than narration. If you have good pictures, editing becomes easy. But when a story doesn't have that knockout photography, then you have to get more creative. This could include things like natural sound, graphics, music, and the like.

Get the story on the air. This really should be the first and great commandment. All the pretty pictures and narration in the world don't do any good if the tape is still sitting in editing at deadline. Some sportscasters make the mistake of trying to be too perfect and do too much, especially with feature stories. Make sure you get a complete, coherent story ready for air, then worry about the rest. Clean the suit first, then press the lapels.

Make sure the style of editing matches the tone of the story. Modern technology allows for all kinds of fancy edits, such as wipes, dissolves, and fades. But make sure you use these in accordance with the story. For example, dissolves and fades work better with slower or more serious feature stories. For highlights or game stories, it's better to stick with traditional hard edits.

When done correctly, the editing should compliment the photography. Many shooters will "edit in the camera," which means they shoot certain sequences and shots with a specific idea of how it will look in the edit booth. Ideally, the photographer should have tremendous input in the editing process, and vice-versa. Obviously, this becomes much easier when the photography and editing are done by the same person, but if not, it's important for the reporter to collaborate with the photographer during the shooting process.

REFERENCES

Strauss, Robert. "One on One: An Empire Built on the Ballet of Football." *Electronic Media,* December 4, 2000, p. 24.

8

Producing

In many ways, producing is the hardest job in sports broadcasting, because it requires the most planning and preparation. The three or four minute sports segment that eventually runs on the evening news is the result of a coordinated effort on the part of several individuals, many of whom have put in hours or even days of planning. But the ultimate responsibility of how the show looks remains with the producer. In larger markets, producers do nothing but produce and spend all day putting the show together. But at smaller stations, producing is just one part of the job, which also includes anchoring, photography, editing, writing, promotion, and almost everything else.

THE BASICS

Every sports production, no matter how big or small, starts with the same basic elements. The producer must be aware of these elements and build the show around them, but must also be ready to change or even eliminate them at a moment's notice (see Figure 8-1).

The first and most important element is time or length. This obviously varies depending on the station, the market size, and the situation. Generally, station executives do not consider sports an important element of the show and almost all research studies confirm their opinion (see Chapter 15). Sports is generally the least watched part of the local television newscast (behind weather and news) and according to consulting firm Frank Magid, up to two-thirds of the audience does not find sports a compelling reason to tune in. As a result, sports is left to the end of the newscast and given less

Figure 8-1 Part of the Production Staff at ESPN (Courtesy ESPN/Rich Arden)

time than the other news elements. This time usually runs about three to four minutes for a weekday sportscast and up to six or seven minutes on the weekends, although a recent trend in several markets has seen sports get cut to two minutes or less. The special weekend wrap-up shows come under a different category and will be discussed later in the chapter.

Coming at the end of the show affords certain advantages, such as having more time to write and edit material. The deadline for getting such material ready for air is usually around 10 or 15 minutes past the hour. But the situation also has several disadvantages. Because the sports segment usually comes at the end of the show, time often gets cut or expanded to make corrections for earlier problems in the newscast. Special situations, such as breaking news or live reporting can often cut into sports time. For an important event like election night, some stations will forego sports coverage entirely. Thus, while the newscast producer will try to stick to the scheduled time as much as possible, the actual time can change often during the day and even during the newscast.

That's what makes preparation so important. Nothing is as important to the success of your sportscast as planning ahead and being ready for almost any eventuality. Television sports is a fluid and dynamic business, where things can and do change at a moment's notice. With the proper planning, you can minimize the damage when equipment breaks down, an interview guest fails to show, or you're stuck in traffic with highlights of the lead story. There are several things to consider when planning out a sportscast:

1. **Always start with a rundown.** A rundown is simply a list of the stories you plan to cover for the day (see Table 8-1). A rundown generally includes the list and names of your stories, how you plan to present them (i.e., highlights only? sound on tape? a full package?) and other important information for the director. Most newsrooms are now computerized and have software programs to use with your rundowns, although in some of the smaller markets you still might have to do your rundown manually on a typewriter.

   The rundown is your blueprint for the show and will often change before the sportscast. Some stories will come in late and have to be delayed, while others will not come at all and have to be dropped entirely. You may also have to drop stories if the news has run long or if your own show has taken longer than expected. Therefore, it's always a good idea to have some sort of backup plan in mind.

   An example of a possible problem in the case of our example rundown is that your reporter could tell you that he couldn't get the interview he needed with the coach. You would have to change the story from a VO/SOT (video with sound on tape) to perhaps just a VO (voice over) and consider adding another short reader or story to make up the time. The key to the rundown is flexibility and being prepared to make changes at any time.

   It's also important to work with the newscast producer and let him or her know exactly what's in your show. He or she should receive a copy of the rundown and be updated on any changes. The newscast pro-

Table 8-1 Typical Sports Segment Rundown

Slug	*Story Type*	*Tape #*	*Still Store*	*Length*	*Total Time*
HS Football	VO	S-147	Football	:40	:40
Scores	CG	—	—	:30	1:10
College Preview	VO/SOT	S-148	Tigers FB	:45	1:55
Coach Jones	PKG	S-149	—	1:50	3:45
Baseball Trade	RDR	—	Cubs	:15	4:00

ducer has the responsibility for the overall newscast, of which your sports-cast plays a part. He or she has the final authority to adjust sports time and approve any last-minute changes.

2. **Make a list of the resources you expect for the show.** What stories you want to cover obviously depend on what's available. How many photographers are available to shoot? How much time will it take to edit? What's coming down on the network sports feed? What's on the national wires? What are the most important local events going on? Does anything warrant live coverage? These are some of the questions you should ask yourself as you plan out your show.

Resources and story ideas come from many different places. Most if not all stations now subscribe to the Associated Press broadcast wire, which transmits global, national, and sometimes local sports informa-

Figure 8-2 Recording Highlights from a Network Sports Feed at a Local Television Station

tion 24 hours a day (see Figure 8-2). Many times, a national story can be localized to attract more interest with the station's audience. For example, if the AP runs a story that says graduation rates for college athletes are falling, you could go to the local college or university and investigate the situation there. The role of the news feed is to provide supporting video and audio material for the bigger stories of the day. In the graduation rate example, the news feed might provide an interview with the head of the NCAA or the person who conducted the study.

Most stations subscribe to some form of news feed, either affiliated with their network or with an independent provider, such as CNN. News feeds come almost continually during the day, although most of the sports content comes at specific times. Usually, news feed organizations provide sports feeds at least three times during the day: in the morning, when the feed includes highlights and interviews from the previous night's games; in the late afternoon, when it includes the major sports news of the day and any afternoon games; and finally in the late evening, when it focuses on highlights of games played that night and updates major stories from earlier in the day (see Table 8-2).

Just as things change quite quickly in the newsroom, material on the news wires and news feeds can change as well. The AP might be slow in getting an update on an important story, or the news feed might be delayed in providing the highlights you need for a particular game. Sometimes, the problems are technical as severe weather can knock out satellite transmission. That's why it's so important to have some sort of backup plan ready, just in case.

Table 8-2 Typical Network Sports News Feed Rundown

Time	Slug	Format	Source	Length
4:30:15	Tyson hearing	VO/SOT		1:30
4:32:05	Yankees parade	VO	WPIX	1:00
4:33:30	FSU preview	VO/SOT	NCAA	3:00
4:37:00	Illinois preview	VO/SOT	NCAA	2:56
4:40:15	Payne Stewart	PKG	WCPX	1:50
4:42:30	Blauser file	VO	MLB	:35
4:43:15	Santiago file	VO	MLB	:30
4:45:00	Cards preview	VO/SOT	KTVK	1:30
4:47:10	Jags preview	VO/SOT	WJXT	1:20
4:48:45	Bears preview	VO/SOT	WFLD	1:45
4:50:45	Chiefs preview	SOT	KMBC	:45

3. **Be realistic about what you can and can't do.** Obviously, you want to give the best possible coverage to each and every story in your rundown, but just as obviously there are technical and logistical handicaps that make your job much more difficult. It would be great to have a live report from the state championship basketball game, but is it even technically possible to get a live shot from the arena? And what's the cost involved? If you don't go live, what's the next best way to cover the game? A package seems logical, but will your reporter have time to drive back to the station and edit a piece? Would a look-live be more appropriate or even a phoner? Sports producers waste a lot of time spinning their wheels because they try to do too much. Certainly, unexpected breakdowns and problems will occur and more often than you like. But pushing the envelope too far only increases your chances for frustration down the line.

4. **Coordinate your coverage as much as possible.** This means coordination at every level—the newsroom, event management, engineering, etc. The news department should be fully aware of what you're trying to do, not only to avoid unnecessary conflict but maybe to provide some unexpected help. If a news reporter is covering a story in the same town where you need an interview with the baseball coach, you might be able to kill two birds with one stone and save yourself the trip. But don't be surprised if you're asked to return the favor someday.

   Many times you'll have to work hand-in-hand with the news department on stories that cross over into both areas. Athletes can become news subjects for their behavior off the field, such as the arrest and trial of O.J. Simpson. In these cases, you will have to work with the news department to decide how best to cover the story. It could involve you anchoring in the news segment or developing sidebar stories (see Table 8-3).

   Many times sports stories become front-page news and it's necessary for the news and sports departments to work together on the coverage. Consider a typical hypothetical example, where a local all-star athlete is arrested on drug charges. Usually news and sports departments will work together to get the pieces of the story. But what are the presentation possibilities for the station?

   The engineering department also needs to know what's going on, especially if there's any satellite or live coverage involved. If you're taking a satellite feed, the engineers need to know details such as coordinates and what time the material will come down. Live shots have to be set up well in advance to overcome possible problems like signal interference.

   As much as possible, you should check with coordinators of the event you're going to cover. Find out about credentials, parking availability, directions to the event, places where you can shoot, and what to do about getting post-game interviews. On the high school and local

Table 8-3 Sports News or News Sports?

Situation	Comments
News anchors throw to sports anchor for story, either on live shot, on set, or in sports office.	This is an extremely popular way to handle the story, although it makes it difficult for the sportscaster to come up with fresh material for his or her own segment. Having the sportscaster in the news segment lends the sports department credibility and lets the audience know this is not just another story. The downside is that it can lead to overkill on a story.
Sportscaster produces some sort of sidebar or related story that runs in the news block.	This is also very popular and allows each department a fresh angle on the story. Usually, the news department would handle the harder edge to the story: the details of the arrest and reactions from community members. The sports department would then handle a related angle, such as the prevalence of drugs in the local athletic community or how the arrest will affect the athlete's status on the team or chances for a college scholarship.
Team coverage of the story, involving both news and sports.	Team coverage involves allocating almost all the station's resources to the story, including reporters, photographers, engineers, and the sports department. At least two or three reporters would provide different reports on the story, all covering a different angle. Proponents of team coverage say it allows a station to give a story the in-depth attention it deserves, while critics simply call it excessive overkill. Again, the main problem for the sportscaster is that it leaves very little new material to use when the sports segment rolls around.
Story runs exclusively either in news or sports, but not both.	This is very seldom done for a variety of reasons. Skipping the story in the news segment sends the signal that it's not a very important story, and also runs the risk of other stations getting the jump on coverage. Running the story exclusively in news might miss the viewers or listeners who don't tune in until the sports segment. It also gives people the impression that the sports department isn't on top of things.

level, many of these decisions are left up to you. But college and pro events have very strict guidelines regarding the media and failure to follow the rules can lead not only to embarrassment, but possibly not getting to cover the game.

5. **Have as many local stories as possible.** Not too long ago, broadcast television stations were the only game in town and the only way for people to see highlights of national sports events like the Kentucky Derby or Indy 500. Now, there are literally hundreds of cable and satellite channels, some of them completely dedicated to sports. Virtually the same highlights run on ESPN, CNN, and the like. Add the Internet and online services, and the viewer can get his or her national sports stories from almost anywhere.

It's essential that you emphasize your local sports scene because it offers your audience something they can't see anywhere else. Certainly, this means the traditional sports, such as football, basketball, and baseball. Many stations have now expanded their weekend shows to 10 or 15 minutes with one goal in mind—show as many high school and local college games as possible.

But local coverage also means nontraditional sports presented in nontraditional ways. Feature stories about inspiring athletes overcoming adversity or unlikely champions have become quite popular because they interest the non-sports fan. The hard-core sports segment (remember, only about a third of the total audience) is going to watch no matter what you show. It's the other two-thirds you need to reach, which can be done with well-crafted feature pieces. Such stories provide much of the real challenge of sportscasting because they force you to get away from scores and highlights and become more of a storyteller (see Chapter 5).

It's also important to keep up-to-date with what's going on in the area. Make a file (sometimes called a "futures" or "tickler" file) of upcoming events and read the local sports section everyday. Develop contacts in the area that can keep you informed of any breaking situations. Many exclusives have been scored because of innocent conversations or phone calls that came in to the sports department.

SHOW-BY-SHOW DETAILS

As a sports producer, you could end up putting together several shows during the course of one day. How you produce these shows depends largely on the time the newscast airs and what kind of viewers you're likely to attract (see Table 8-4).

Morning Shows

Some stations allow time on the early morning wake-up shows for a few minutes of sports. This is not all that common and is usually taken care of by nonsports personnel, but if it ever falls in your lap there are some key elements to consider. Your audience will consist of a wide variety of demographic segments, including men and women on their way to work, kids on their way to school, and stay-at-home moms or dads. None of these groups should be considered hard core fans; the hard core fan stayed up late to watch ESPN or got up early to look on the Internet.

The morning group is mainly people who want to check out a particular score or see if anything interesting happened since bedtime. Therefore, make sure you get all the scores on, especially the late games from the West Coast and try to find at least one unusual or interesting piece of video. The video could be a great play from a game or it could be a blooper or lighter moment. The idea is to provoke reaction from the viewers and give them something to talk about during the day. "Did you see what happened last night in the football/basketball/baseball game?" is a typical question asked at thousands of businesses across the country. Sometimes, these are called "water cooler" stories, because people talk about them around the water cooler at work.

There's really not enough time in this type of show for anything other than the scores and a highlight or two. Your segment should give the viewers what they want, along with the reassurance that they haven't missed anything important.

Table 8-4 Considerations for Sports Producing

Show	Primary Audience	Elements
Morning	Men and women headed to work, some kids	Late scores/highlights, unusual or interesting video
5:00 P.M.	Women, elderly, kids, casual fans	Longer feature stories, packages, personality-oriented stories, visually interesting
6:00 P.M.	Men, hard-core fans	Harder stories, fewer packages, higher story count, more VO and VO/SOTs
10/11:00 P.M.	Wide range, usually more interested fans	Scores, highlights, reaction

5:00 P.M. Shows

Almost unheard of 20 years ago, early afternoon newscasts have become almost a standard at every station in the country. Some of the larger markets start their newscasts at 4:00 P.M. and go straight through until 6:00 or 6:30 P.M.

The audience for these types of shows varies almost as much as for the morning shows. People who work usually haven't arrived home yet, so that leaves stay-at-homes (mostly women), the elderly, and a few kids. Many of these people are serious about their news, but again are just casual sports fans. And that means you should produce your sportscasts with them in mind.

Primarily, the show should be lighter and have more features than a typical sportscast. That means more feature-type packages, more emphasis on live shots and visuals, and more personality-oriented stories. The housewife or grandmother at home does not really care who won last night's game between the Kings and Mavericks. But as previously noted, nonsports fans will watch if the show involves good story telling with an interesting presentation. You certainly can use stories from the night before, as long as they're fresh or involving. And it's also a good idea to use some of the time to promote what's coming up in later sportscasts.

The trick is to avoid repeating what you're going to do at 6 or 11 P.M. Research shows that each of these shows has a different audience, but even so you don't want your sportscasts to become stale and repetitive. You will likely cover the same stories for all three (or more) shows, but the solution lies in finding different ways to present them. A feature package on the 5:00 P.M. show may rate just a VO/SOT at 6:00 P.M. and may not be included at all at 10:00 P.M.

6:00 P.M. Shows

This is usually the bread-and-butter show of the day because it's where you have your most interested audience. Most of your hard core audience tunes in at 6:00 P.M., which means a completely different way of thinking from 5:00 P.M.

Now is the time to use the more serious sports pieces with a harder edge. It also means a faster pace than at 5:00 P.M., so you might want to consider cutting down packages or longer stories in favor of more VOs and VO/SOTs to build a higher "story count." Typical stories in this type of sportscast include previews of games coming up that night, interviews with players and coaches on a particular game or subject, and a roundup of the major national sports news. You don't necessarily have to shy away from features or similar stories, but try to keep in mind your primary audience. If you run anything from the night before, it should be something so outstanding or unusual that the audience expects to see it again. And as with earlier shows, you'll probably want to promote what's coming up at 11:00 P.M., especially stories of local interest you're planning to cover.

Just because the show is a little more serious during this hour compared to earlier shows doesn't mean it has to be humorless. We've already discussed the role of style and personality in a sportscast and we'll continue to address it in later chapters.

10:00/11:00 P.M. Shows

This is usually the most hectic and frantic show of the day because the preparation time is significantly shorter than your other sportscasts. For a 5:00 or 6:00 P.M. show, you have most of the afternoon to produce and get things ready. But the late show gives you only a few hours of turnaround time, which is quickly filled watching and logging games, coordinating local sports coverage, checking satellite feeds and highlights, writing the show, and maybe even going out to shoot. Often times, stories and highlights will change right up until deadline.

As a result, it's very difficult to put together an elaborate sports production filled with perfectly timed highlights and fascinating features. You're better off keeping it simple and concentrating on getting the basics—the scores, the highlights, and some reaction. This works particularly well because that's what most of the audience wants to see on a late sports show. They want to know who won the important games of the night, see a few key plays, and maybe hear some post-game interviews. And by the time you've done all that, you've probably filled up your allotted time.

Obviously, by scores and highlights we're talking as local as possible. Don't forget, the viewer can see all the national stuff on cable and the Internet. But he or she can't see local high school or college action and that's probably the main reason most local viewers tune in. Don't shy away completely from national events—there are still a lot of people out there without cable hookup or personal computers and you're their only source of sports news. But build your sportscast around the local stuff first, and then let everything else fall into place.

RUNDOWN ROULETTE: PUTTING IT ALL TOGETHER

Spacing out stories for three or four different sportscasts is one of the main responsibilities of producing. To get an idea of how this is done, let's assume you come into the station on a summer Thursday afternoon. Let's say you work in the Rockford, Illinois market, with no major league teams, but close proximity to Chicago. A scan of the paper, wires, and other sources reveals the following possibilities for the day:

- Local junior golf tournament begins
- First round of PGA stop (Greensboro, North Carolina)
- Area high school hires new football coach
- Afternoon baseball highlights (Cubs–Brewers)
- Evening baseball scores and highlights

Right off the top, the new coach story sounds interesting. Much depends on the school, its history of success, and its importance in the community. This could be the lead. The local golf tournament doesn't sound exciting, but you may need to fill some time. Is there any way to find an engaging story for a package? Maybe there's a precocious talent playing (a young Tiger Woods?) or some other interesting angle. The PGA story is nothing more than short highlights or a VO, unless something unusual or interesting happens. You know your audience is interested in the Cubs and probably the baseball scores. It also looks like you'll have to fill out the rest of your time with other national stories or some local item of interest.

Given these factors, we could come up with the following rundowns:

5:00 P.M.

1. New coach	SOT
2. Cubs	VO
3. PGA	VO or Reader
4. Local golf	PKG (Live?)

Remember, our audience is primarily women who are more interested in feature-type stories. We can lead with the coach, but keep it short and to the point. Maybe include some highlights on the Cubs or the PGA event. The main focus of the show could be the junior golf tournament. There's a chance to turn an interesting angle into a good story. You might even consider a live shot if the situation warrants.

6:00 P.M.

1. New coach	PKG/live/phoner/in-studio interview
2. Cubs	VO
3. PGA	Reader
4. Local golf	VO or VO/SOT

This is a more hard-core audience, so it's appropriate to extend the coach story into a package. You might consider a live shot, live talk-back, or even a live, in-studio interview if the story is important enough. People still want to know about the Cubs, and you can go a little longer with the highlights. You have to cut something, which means less time for the golf stories.

10:00 P.M.

1. Night baseball highlights/scores	VO/Scores
2. Cubs	VO
3. New coach	SOT
4. PGA	VO/Reader
5. Local golf	VO/Scores

It's important to lead with something new at 10 o'clock, simply because viewers have already seen your other stories at least twice. Unless the coach story is of paramount importance, you should probably drop it in the rundown. You don't necessarily have to lead with baseball, but you should offer something new and different. Maybe you could show highlights of a local game of interest. The other stories are reduced accordingly, if only because by 10 o'clock they have almost become old news.

LONGER PRODUCTIONS

It has become quite common for sports departments to expand coverage for some shows to 15 or 30 minutes. Sometimes, these shows cover a particular event or topic on a weekly basis, such as a NASCAR weekend wrap-up show or a weekly show devoted to sports coverage of a particular team or city. In some cases, the shows are simply special productions to take advantage of increased demand for a particular event. Super Bowls, college bowl games, and local PGA tournaments certainly fall into this category. Another type of longer production is built around a theme of local interest, such as fishing, outdoor activity, auto racing, or bowling. But no matter what type of show, longer productions all aim to satisfy an increased demand for sports coverage that viewers can't get during a normal weekday newscast.

Obviously, how these shows are produced depends on the money and resources available to the producer. When a big-market team goes to the Super Bowl or the NCAA basketball tournament, stations usually spare no expense in their coverage. This includes sending dozens of reporters, photographers, and anchors to the scene for extensive live reporting, such as when WTMJ-TV in Milwaukee sent 31 people to cover the Packers in Super

Bowl XXXI. A smaller station faced with a similar event would have a much more scaled-down effort, likely including only one or two people at the scene and some live satellite transmission. But no matter what the market size, sports producers must approach the production in much the same way.

The most important consideration is to make sure there's enough interest to justify extended coverage. Even simple productions cost extra money for personnel, equipment, and salaries. If the production has to go out of town or out of the country, the cost can run into the many thousands of dollars. For that kind of investment, news directors want to know there's going to be enough audience and advertiser interest in the project. The key is getting the advertisers, because they'll have to contribute above and beyond their normal financial commitment. Often times, a station will sign up an exclusive or single sponsor for an event, resulting in things like the "Jones Chevrolet Post-Game Show" or "Channel Two's Rose Bowl Show, brought to you by Kroger." Single sponsorships increase visibility for the advertiser, but also increase the possibility of excessive demands or a desire to influence the editorial content. Enlisting the help of several different sponsors is also quite common.

Generally speaking, stations will not undertake a special sports production unless they know they have advertisers in place. However, in some cases stations will take a financial loss in exchange for the promotional value and credibility associated with the production. There's also a danger of listening to the advertisers instead of the audience. Many times, a station will get involved with a production because the sales department has several interested sponsors lined up. But if these advertiser-driven shows don't have enough audience appeal, they usually don't last very long. The ratings will suffer and the advertisers will eventually drift away.

Another important consideration is the interest level of the production. An hour or even a half-hour is a long time for a specialized content show that appeals to only a small segment of the audience. For years, one of the more common types of special sports productions has been the "coaches show." A university or college coach usually co-hosts the show with a local sports personality and reviews plays from the previous game. But that combination has proven to be extremely and excruciatingly boring. The coaches are generally not very effective media communicators, the highlights are repetitive, and the in-studio interview guests come across as uninteresting. A cheesy show open or graphics package can also send a signal to the viewer that the production is not worth watching.

The challenge for the producer is to find a way to liven up the format and keep the show from getting dull. This can include such things as high-energy music and graphics, adding more segments to the production, and getting out of the studio setting. By its nature, the studio lends itself to familiarity with the viewer, who sees the show as just the same old stuff. Going out on location helps add freshness to the presentation, as does the addition of feature-type elements. Many stations will include news and feature reports in a sports production to broaden the appeal of the show. So when a local team goes to play in the Sugar Bowl, the extended sports show could also include reports of the New Orleans nightlife or interesting restaurants. Another way to help liven up the show is to either reduce the static one-on-one interviews or present them in a different format.

The challenge for the producer is to focus on the local angles and yet still make the presentation unique. Realize that other stations and outlets in the market are probably considering or doing much the same thing. If there's a big PGA tournament in town, chances are all the other stations will have some sort of extended sports programming. That's why it's important for the show to have its own unmistakable identity and something that separates it from the competition. This can be accomplished in several different ways, including emphasizing the personality of the anchors, the quality of the photography and graphics, or the type of stories presented. Much of this can be accomplished through planning and preparation and more than any other sports effort, the extended show requires the cooperation and coordination of all other departments. The sports producer should consult with the news director, engineers, and other station personnel to map out a strategy for the entire production. The ultimate success or failure of the production depends largely on planning done ahead of time.

FINAL ADVICE

No two people would put together a sports show the same way. Some would go heavy on the visuals, with lots of live shots and graphics. Others would go for the humorous stuff, making every story into a reflection of their personality. And many prefer the more traditional way of delivering sports in a straight and no-nonsense fashion.

Much of the sports production depends on other factors, such as budget, equipment, and certainly the attitude of the news director. But no matter what situation you find yourself in, some basic guidelines can help make your sportscast better.

Think big and push the envelope. This presents a special challenge for producers in small markets with small budgets and limited resources. If you're covering only two high school football games on Friday nights, is there a way to get to three or even more? Who says you can't cover the major university on a regular basis, even if it is a couple of hours away? Viewers will always notice if you do something different and try something new, especially if it involves a major effort. Sometimes thinking big means nothing more than breaking away from the traditional way of doing things. Just because things have always been done a certain way at a station, doesn't mean you can't try something new.

Be unique and do something different. Find a way to present a show that carves out your own identity in the market. So many local sportscasts have become cookie-cutter presentations; they all look and sound the same. Several years ago, a few stations began doing a "Team of the Week," or "Athlete of the Week" type story. Now, so many have copied the idea that it's lost its originality and freshness. Your sportscast should have its own feel and flavor, so that when anyone in the audience sees it, they immediately think of your station.

Save something for a rainy day. If you're producing three shows a night, five days a week, that adds up to a lot of minutes to fill. Even the best producers run out of ideas, especially during the hot, boring summer months. The most experienced producers never throw anything away or erase any tapes (if they can afford it). Putting stuff away on the shelf can save your bacon on a slow day and might even produce an award-winning story. For instance, you may have done several interviews with the local football coach who finally retired after 40 years at the high school. Six months later, the coach unexpectedly passes on. If you saved your tapes, you could produce a quite effective and moving obituary, given in the coach's own words. It doesn't even have to be anything that dramatic. Interviews and other features have a long shelf life and can last for months, or even years.

Try to make the show interactive and give the viewer a tangible reason to watch. It's no accident the Internet has become so successful, because it allows the audience to actively participate in the communication process. There are all kinds of ways to do this in television—quizzes, sweepstakes, giveaways, phone polls—anything to give the viewer a sense of participation. At KCRG-TV in Cedar Rapids, Iowa, sports director John Campbell runs a feature called "Big Ol' Fish." Viewers will send in pictures of the big catches they made and Campbell will add some music underneath and the voice-over work. It sounds almost too simple to work, but over several years "Big Ol' Fish" has become the most popular segment of the sports show and Campbell has a six-month backlog of pictures to sort through.

Don't be afraid to experiment. We've already talked a little bit about trying new things. The only stories that always fail are the ones you don't try. A small-market station in Ohio wanted to find a way to beat the competition in Friday night football coverage. The sports director suggested a "sports ticker," that continuously ran scores at the bottom of the screen during the entire length of the 30-minute newscast. That way, the news could promote the sports and vice-versa. Other ideas could include covering unusual sports or trying different camera angles. Experimentation means nothing more

Figure 8-3   The Final Goal of the Production Process—Putting the Show on the Air

than trying something different or doing something in a new way. Often times it doesn't work, but sometimes it can really pay off.

Find ways to reduce the time devoted to giving scores. Scores are the lifeblood of the sports show and one of the main reasons viewers tune in. But to simply put up a graphic and repeat the scores everyone can see on the screen wastes a lot of precious time. And every year, news directors become more willing to cut time from the sports show. You've got to give the scores, but experiment with different ways of doing it. Many station executives find the "ticker" mentioned earlier too distracting, but at least it saves precious time that could be used for something more important (see Figure 8-3).

REFERENCE

Rosenthal, Phil. "Everybody's a Comedian." *Electronic Media,* March 22, 1999.

9

Live Event Production

When the very first sporting events were televised back in the 1930s and 40s, the technology was still extremely primitive. It limited the type and location of events, and necessitated simple, no-nonsense coverage. As a result, most events were televised with only a single camera and hardly any frills. The equipment was big, bulky, and inconsistent, resulting in several breakdowns and other accidents. Many people remember the 1958 NFL Championship game between the Colts and Giants as one of the most dramatic games in football history and the landmark television sports event of its era. But fewer people remember an incident that happened near the end of the game, when NBC television cables accidentally got dislodged, knocking the signal off the air. Luckily for NBC, a fan ran onto the field, creating a distraction that allowed engineers to fix the problem just before the winning touchdown was scored. According to an apocryphal story, it was an NBC employee who created the distraction to save the network from 45 million angry viewers.

Flash forward to the NFL championship game in January 2000, Super Bowl XXXIV. In two weeks, ABC technicians transformed the Georgia Dome in Atlanta into one of the most sophisticated broadcasting venues in history. The production included 23 pedestal cameras, 6 hand-held cameras, 2 remote control cameras, and another camera on a blimp. Another seven high-definition cameras were used in conjunction with the traditional cameras. The ABC production crew also utilized 75 monitors, 30 video tape recorders (VTRs), 60 microphones, 20 miles of cable, 35 production trucks, and a crew of more than 300. The Super Bowl is no ordinary show, but clearly, producing live sports events has become much more complicated, time consuming, and expensive. And it is a frontier that is constantly changing and updating, especially with the impending arrival of digital broadcasting.

TELEVISION PRODUCTION

There are certainly many variables to live television sports production, including the type of event, the venue, and the resources available for coverage. But no matter what the circumstances involved, production actually starts days and even weeks before the event takes place. Once an organization decides to have its event televised live, it usually contracts out the work to a company that specializes in sports production. Several such organizations exist throughout the country and they usually work events on a regional scale, which allows for transportation of the equipment by large trucks. For example, Metro Sports in Kansas City will handle live events in Missouri, Kansas, Arkansas, and Illinois. Companies like Metro Sports own much of the equipment they use, but often will have to borrow facilities to help meet the demand for their services.

The production company is responsible for almost every facet of the live telecast, including satellite truck and uplink facilities, equipment, and crew (although in many cases, the organization that sponsors the event will arrange its own talent for the broadcast). The size of the crew depends on the size of the event, but for a regional event like a college football or basketball game there are usually two dozen or so crewmembers involved. With a few notable exceptions, most of the crewmembers are freelancers and contract their services out on a per-event basis. Each crewmember usually gets around $250 or $300 per day plus expenses, and the cost can go even higher in places that require union labor. The cost of the crew is one of the major expenses of a live sports production and can easily run between $5,000 and $10,000 for a single game. Uplink time and the use of a satellite truck runs around $3,500, while the production truck and the use of an engineer usually costs another $5,000. When you consider miscellaneous expenses and overtime costs, it's not unusual for major sports production costs to run about $20,000 per event (see Figure 9-1).

Typical Sports Production Crew List

1 producer

1 director

1 technical director

2 audio operators

1 graphics operator

3 tape replay operators

5 camera operators

1 engineer

(a)

(b)

Figure 9-1(a) and (b)   Exterior and Interior Views of a Typical Sports Production Truck

2 statistics operators

1 time out coordinator

2 utility coordinators

Production trucks usually come at a high price because they contain extremely sophisticated and expensive equipment. Each truck is in effect a mobile television studio. It has dozens of monitors, cameras, cables, and microphones necessary for the production of any live sports event. Production trucks literally come in all shapes and sizes. Jefferson-Pilot Sports produces hundreds of live sporting events every year. One of the company's medium range 48-foot trucks includes the following:

Cameras

5 HK-366 cameras

3 Canon 55:1 lenses with 2x extender

2 Canon 55:1 tele super lenses with 2x extender

3 HK-355PA handhelds

3 Canon 18:1 lenses with 2x extender

1 studio configuration

1 betacam (by request)

2 Panasonic CCD LPS cameras

Production Switcher

3000-T Grass Valley

36 inputs

3 mix effects

Routing Switcher

SMS 64 x 64 Grass Valley

48 x 48 video

32 x 32 audio

Special Effects

Abekas A-42 still store

Abekas A-51 dual channel DVE

Videotape

2 Sony DVW-A500 digibeta videotapes

4 DNF slo-mo controllers

1 Lance slo-mo controller

4 Sony BVW 75 beta SP videotapes

1 drastic disc recorder

Production

58 monitors (monitor wall)

2 Ikegami 19" color monitors

4 color 9" monitors

42 b/w 9" monitors

2 b/w triple monitors

1 b/w quad monitor

Additional Monitors

3 color 13" monitors

4 color 11" monitors

5 color 9" monitors

2 b/w 9" monitors

Other Equipment

7 frame syncs

2 Lowell-D light kits

Audio

Yamaha PM 4000 console with 52 inputs and 24 outputs

2 6-input sub-mixers

8 compressors

1 2-channel Yamaha digital

Effects

1 Digicart II

1 360 digital audio editor

1 CD player

1 DAT recorder

Microphones

4 Sennheiser 816 (shotgun)

7 Sennheiser 416 (shotgun)

6 ECM 44B lavs

1 Lectronics HH mic

3 Lectronics body packs

A full complement of hand mics

18 Bantam patch panels

40 Audio DAs

4 QKT lines to patch field

Gentner digital telephone

Interface

Communications

RTS 9-channel intercom

RTS IFB

Intercom with 4 stations

1 wireless IFB with 2 receivers

Receivers

2 Telos links

4 Clear Com Adaptacom

6 walkie-talkies—5 watts

2 base units—45 watts

11 10-line AT&T telephones

Graphics

Chyron Infinit! 13.5 MHz/68060 CPU

Bernoulli 230 meg drive

1 gig JAZ drive

General

Power requirements: 220 volt/200 amp

Source: Courtesy Jefferson-Pilot Sports

CHAIN OF COMMAND

Everything in live sports production begins and ends with the event producer. The producer is ultimately responsible for every component of the telecast, although much of his or her work is done before the event ever begins. Producers often work three or four games a week and have a heavy travel schedule. As a result, they usually don't get to a venue until the night before the live production, when they schedule meetings with the crew and talent. This is a run-through to make sure everyone is on the same page and to go over important points that the producer wants to emphasize during the telecast.

Most of the producer's work is done the next day in the hours leading up to the event. During that time, the producer will make sure the cameras are positioned properly, do all the pre-production work for the telecast, work on commercials, and make the final decisions for any questions regarding preparation for the telecast. Pre-production work takes up the bulk of the producer's time and includes all the prerecorded elements that will go into the show, including previous highlights, game day interviews, and special feature segments. For a large-scale event, it's not unusual for the pre-production to take three or four hours or longer. The producer must also make sure that the commercials are ready to go and positioned in the proper place. Depending on the type of event, the length of preparation before a telecast can run anywhere from three to six hours. For televising games of the Chicago White Sox, Fox Sports Chicago starts its pre-game production process about seven hours before the game starts.

Once the game starts, the producer serves mainly as an overseer for the telecast. Again, one of his or her main responsibilities is making sure the commercials run in their proper places. The producer also helps the director run the telecast and communicate with the talent. The latter mainly involves keeping the announcers informed as to the general direction and flow of the telecast.

While the producer does most of his work before the game starts, the director does all his work after the game begins. The director charts the pattern of the game by calling the sequence of cameras to be used, an often difficult job that involves a half-dozen or so cameras placed in various positions around the event. The director must be aware of not only what is going on, but also what is coming up, for he or she has to decide which cameras to use and for how long. In addition to cameras, the director must also integrate other elements of the telecast, such as videotape, replays, audio, and the like.

While the director calls the shots, the technical director actually pushes the buttons during the telecast. Also called a technical manager, this person also checks out all the monitors and equipment inside the production truck to make sure they're working properly. As many times as the crew has to set up and break down the equipment, the settings often change or something simply malfunctions. The technical director must also make sure all the equipment is set to his or her specifications (see Figure 9-2).

Each event generally has two people working audio. The first person (often called A1) is responsible for the internal audio in the production truck. This person must make sure that all the audio settings inside the truck are correct and allow for proper internal communications and processing of the live signal. The second audio person (A2) usually handles the external audio at the event site. This would include the proper positioning of all the audio cables and microphones related to the event. Audio can be a difficult job because every venue is wired differently and requires a unique set up. Cables that fit together in a certain way at Yankee Stadium in New York could be completely different than the set up at Shea Stadium across town (see Figure 9-3).

Also inside the production truck are the graphics operator and the tape replay operators, two positions that are fairly self-descriptive. The graphics operator is responsible for all the printed information that appears on-screen during the telecast. This means loading the graphic information in the hours before the game, including names, statistics, and the like. During the game, the graphics operator works with the director and technical director in getting the proper graphics on the screen at the right time. Tape replay operators are responsible for capturing, loading, and displaying video replays during the game. Again, these positions work with the director and technical director. Because of the frequency of replays in live sports events, it usually takes more than one or two replay people to handle the load (see Figure 9-4).

Some of the most visible members of the crew are the camera operators. With the exception of major events like the Super Bowl or World Series,

Figure 9-2 A Director Goes Over the Board in the Hours Before the Start of the Game

Figure 9-3 Built-in Configurations for Video and Audio Hookups

Figure 9-4 A Graphics Operator Loads Information Several Hours Before Game Time

most live sports productions use six or fewer cameras per game. The camera locations are fairly static, although much depends on the configuration of the venue and some cameras may have to be repositioned or moved slightly (see Figure 9-5).

Camera operators listen to the director to help them figure out what shots to get. A director might say that he or she needs a player close-up on a particular camera and a wide shot of the arena on another. But most experienced operators already know what shots they need ahead of time. Either way, it's important to remember that the camera operator is not freelancing to shoot whatever he wants. Usually, the operator has very detailed and specific instructions on how to shoot from his or her particular location. These instructions are discussed in the hours before the game and vary depending on where the camera is located. The camera operators also need some sort of basic knowledge about the game or the sport that they're shooting. If the director calls for a wide shot of a possible suicide squeeze play, the camera operator has to know exactly what to look for to set up the shot properly (see Figure 9-6[a] and [b]).

Every crew must have an engineer, but it hopes to never use him or her. An engineer must be available to repair any equipment breakdowns or malfunctions, and there are very few times when a crew will not need his services. "We deal with very expensive and finicky equipment," says Curtis

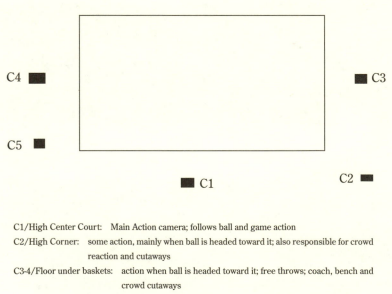

C1/High Center Court: Main Action camera; follows ball and game action

C2/High Corner: some action, mainly when ball is headed toward it; also responsible for crowd reaction and cutaways

C3-4/Floor under baskets: action when ball is headed toward it; free throws; coach, bench and crowd cutaways

C5: Mobile/handheld: floating camera responsible for action, cutaways and shots of talent

Figure 9-5   5-Camera Basketball Positions

(a)

(b)

Figure 9-6(a) and (b)   Camera Operators Must Know Their Exact Assignments

Lorenz of Metro Sports. "Things are bound to break down and go wrong." An engineer must not only be available at a moment's notice, but he or she must also have a current and in-depth knowledge of a wide variety of broadcasting equipment. Technology changes constantly and the engineer must keep on top of the latest developments. Like much of the crew, most engineers work on a freelance basis.

Each crew usually has two people to handle the statistics involved with the game. It generally requires more than one person because the flood of numbers can overwhelm a director—averages, ages, heights, weights, personal histories, and the like. All of it must be sorted through and presented in a coherent fashion for the broadcast. The production truck also has at least one liaison that works down on the field. For a basketball game, it's the time out coordinator, who notifies referees and game officials about designated breaks in the game for commercial spots. The time out coordinator or liaison also keeps officials aware of any situations that necessitate a change in the action. One of the more famous examples came in Super Bowl I, when broadcast networks stayed too long in commercial and missed a kickoff. After notification, the referees simply ordered the teams to kickoff again. Such instances are extremely rare, but the production crew must have a way of communicating with the officials in charge of the game.

The final members of the crew are the utility people, usually about a half dozen or so for each game. Their responsibility is to do all the necessary but unglamorous work associated with the telecast. This includes such things as handling cable, keeping track of certain pieces of equipment, or running errands for other members of the crew. Utility crewmembers are usually local volunteer workers who take the job more for the experience than the pay. Many times they are students from the local university or college.

RADIO PRODUCTION

As with the medium itself, live sports production on radio has a much longer history than events on television. Accounts vary as to the first sporting event broadcast on radio, but live production of such events goes back to 1921. Interestingly, although the technology has dramatically improved, the basics of radio sports production remain very much the same.

Most radio sports coverage still depends on transmission through telephone wires. In the earliest days, a radio station would order a telephone line a couple of weeks in advance of an event and the phone company would string a line into the event venue. Once the line was strung, the announcer would attach a telephone and use the handset to give the play-by-play. This process proved to be quite a challenge when there were no existing lines or the venue proved difficult for technicians to reach, and it eventually led to the development of permanent, dedicated phone lines. Because of the simplicity and low cost of this system, the production did not require a large crew. Many sports broadcasters covered events by themselves or occasionally used the services of engineers. The development of remote trucks for long-distance coverage added a few more people to the mix, but sports broadcasting on radio remained very much a one- or two-man operation.

Despite all the technological advancements of today, many stations still follow this production process. It is especially helpful for smaller stations because of the costs, which usually only involve paying the talent and the cost of the phone service. For a typical out-of-town game that requires long-distance service, a two- or three-hour radio sports broadcast normally runs between $100–$150 in phone charges. A local broadcast using only local lines would obviously cost much less. Thus, any radio station in America, regardless of size or finances, can broadcast live sports events using only one person and a phone line. Today's stations often utilize a phone with a jack on the side to send its signal back. The production is simple, effective, and inexpensive, but it does not offer the best sound reproduction. Using phone lines in such a manner usually results in tinny or scratchy audio. Yet, such a means of transmission remains a staple for thousands of small stations across the country.

For bigger stations that can afford better equipment, there are a variety of options. For years, the Marti was the basis for much radio sports production. The Marti does not depend on telephone relay, but sends the signal back to the station via a microwave signal. This provides the advantages of broadcasting from venues where telephone lines are unavailable and because it does not require lines, the costs are almost zero. But the Marti also requires a line-of-sight relay connection to the broadcasting station and the path must be free of obstacles which could impede the signal, such as buildings or trees. It also is considered somewhat big and bulky and has a dependable range of only about 20–25 miles.

Another development along these lines is known as the Cellcast. Since the Cellcast uses cellular phone technology it can go anywhere in the country where cell phone service is available. The obvious drawbacks are the uncertainty of cellular service and the expense associated with it.

The advent of digital technology has also led to the development of the Comrex. It works very much like other forms of transmission in that it sends the signal out over telephone lines. But the Comrex digitally compresses the signal, which is sent back to the station for decompression and transmission. As a result, the audio signal has the highest professional quality and sounds much better than traditional transmission methods. The Comrex system also allows for closed-channel communication between people at the studio and the broadcaster at the event. Workers back at the station can inform the broadcaster of score updates from other games or other important information related to the broadcast. Such communication is impossible with the standard phone line using a Marti or similar device. In those situations, the broadcaster must rely on the over-the-air game broadcast to know what's going on and when to run commercials.

Regardless of what system the radio broadcaster uses, almost all stations have some sort of mixer as part of their production. A mixer is a device that lets the broadcasters on the scene mix in other sound elements besides their own voices. First and foremost, this includes other microphones at the event. Besides the ones used in the booth by the broadcasters, a station will place a variety of microphones at an event to capture crowd noise, sideline activity, and the like. The mixer allows the broadcasters to control the type and amount of extraneous noise going on the air. It also allows them to record audio at the event for delayed playback or playback previously recorded material as part of the broadcast. Many stations handle this with cassettes, but more and more are switching to digital discs or mini-discs because of the better sound quality. With such technology, broadcasters can instantly replay any key moment or any other sound element from the game.

Despite such sophisticated technology, radio sports production still does not require nearly the amount of support personnel as television. Many stations continue to utilize two- or three-man crews, primarily the people who handle the play-by-play and color duties. These same people take care of the technical details as well, although they may consult a radio engineer for an especially difficult situation. The third person is usually someone back at the station who handles the incoming transmission for rebroadcast. That same person punches the audio board, runs the commercials, and makes sure the broadcast conforms to the pre-arranged format found in the broadcast log. Bigger stations with more elaborate productions may require dozens of support personnel. A typical NFL radio pre-game show, for example, can involve switching back and forth from several live venues involving half a dozen performers. Such a production obviously requires much more planning, technical support, and, of course, comes at a higher cost.

THE FUTURE

There is no reason to think that the demand for live sports production will do anything but increase in the coming years. Deregulation and legislation have opened the door for more and more opportunities in the industry. The proliferation of new media, such as the Internet, satellite, and cable has provided the means to satisfy growing consumer demand. And as technology continues to improve, it will make live sports transmission both cheaper and more feasible. This is especially true as more and more productions covert to the digital format. "Digital will mainly affect the industry in relation to transmission costs," says Leo Gher, who has 25 years of experience in sports production and broadcasting. "Digital compression has reduced the rates by some 75 percent, at last estimate."

"Digital gives a better picture, no doubt about it," says Lorenz. "The cameras are smaller and easier to work with, the audio is better sounding, and the entire size of the operation shrinks down. But we need to get ready for this digital revolution and rethink the way we do things. For example, there are only five HDTV production trucks in operation now. Five years from now, live sports production will be completely different than it is today."

REFERENCES

Catsis, John. *Sports Broadcasting*. Chicago: Nelson-Hall, 1993.

Grant, Jim. "The Dual-Cast in Atlanta Held Many Challenges, but ABC Technicians and Crew Were Up to the Task." [Online]. Available: www.tvbroadcast.com/issues/2000/0225/02.25.4.htm, February 25, 2000.

10

Media Relations

When a sports director or reporter sits down at a computer to produce a show every day, he or she faces an endless array of choices. Much of his or her information comes from the local news wires, the daily video news feeds, and even the local sports section of the newspaper. But there's another source of information to consider: the professional media specialist. Media-relations organizations employ thousands of people and spend millions of dollars every year with one goal in mind—to get their products or services mentioned on the air in the best possible way.

Sometimes, their efforts are nothing more than blatant attempts to pitch products. The sports reporter often receives unsolicited video news releases (VNRs) in the mail, usually in the form of a tape already prepared for broadcast. These VNRs have video and interviews on the new golf ball that will travel 500 yards or an unbreakable wooden baseball bat. Sometimes, they include items of genuine interest to the public, but one should always keep in mind where the VNR comes from and who's distributing it.

It's relatively easy to spot a VNR and decide whether it presents any useful information. But the sports reporter receives thousands of bits and pieces of information every day—reams of paper and information from genuinely legitimate sources, like high schools, colleges, and professional organizations. And this makes it much more difficult to determine what goes on the air and what doesn't.

LOCAL INFORMATION

Generally speaking, there are very few media organizations dedicated to promoting purely local events. Most fall in the category of "event-specific" organizations; groups devoted to promoting one particular event, such as an annual triathlon or golf scramble. In such situations, the publicity is usually handled by a part of the sponsoring organization. For instance, if the local United Way has an annual charity "fun run," someone from the United Way serves as a contact point for the organization and is responsible for working with the media.

It's important to remember in such situations that these organizations don't view the event the same way you do. To them, it's the most important thing going on and merits lots of coverage. To you, it's just another event competing for space on your nightly sportscast. This can create some obvious tension, especially if the organization doesn't think you're giving the event the coverage it deserves. Your job is to balance the needs of the organization with the best interests of the station and the viewers. And sometimes that means saying "No thanks." Much of the coverage issue has to do with timing. A local event planned during Super Bowl week or the state basketball tournament will not get as much coverage as it would during the long, boring summer months. Most organizations recognize this and try to schedule accordingly.

Another source of tension occurs when the event itself becomes less important than something that happens during the event. Every year, Wichita Falls, Texas hosts a bicycle race called the "Hotter 'n Hell Hundred." One year, the course was poorly marked and several of the race leaders became lost, resulting in enormous confusion at the finish line. Thus, the major story shifted from the race itself to the confusion surrounding the winner and the local media rightly played up that angle, much to the frustration of the event organizers. The issue is one of control and at such times, organizers lose control of event coverage.

Most high schools do not have full-time personnel dedicated to event promotion and so the responsibility falls with the sports reporter. Coaches and administrators can be extremely helpful in delivering information on schedules, scores, and athletes, but they usually don't come to you. It's wise to develop contacts at the school that can provide this information. Sometimes this contact is the head coach or athletic director, but it can also be other school officials or even parents of the players. The local newspaper can also provide valuable information in this area.

Again, it's important to remember that local schools have the same vested interest that other organizations do and want to see themselves presented in the best possible light. No school wants viewers to hear about its drug problem or an abusive coach, which can create very difficult situations for the sports reporter (see Chapter 5).

ON CAMPUS

Almost every broadcast market includes a major university, college, or junior college. And unlike high schools or other local organizations, all of these institutions have full-time, professional staff to disseminate media information. A few of these people work for university public relations, but most work in the sports information department.

The sports information department varies in size, depending on the size of the school. Larger schools will have dozens of employees, each with a specific area of responsibility. Some will be in charge of certain sports, while others work on publications or behind the scenes. Smaller schools may only have a few people who have to do everything. But no matter what the size, sports information departments all perform the same basic functions.

The primary function is to keep the media informed of upcoming events and provide necessary information. The sports information department is responsible for keeping track of all the facts and figures related to the school, the players, and the coaching staff. This involves sending out enormous amounts of printed information—box scores, statistics, feature stories, media guides, and the like. And now most schools have added a Web site to include much of the same information on the Internet. Bobby Parker is a typical sports information director (SID) at Bradley University. He says, "My primary duties involve producing media guides for volleyball, soccer, men's and women's basketball, baseball, and softball, as well as keeping our official Web site up-to-date, maintaining statistics and records for all sports in general and sport-specific release writing."

But perhaps a more important function is acting as a liaison between the university, the media, and the school's athletic teams. Bill Lamberty, SID at Montana State University, says, "The most difficult component of the profession, I believe, is to balance the needs of the media with what is best for the coaches and athletes. In a sense, the SID must maintain a loyalty to the media without sacrificing the best interests of the school." Oftentimes, the balancing act becomes extremely difficult, especially in the case of a negative story. It's important to remember that sports information people work for the school and will always put that interest first, but they also recognize the media's responsibility. "There has been a big change in the way the local media report events," says Washington State SID Rod Commons. "They are much more critical than in the past, which isn't always bad." Maxey Parrish, the SID at Baylor University, says, "I've been in the business long enough to remember when sports writers were friends with whom you could share just about anything. Today, there are only a handful still like that. Almost everybody is out to move up the ladder by breaking the big story; the worse the circumstances, the bigger the story."

Interestingly, many SIDs say their own coaches are harder to work with than the media. Ohio University SID Heather Czeczok says, "For the most part, the media are only difficult when they're snooping or you have a bad situation to deal with. Athletes can be temperamental, but I really think coaches are harder to deal with in most cases, because his or her sport is the most important thing and no other sports matter."

Media and industry professionals say the key to working in this atmosphere is to develop trust, especially difficult in this age of increased media attention and emphasis on celebrities. "Trust is huge," says University of Arizona SID Tom Duddleston. "The SID must be able to convince the staff at the university that the media are not a necessary evil, but a fun part of the whole experience." Parker says, "Trust remains the foundation. The media trust that the SID is providing accurate information in a timely fashion and the SID must trust the media to report on that information fairly."

To develop this trust, it's important for the sports reporter to develop a good working relationship with the sports information department. Not necessarily a friendship, but both sides can develop a situation where they make clear their expectations. Trust also involves respecting the guidelines and restrictions imposed by sports information departments, most of which come directly from the coaches. Almost every school has certain restrictions on when you can cover practices, games, and athletes. This could involve conducting interviews only on certain days or not being able to photograph certain practice sessions. Sports reporters should observe and respect these conditions, despite the obvious temptations not to do so. Circumventing the rules may work in the short run, but it will destroy the trust of the sports information department and have serious consequences down the line. Sports information departments will be much less willing to share information and work with reporters who have "burned" them.

This does not mean that reporters should fail to investigate serious stories or allegations regarding the school, especially if they feel they're getting stonewalled. But such situations are rare and certainly don't fall within the bounds of everyday coverage (see Figure 10-1).

THE BIG LEAGUES

Ask any athlete and he or she will tell you the difficulty in moving from college to the pros. The players are bigger, the game is faster, and it's a completely different culture. Much the same can be said when comparing media specialists who work for colleges with those who work for professional organizations or teams. It's a whole new ballgame.

The biggest difference is one of control. At the college level, the university (meaning the coaches and the sports information staff) has a strong degree of control over the athletes. When a coach tells the player to talk to the media (or not to talk), the player usually complies. When someone from sports information sets up an interview with a player, that player usually

(a)

(b)

Figure 10-1(a) and (b) SIDs Decide Who Gets Credentials to the Press Box and Who Doesn't (Courtesy Mary Lou Sheffer)

shows up and does the interview. Only in rare circumstances does the player (or the coach, e.g., Bobby Knight) rebel against the system.

Not so in professional athletics. Players make a lot of money and enjoy a tremendous amount of personal freedom. Whether or not they cooperate with the media and to what degree is entirely up to them. Several athletes, most notably people like Steve Carlton and Albert Belle, have simply refused to have any dealings with the media, except on their terms. Other players will cooperate to a degree, but show open hostility to reporters. The relationship between the media and athletes, which once bordered on friendship, can now best be described as cautious, or even adversarial (see Chapter 5).

This puts team media specialists in a difficult situation. Every professional team has someone in charge of dealing with the media, but in no way can that person control or dictate to the athletes. By way of example, the 2000 Boston Red Sox clubhouse became something of a war zone among players, the manager, and the media. One of the main instigators was moody outfielder Carl Everett. In late September, according to writer Peter Gammons, "Carl Everett had launched into an obscenity-filled, threatening tirade at *Boston Globe* writer Gordon Edes. There were club officials present, but they did nothing until Edes replied, 'Nice game, Carl,' and walked away so [Everett's] teammates could have some peace. Edes was then confronted by those club officials and accused of a cheap shot." When you're in the big leagues, you're on your own.

Control is also a two-way street. At the college level, if a reporter violates media policy it could result in serious repercussions, which range from loss of credentials to simply getting cut off from information and stories. But at the professional level, media managers have no such control. In some dire situations, teams have barred certain reporters from practices and other events, but it's certainly not a major threat. At this level, most reporters simply ignore the team media specialist and get stories on their own, especially if it's a controversial or sensitive topic. Reporters realize the team media specialist doesn't have the power to give them the coverage or the access to the athletes they need.

That is not to say that such media specialists are powerless in these situations. They can establish and try to enforce guidelines for interviewing coaches and players, but their abilities in this area are often hampered by situations outside their control. In certain situations, such as "media day" at the Super Bowl or NBA Finals, the league will step in and order players and coaches to cooperate with reporters. Failure to do so usually results in a fine, but given today's huge salaries, it's not unusual for players to simply refuse to show up.

Despite such lack of control, professional media specialists still have many of the same responsibilities as their collegiate counterparts. Mainly, this includes preparation and dissemination of information. Sports reporters need to know statistics, facts, times, and other pertinent information, all of which comes from the team's media director. Another function is "credentialing," making sure supply for game credentials meets demand. Media organizations that cover teams on a regular basis will take up the bulk of the credentials, sometimes up to a dozen for each game. The rest go to reporters in town for special assignments or stories. There are very specific rules for getting game credentials and each organization has its own way of handling the situation.

Sometimes, the job involves public relations in its purest form—simply trying to get reporters out to cover the team. In the 1940s, when interest in pro football still lagged behind the college game, Tex Schramm of the Los Angeles Rams wrote stories for local newspapers that didn't bother to send reporters to training camp. Obviously, the NFL doesn't need any more publicity today, but dozens of other fledgling sports do. Professional soccer, women's basketball, arena football, and similar ventures have all suffered attendance and financial problems. In these situations, the work of the media or publicity director can have a huge effect on the success of the team or even an entire league.

The key to a good working relationship with media specialists of professional organizations is to realize that fundamentally they have very little power. Media directors can supply important information, but remember that they have a vested interest in their own position and their own organization. The big stories and the important stories are going to come from old-fashioned reporting—day-to-day coverage of the coaches, owners, and athletes involved with the team. New York reporter Dick Young had a reputation as one of the best baseball writers of the 1950s, 60s, and 70s. Young passed away several years ago, but his advice on good reporting still applies today—not only for writers but sports broadcasters. "If you put in time, if you're there, you'll get things that other guys don't get. [The team] won't call you up and tell you. There are no shortcuts. You get stories by working. There's no substitute."

ADVICE FROM PROFESSIONALS

Work as a college or university SID has changed from a 9-month job to a position that demands 60- to 100-hour work weeks almost year round. The people who work in sports information have a unique and demanding position that provides them special insight into the relationship between athletes and the media. Several college and university SIDs offered their opinions on a variety of topics, which media practitioners will hopefully find useful and thought provoking.

How would you describe the duties of a SID?

"Years ago it was much more of a public relations position than it is now. Today, all athletics departments have promotions and marketing directors, jobs the SID did in years past. Now, the SID is more responsible for NCAA reports, conference reports, and the like. It's much more demanding." *Fred Huff, Southern Illinois University*

"Our primary area of responsibility is with the media and good public relations can't be beat. We also work a lot with coaches and a willingness to work with them is critical." *Rod Commons, Washington State University*

"Sports information is at its essence a service industry. The first and foremost function is to disseminate information, but at the same time to maintain relationships with media members and provide them with the information they need in a manner which fits their needs." *Bill Lamberty, Montana State University*

What is the most difficult part of your job?

"Typically, SIDs put in stretches of about 100–120 days twice a year in which they work seven days a week without a break. That's 60–70 hours a week. And time and circumstances make it impossible to please everybody." *Maxey Parrish, Baylor University*

"Time management. No one other than other SIDs realizes the amount of time required for the job today. I'm in the office or on the road with the team every day, including Saturdays and Sundays, from August to April." *Fred Huff, Southern Illinois University*

What is the ideal relationship between a SID and the media?

"The ideal relationship is built on trust. The media have to trust the SID to be fully factual, whether the news is good or bad. The SID has to trust the media to treat his school fairly." *Maxey Parrish, Baylor University*

"There needs to be a personal element to the relationship. This has lessened over the years with the move to faxes, fax-on-demand, e-mail, and the Internet." *Heather Czeczok, Ohio University*

How has the media changed in the way it covered sports over the years?

"The growth of sports talk radio and the Internet have created a more negative approach to coverage. The Internet has provided another avenue for the media to get information, but it's not always reliable." *Bobby Parker, Bradley University*

"Media demands have changed dramatically. With the advent of the fax machine, e-mail, and the Internet, the world wants news faster and faster. The technology has caused more and more media outlets to arise and require information." *Joe Hernandez, Ball State University*

"A whole lot of technological improvements keep the business changing all the time. But a good reporter still covers an event the way a good reporter did 30 years ago—with an objective mind and hopefully some writing talent." *Tom Duddleston, University of Arizona*

REFERENCES

Gammons, Peter. "The Mess Grows in Boston." ESPN. [Online]. Available: www.espn .go.com/gammons/s/0923notes.html. September 23, 2000.
Golenbock, Peter. *Bums.* New York: Pocket Books, 1984.
Seventy-five Seasons. Atlanta: Turner Publishing, 1994.

Ethics

11

When Michael Jordan retired from the NBA for a second time in 1999, he passed from a basketball superstar to a larger-than-life legend. Sports journalists and broadcasters were effusive in their praise for Jordan as a man above mere mortals who transcended the game. Much of this has to do with the tendency of modern-day sports journalism to focus on celebrity and sensationalism (see Chapter 3). But it raises the larger issue of ethical sports reporting. Former sports writer Gene Collier criticized the coverage of Jordan as "embarrassing, even sickening. It was a hurricane of idolatry that devastated all perspective." The point is, how can we simultaneously praise and worship Jordan, yet report on him critically and truthfully? Those writers and broadcasters closest to Jordan, who followed his career for several years, admitted after his retirement that they had probably protected him too much.

It is not hard to find books, articles, and theories about journalism ethics. There is a tremendous interest in the industry and many major universities now teach classes in the subject. But the narrower focus of sports journalism ethics is a little more shadowy and harder to define. Certainly, many of the ethical dilemmas that face news departments also pose problems in sports. For example, hidden cameras and checkbook journalism have long been hot topics of debate in television newsrooms. The issue came to a head in sports in 1996 in a situation involving KXAS-TV in Fort Worth, Texas. The station paid $6,000 to a friend of Dallas Cowboys receiver Michael Irvin for footage of Irvin allegedly handling illegal drugs. In a panel discussion that took place after the story aired, Dallas mayor Ron Kirk called it "the most disgusting thing I have seen on TV."

GO TEAM GO

A much more common type of ethical dilemma in sports is conflict of interest, which can take many forms. An obvious situation arose when the A. H. Belo Corporation acquired a minority interest in the NBA's Dallas Mavericks. Belo also owns the *Dallas Morning News* and the Dallas TV station WFAA, which presented obvious ethical problems. In the summer of 2000, Belo announced plans to sell the minority share, not because of any conflict of interest, but rather for financial reasons. According to *Mediaweek*, Belo wanted to sell off the interest "to raise money for a stock repurchase and boost its sagging share price."

At its most fundamental level, conflict of interest can be nothing more than boosterism. The theory goes that local fans and viewers want the local teams to win. When local teams win it creates excitement in the community and generates much more interest for local papers and broadcast outlets. Players on winning teams are much more relaxed and media-friendly. It certainly makes the job more fun and prestigious for the local media to cover a winning team. What newspaper or station wouldn't want to follow the team to a Super Bowl or World Series? When the team is winning, it seems everyone else wins as well.

But this situation also carries with it several ethical considerations. Namely, how can a reporter or broadcaster report truthfully or critically against a popular home team? In the early 1970s, a sports writer in Oklahoma named Frank Boggs uncovered a NCAA investigation into the football program at the University of Oklahoma. Boggs published a series of articles detailing the investigation, which centered on an alleged ticket-scalping scandal. But he severely underestimated the popularity and power of the Oklahoma football program, which had regularly contended for the national championship. The criticism began when Oklahoma coach Barry Switzer called the reporting a "conspiracy" and angry fans turned against Boggs. He and co-writer Jack Taylor received 30 death threats in one hour. Even friends and co-workers avoided him. The situation got so hot, Boggs eventually transferred to another paper in Colorado.

There aren't many courageous sports journalists today like Frank Boggs. Most writers and broadcasters feel it's better to get on board than to face the unpleasant alternatives. In 1999, the *Los Angeles Times* admitted ethical wrongdoing on a series it ran on the city's proposed sports arena. The paper had agreed to become a founding partner of the $400 million Staples Center, but failed to tell readers about the arrangement. The deal included working with the arena on a joint project and splitting ad revenue from a special newspaper issue. In return, the *Times* got signs, vending rights, a luxury skybox at the arena, and a record $2 million in advertising revenue. *Time* magazine said it "seemed like a dangerous compromise of the paper's objectivity." *Forbes* magazine called the deal "bad for business and bad for journalism, but boosterism as usual."

With the huge amounts of money involved these days, it's easy to see why some media choose to take sides. If media criticism becomes too hot, a popular star player might decide to leave town for another team. If the team itself decides to leave, it can create an economic vacuum that could cost the community millions of dollars. When a new team moves into town it usually enjoys a honeymoon period, where the owners, players, and coaches receive continuous praise for their courage in making the move. But when a team leaves town, like the Cleveland Browns did in the mid-1990s, then the media criticism comes out full force. Browns owner Art Modell was generally vilified by the Cleveland media for moving the team to Baltimore, although some reporters made an effort to include all sides of the story.

It's also ethically questionable to take the opposite approach, which is to be critical just for the sake of ratings or readers. This is especially dangerous given today's media climate, where dozens of voices now feel they have to be as outlandish and negative as possible to be heard above the competition. Veteran sports talk show host Mike Gastineau of KJR-AM in Seattle admits, "There can be a negativism that is really discouraging at times [and] there are too many guys in the business trying to build careers on that. I've heard guys in the business refer to themselves as 'coach killers.' I think that's wildly out of line. It's not our job to get guys fired. I think it's egomaniacal to think you know as a talk-show host everything that's going on. I don't care how much research and behind-the-scenes privileges you have."

FRIEND OR FOE?

Another common conflict of interest is the personal relationship between the media and players, owners, and coaches. Sports writers and broadcasters have almost unlimited professional access to athletes. They often travel together on the same plane or bus, they obviously spend time together at the game, and then many times they will see each other afterwards. This can create a situation where the business relationship can become more like a friendship, with its obvious ethical considerations.

We have already discussed how players and reporters had a much closer relationship several years ago (see Chapter 3). Back when the media wasn't so sizeable or sophisticated, players and reporters could develop strong attachments. Reporters would often protect players, sometimes from themselves and the things that might end up in print. The times when reporters did say something critical, they could often cool off the offended player with a round of drinks at the local bar.

This situation has changed drastically in recent years, thanks greatly to the proliferation of media. Broadcasters have become just one of thousands of microphones vying for the attention of a player, who naturally became more defensive and distrustful. But even without the close relationship, reporters still have good reason to stay in a player's good graces. There's always the danger of a player cutting off a reporter and simply not talking to him anymore, which can be quite difficult if it's the star player of a popular team. Reporters also face the possibility of verbal or even physical abuse from players.

All of this adds up to a situation in which the sports reporter or broadcaster might feel compelled to report more favorably on a player or omit damaging information. In January 2000, New York Rangers hockey player Kevin Stevens was arrested on charges of drug abuse and prostitution. That combination might seem like a sure-fire screaming headline, but the reporting was somewhat low-key. An article in *Sports Illustrated* described Stevens as someone "(who) ... carried sunshine in his back pocket. He never big-timed anyone and he laughed loudest and longest in the dressing room." Author and journalist David Krajicek called the coverage "surprisingly tame," because of Stevens's reputation as one of the league's most popular players. Krajicek went on to say that of the four beat writers covering the story, only one mentioned the fact that Stevens had already spent time in the league's substance abuse program. "The ribald tabloids that usually go nuts on sexy celebrity stories, displayed uncharacteristic reserve," he noted. "The pussy-footing stories could be seen as suck-up journalism by the beat writers."

Such situations probably happen more in regards to coaches and owners than the players. From the reporters' standpoint, players are expendable commodities; they come and go frequently. But coaches and owners have much more longevity (relatively speaking) and considerably more power. Thus, many broadcasters find it profitable to develop stronger ties in this area. One of the most famous reporter-coach relationships involved former Indiana University basketball coach Bob Knight and Bob Hamel, a long-time reporter for the *Bloomington Herald-Telegraph*. In his excellent book, *A Season on the Brink*, author John Feinstein describes the relationship between the two as unusually strong, almost like brothers. They would take long walks together the night before road games and Knight would often volunteer information to Hamel before he told other media members. In this situation, one could understand how Hamel would be reluctant to report any damaging information about Knight or the basketball program. According to Feinstein, Hamel never considered it a serious ethical issue, although he admitted to having a rooting interest in the games.

Either Knight or Hamel could have abused the situation to his own benefit, although apparently neither one did. But other coaches and players have no reservations about using a relationship with a reporter to further their own cause. Coaches routinely plant stories with reporters when they want to send a message to a player without confronting him directly. The reporter becomes an unwitting agent, caught in the middle of team dynamics. Owners can also use the media for a very simple reason: to blunt the sharp edge of a reporter's sword. Sports writer Dick Young had one of the keenest, most critical writing styles in all of baseball. But according to Roger Kahn, once new owners took over the Dodgers in the 1950s, they began cultivating a personal relationship with Young and feeding him exclusive information. As a result, said Kahn, "[Young] was in the Dodger pocket all the time. Young gave the Dodger line and the guys he liked were the guys management liked. The [*Daily News*] became a Dodger house organ."

A much more subtle way to influence is all the free perks that go to sports reporters. At almost every event, reporters enjoy access to all kinds of goodies, the most common being the free meal. Free food has become the standard at professional and college events and has now even become common on the high school level. While most organizations offer the food as a common courtesy, it does come with its own ethical implications. Are reporters more willing to speak favorably about the event on a full stomach? When the event does not offer food, does that make the reporter more suspicious or critical? Often times when teams skimp on the meals, they gain a reputation in media circles as being "cheap" or "low class." Some organizations, most notably major league baseball teams, have cut off the ethical debate by charging for food in the media room (which has caused more than its share of grumbling by reporters). On the other side, the *St. Petersburg Times* decided the free buffet at Tampa Bay Buccaneer football games was a conflict of interest, and paid the team for meals eaten by its sports staff.

At the other end of the scale are the more permanent gifts, which come in all shapes, sizes, and colors. Teams and organizations routinely shower media members with hats, jackets, bags, briefcases, pens, pencils, coasters, and thousands of other mementos to mark a particular occasion. Most of the items are relatively inexpensive and usually end up in the bottom of the reporter's closet, but the ethical questions remain. And yes, sports reporters look at these gifts the same way they view the food—almost like an entitlement program.

Many organizations have made serious effort to cut down on freebies. Several professional teams used to give free tickets to sports personnel who wanted to go to a game in their spare time. Now, most teams have ended the practice and extend courtesy privileges only to working media.

WHO SIGNS THE CHECKS?

One of the most confusing examples of conflict of interest are the play-by-play announcers, many of whom work as employees of the team they cover.

Organizations are usually very open about this and provide a disclaimer for each game that indicates the broadcaster works for the team and not the broadcast station.

But disclaimers aside, the practice is loaded with ethical problems. How can any broadcaster criticize or downgrade a team that signs his or her paychecks? The temptation is to become a homer, an unabashed and usually uncritical fan of the home team (see Chapter 6). Bob Prince of the Pirates and Harry Caray of the Cubs are just two examples of broadcasters who had no trouble taking sides. The situation becomes even more confusing when you consider how sports and broadcasting entities have merged in recent years. The Tribune company owns not only the Cubs, but also WGN-TV, which televises many of the games. So does a Cubs announcer work for the Tribune, for WGN, or for the team? And how can one remain independent in that situation? The same scenario exists in other cities, where Cablevision owns the New York Rangers and Knicks, Fox owns the Los Angeles Dodgers, and Disney owns the Anaheim Angels and Mighty Ducks (see Chapter 2). Even when the media doesn't have an ownership stake other problems can arise. Several media outlets offer partial or full sponsorship of events, such as the ties between the *New York Times* and the U.S. Open tennis championship.

Local teams have always believed it's important for their own broadcasters to present the team in the very best light. Red Barber finished up his distinguished career with the Yankees in the mid-1960s, when the team fell apart on the field after decades of dominance. Barber was uncompromising in his description of the team and the lack of fans in the stands, and for that Yankee management forced him out. Popular play-by-play announcer Jon Miller left Baltimore for San Francisco, rather than deal with team ownership that felt he was too critical. Another interesting situation developed in June 2000, when the Atlanta Braves banned four of their own TBS broadcasters from riding on the team plane. The incident stemmed from on-air comments the broadcasters made regarding how the local grounds crew may have altered the catcher's box to help the Braves pitching staff. Ironically, both the Braves and TBS were owned at the time by media conglomerate Time-Warner.

Such occurrences are a disturbing trend in the industry, which has seen much more tolerance of critical announcing in recent years. Today, if an announcer wants to become a homer, he usually does so out of choice, not because he feels pressure from the home team to do so. Men like Caray and Prince had personalities that suited rooting for the home team and they used it to their advantage. But the ethical dangers still exist, especially at the college and high school level. In those situations, the pressure comes more from listeners, viewers, and station management. An announcer who doesn't back the home team may get himself in trouble for the most basic of broadcasting reasons—not enough people will watch or listen.

THE BUCK STOPS HERE

The influence of advertising has long been a concern among professionals in the broadcasting business, and certainly sports is not immune. Advertising and sports have gone hand-in-hand almost from the very beginning, but we seem no closer today to answering the same old ethical questions.

To an advertiser, sports provide a vehicle to reach potential customers. It can be something as covert as putting ads on the outfield wall at a baseball game, or something more obvious like outfitting tennis and golf players as walking billboards. However advertisers go about it, their main goal is to present their product in the most favorable light to viewers and listeners. And they spend millions of dollars every year to do it.

This can present all kinds of challenges for the broadcaster, who may feel pressure to protect or promote important advertisers. It has become routine for play-by-play broadcasters to give a list of sponsors during the telecast. Who hasn't heard an announcer say, "Today's game is brought to you in part by Budweiser, the King of Beers"? Usually, broadcasters have no problem with this arrangement. But what happens if a broadcaster has moral reservations about promoting certain products, like beer? What if the broadcaster drinks beer, but hates Budweiser?

Huge conglomerates like Anheuser-Busch and R. J. Reynolds often spend money for sponsorship of an entire event, a common practice on the professional golf and tennis circuits. How often does a broadcaster feel compelled to repeat the name of the "Fed Ex St. Jude's Golf Classic," or the "Nokia Sugar Bowl"? R. J. Reynolds has become the driving force and principal sponsor of the NASCAR auto racing league. Winning drivers compete for the Winston Cup, symbolic of the sport's national champion. Does this mean that auto racing broadcasters must promote or endorse cigarettes or tobacco? More importantly, what happens if the broadcaster says something the sponsor doesn't like?

A partial answer came at the Masters golf tournament in Augusta, Georgia. The Masters has positioned itself as an upscale sporting event, attractive to sponsors like Cadillac. CBS has an annual contract to televise the event and uses a dozen or so broadcasters positioned in different places around the course. One of these broadcasters was Gary McCord, who has a rather relaxed and flippant attitude about golf. One year, McCord made several comments about the course conditions, including a reference to the Augusta greens as looking like they were "waxed with bikini wax." After the tournament, Masters organizations made the decision to ban McCord from further telecasts. It's not known whether Cadillac or other sponsors brought pressure in this instance, but Masters organizers said McCord did not fit in with the atmosphere of the event.

At the other end of the spectrum are the broadcasters who openly embrace endorsements. Usually, the spots are for innocuous products, for instance John Madden's pitches for Ace Hardware or Terry Bradshaw's ads for a long distance phone service. Madden or Bradshaw would never think about openly endorsing the products during a game telecast (there are very strict broadcasting rules against practices such as plugola and payola), but they would certainly never criticize the products either. It's also very difficult to determine exactly what crosses the line. Veteran broadcasters acknowledge that no one could work a commercial into a game telecast better than Mel Allen. Allen would say something like, "A great defensive play there for the putout . . . and fans, make a great play for yourself by going to the refrigerator for a delicious Ballantine beer."

For these and other reasons, the very idea of broadcasters doing commercials has raised serious ethical issues. When broadcasters align themselves with a certain product or service, it automatically effects their credibility and integrity. Broadcasters and reporters have reputations based on neutrality and impartiality. Those reputations can take a serious hit when they step into the world of commercials, such as when Dan Patrick of ESPN received criticism for a series of beer commercials that he did with former Denver Broncos quarterback John Elway.

But at least Elway was retired. A much more serious situation arises when broadcasters appear in promos or commercials with active players. ESPN runs a series of very creative promotions for its *SportsCenter* shows, many of them involving current players. To Al Tompkins, former TV news director now with the Poynter Institute, this is an uncomfortable situation. "How would it be if you appear in a promo with an athlete one day," asks Tompkins, "then the next day you have to do a difficult story about that athlete's cocaine use? It would be quite difficult." Responds Bob Eaton of ESPN, "We had some questions about the promos. We ultimately structured it so we make a donation to the charity of the athlete's choice. We don't pay them and don't give them any special treatment."

Almost every station and news organization has strict rules against plugola and payola, forms of ethical violations that go back to the very beginning of broadcasting. The announcer in exchange for behind-the-back compensation would plug, or promote, the advertiser's product on the air. And despite today's legal safeguards, plugola and payola still present serious problems. It's not unheard of, for example, for a sportscaster to cut a side deal with a local advertiser. In one such instance, a sportscaster featured a series of tips from the local tennis pro in exchange for membership in an exclusive tennis club. Another sports person used his position to reward certain friends with Masters golf tickets. In each case, the offender was discovered and punished, but the practice and the temptation remain.

The endorsement doesn't have to be so sinister to raise ethical eyebrows. In 1999, ESPN anchor Robin Roberts emceed a fundraising event for presidential candidate Bill Bradley. Roberts later said that she was surprised at receiving criticism for the appearance. Tompkins says anything that waters down or damages credibility hurts in the long run. According to ESPN executive editor John Walsh, "Certainly the fallout has given us cause to look at the issue. I think Robin was a bit naïve."

A DOUBLE STANDARD?

Many of the issues under discussion are not unique to sports. Television and radio news departments often struggle with the same problems. But does one set of ethical rules exist for sports and a different one for news?

Many long-time journalists think so. Tompkins says, "I come from 25 years in television [and] I personally treated sports more leniently than news. I let my sports guy do stuff I wouldn't let the news anchors do." Sports writer and broadcaster Frank Deford says, "Sports journalism is held to a different standard. Visualize Tom Daschle and Trent Lott teaming up to do a promotion on ABC for Peter Jennings. That's the equivalent of what ESPN is doing [with its promos for *SportsCenter*]."

The other argument is that sports simply isn't on the same level with news because of its relative unimportance. Don Skwer of the *Boston Globe* says, "Sports isn't politics and that's where I draw the line. There's a public trust involved, but it's a totally different thing." Many sports broadcasters agree. "Stuart Scott and I have the same philosophy," says ESPN's Rich Eisen. "This is just sports. It's serious at some point, but it's still just a game."

THE BOTTOM LINE

There are no simple answers to these ethical problems, which the industry continues to debate. Almost every newsroom in the country has ethical guidelines in place, but such guidelines don't address all the important issues, aren't consistently applied, and usually don't carry a mechanism to punish offenders. As a result, serious ethical decisions still remain in the hands of the individual. "Every person in this business has to answer to himself," says ESPN's Bob Ley. Most ethical decisions will continue to be made by each sports person on a case-by-case basis, given the lack of a standard body of codified conduct. But there are several resources available to help in the decision-making process.

Professional organizations such as the Radio Television News Directors Association (www.rtnda.org) and the Society for Professional Journalists (www.spj.org) devote regular columns and forums to ethical issues. The same can be said for journalism industry and watchdog publications like *Broadcasting and Cable* (www.broadcastingcable.com), *Electronic Media* (www.emonline.com), the *Columbia Journalism Review* (www.cjr.com), and the *American Journalism Review* (www.ajr.com). Other organizations have also emerged to include discussions of ethical sports reporting and broadcasting. JFORUM (www.jforum.org) was launched in 1985 by former NBC news director Jim Cameron and now lists 42,000 subscribers worldwide.

Even so, these resources can provide only guidance and can't begin to answer the difficult kinds of ethical issues that sports people face everyday. For the foreseeable future, those remain newsroom and individual decisions. The problem is that today's sports and news journalists aren't getting much in the way of ethical training. In a recent study conducted by the Radio and Television News Directors Foundation, 65 percent of news directors say their organization has some formalized code of ethics. But only 59 percent of news directors feel such training is "very necessary," and only 56 percent of the news executives require their reporters to take some sort of ethics training. Perhaps more telling, the plurality of news directors say their new employees do not go through formal ethical training.

That pretty much leaves it up to the individual sports reporter, who must either learn ethical codes of conduct in school or, more commonly, in his or her first job. "The ethics situation is finally being addressed by the entire industry," said Tom Tebbs, sports editor of the *Monterey County Herald* (California). "The public's image may not improve because of their view of our integrity, which they assimilate to that of lawyers. This, however, cannot be fought." The fight, it seems, has really just begun.

REFERENCES

Bassman, Virginia. "Irvin Debate Reborn with SPJ Chapter." *Dallas Morning News*, June 6, 1996.

"Belo Dumps Dailies, Mavericks Stake" *Mediaweek*, July 3, 2000.

Booth, Cathy. "Worst of Times." *Time*, November 15, 1999.

"Braves Tell Broadcasters to Fly Commercial." *Associated Press*. [Online]. Available: http://www.espn.go.com/mlb/news/2000/0626/605703.html, June 27, 2000.

Collier, Gene. "The Ex-sportswriter: 'I Was Looking for Heroes in All the Wrong Places.'" *Columbia Journalism Review*, January–February 2000.

de Turenne, Veronica. "Dodgers and Scully Still Moving On." *Scripps Howard News Service*, October 1, 1996.

Farber, Michael. "Life of the Party." *Sports Illustrated,* February 14, 2000.

Feinstein, John. *A Season on the Brink: A Year with Bobby Knight and the Indiana Hoosiers*. New York: Simon and Schuster, 1989.

Golenbock, Peter. *Bums*. New York: Pocket Books, 1984.

Heard, Robert. *Oklahoma vs. Texas: When Football Becomes War.* Austin, TX: Honey Hill Publishing, 1980.

"Journalism Ethics and Integrity Project." *Radio Television News Directors Foundation*. [Online]. Available: www.rtnda.org/issues/survey.htm.

Krajicek, David. "Sportswriters Need to Take Kid Gloves Off." [Online]. Available: www.apbnews.com, January 27, 2000.

Postrel, Virginia. "The Ethics of Boosterism." *Forbes*, February 7, 2000.

Salwen, Michael and Garrison, Bruce. "Survey Examines Extent of Professionalism in Sports Journalism. *Editor & Publisher*, January 15, 1994.

Scanlan, Christopher. *Reporting and Writing: Basics for the 21st Century.* Orlando: Harcourt, 2000.

Shea, Jim. "The King: How ESPN Changes Everything." *Columbia Journalism Review*, January–February 2000.

"Sports-talk Radio Host." ESPN. [Online]. Available: http://espn.go.com/special/s/careers/sptalk.html, September 7, 1999.

Employment

12

If you took an economics class at school, you know about the basic laws of supply and demand. As the supply of any product rises above demand, there is a surplus and the price charged for the product drops accordingly. The same situation applies in the world of sports broadcasting. Every year there is a tremendous supply of eager college graduates looking to make their mark in the business. Think of how many people at your school alone are interested in sports broadcasting, then multiply that number by hundreds of thousands of colleges, universities, and trade schools all across the country. According to a report in the *American Journalism Review*, more than one-half of all the males surveyed at three major broadcast journalism schools (Syracuse University, the University of Missouri, and Ohio University) wanted a career in sports broadcasting. That compares with just 27 percent who want to go into television or radio news. "It supports my gut reaction that most of the males come to Ohio University to be about sports," says Eddith Dashiell, associate professor in the university's E.W. Scripps School of Journalism.

Those who do graduate must compete with the thousands of other people already in the business, but looking to move to a new situation. Unfortunately, the demand for such talent can never keep up with supply. Sports broadcasting positions, even in the smallest and poorest markets in the country, are rare and highly coveted. The growth of cable and other alternative outlets has eased the situation somewhat by creating more positions. But the fact remains that getting a job in sports broadcasting, especially in front of the camera, remains a difficult and frustrating endeavor.

THE BAD NEWS

Probably the most important hurdle to get over is your own perception of the sports broadcasting industry. Most people get interested in the business with the idea that they will become the next John Madden or Dick Vitale. They envision themselves traveling first-class to cover huge events, interviewing and hanging out with famous athletes, and becoming a household name.

Certainly that is the case for a select number of sports broadcasters who have reached the very top of their profession. But the reality is very different for everyone else in the business, especially those just starting out. Sports broadcasting is difficult and often monotonous work. Instead of covering the Super Bowl, you'll probably be covering high school swimming or tennis. The hours are long and the pay is low, leading to cases of burnout for many people in the business. Sports doesn't seem as much fun when it's no longer just a hobby and becomes a career. Griff Potter, news director at WQAD-TV, in Moline, Illinois says, "It's about journalism, not sports. If you are in it for the sports, you're not a journalist but a fan. Get a job in another industry and buy season tickets." News director Dennis Fisher of WOWK-TV in Huntington, West Virginia is even more blunt. "Don't get in the business," he says. "There is too much competition and not enough jobs to go around. If you insist on going into it, then be resigned to hard work and little glory."

The Numbers Game

Thanks to new outlets and the increasing popularity of sports, more and more sports broadcasting positions continue to open up. Vernon Stone, professor emeritus of journalism at the University of Missouri, specializes in broadcasting employment trends. According to his research, by the late 1990s nearly 42,000 people were working in commercial radio and TV newsrooms, as cutbacks eased and the work force boomed to an all-time high. The TV newsroom work force also continues to grow, up to nearly 26,000 by the mid-90s. Stone says that the TV news work force grows every year, in part because people hold on to jobs for only a few years or so before moving on.

But as mentioned, supply still far exceeds demand. Research from Stone and Lee Becker shows that entry-level applicants outnumber hirings by 3-to-1 in radio and a whopping 10-to-1 in television. And even that probably underestimates the situation in sports broadcasting. Stone says that for every entry-level position in a TV newsroom, the typical news director gets 60 to 70 resume tapes. News director Jeff Kiernan of WTMJ-TV in Milwaukee says whenever he has a sports opening, which is rare, he usually get around 200 resumes. It's a much brighter situation for behind-the-scenes personnel such as photographers or editors. For those openings, a news director might get only a dozen or so applications.

The Money Pit

Because there are so many people applying for positions and so few positions available, entry-level salaries remain depressingly low. Station management knows it can pay low salaries because it has an inexhaustible talent pool. As the market size and responsibilities increase, so does the pay. But entry-level sports broadcasters often find it difficult to survive the beginning years when they are expected to "pay their dues." Ball State University professors Mike Gerhard and Bob Papper have confirmed this with their research into industry salary levels. The most recent numbers for the late 1990s show that salaries have increased about 4 percent to keep ahead of inflation. But a closer look at the figures reveals some disturbing information for sports broadcasters (see Table 12-1 and Table 12-2).

Two things jump out immediately. First, sports broadcasters make a lot less than their counterparts in news and weather, a fact that is consistent at every television station in the country. As previously discussed, research shows that sports is the least-watched segment of the newscast. Because of its relative lack of respect and importance, sports broadcasters are generally not as highly paid as news or weather talent. This obviously does not apply to all-sports outlets, such as ESPN or sports talk radio.

The second observation is that while some of the salaries seem impressive, keep in mind that most of the gains and the big numbers come from the bigger markets. Sportscasters in New York, Los Angeles, and Chicago make a very good living in the business, as do industry professionals in places like Minneapolis, Nashville, and Miami. But it usually takes years to work up to such a professional level. Of greater importance are the figures for the smaller markets, places like Tupelo, Mississippi, or Lawton, Oklahoma, where entry-level graduates are likely to start out. In those markets, you can

Table 12-1 Television Salary Comparison

	Average	*Median*	*Low*	*High*
Sports reporter	$27,600	$22,000	$7,000	$153,000
Sports anchor	$46,000	$33,000	$15,000	$260,000
News anchor	$62,100	$44,000	$9,000	$800,000
News reporter	$29,200	$24,000	$14,000	$130,000
Weather anchor	$51,500	$40,000	$14,000	$250,000

Source: "Salary Survey Statistics," *RTNDA Communicator*, May 1999

Table 12-2 Television News Salaries by Market Size

	Markets by Size (1 = Largest Market)				
	1–26	*26–50*	*51–100*	*101–150*	*150+*
Sports anchor	$100,000	$64,000	$40,000	$28,500	$21,000
Sports reporter	$46,500	$26,000	$26,000	$21,000	$17,000
News anchor	$148,000	$90,000	$50,000	$37,000	$24,500
News reporter	$61,000	$35,000	$25,500	$20,000	$17,000
Weather anchor	$82,500	$75,000	$45,000	$35,000	$25,000

Source: "Salary Survey Statistics," *RTNDA Communicator*, May 1999

expect to start under $20,000 a year, no matter what the position. Bill Evans, now the news director of WPSD-TV, in Paducah, Kentucky started in 1982 as a sports director in El Dorado, Arkansas for $11,500 a year. Today, that's equivalent to about $20,000 or what Evans pays now for experienced reporters. "Many of the starting salaries today are what I was getting in the late 70s," says news director Dean Adams of KAAL-TV in Austin, Minnesota. "That just amazes me." According to news director Bob Freeman of WFIE-TV in Evansville, Indiana, "People getting out of school feel they shouldn't have to work for $18,000 a year. They think they should make $25,000 or $30,000. Frankly, a market this size can't bear that kind of starting salary." Sports director Cory Curtis of WOLO-TV in Columbia, South Carolina says young sportscasters can handle the low pay, if they're willing to make sacrifices. "I have a saying, 'short-term sacrifices for long-term gains.' That means moving to Billings, Montana if you have to. That means making $13,000 a year if you have to."

Sometimes it means working additional jobs just to make ends meet. The weekend sports anchor at WSIL-TV in Carterville, Illinois (market 74) works at Wal-Mart on his days off. At WCJW-AM in Warsaw, New York news and sports director Mike Holmes has a salary of $16,000. He also has to write for a small local paper and has considered getting his teaching certificate, which would allow him to stay in the area. Holmes's dilemma points out that the situation is not much better in radio. The same Papper and Gerhard survey showed that a small market sports anchor can expect to make in the range of $24,000 a year. That sounds like a lot, but consider all the other duties involved.

The Minority Report

Minorities continue to make small gains in overall broadcast employment, including sports, but whites and males still dominate almost all areas of the industry as you can see from recent RTNDA figures (see Table 12-3 and

Table 12-4). In 1971, minorities comprised only 9 percent of total news employment. Today, that has more than doubled to 20 percent. Much of the gain can be credited to a landmark case filed against the FCC in 1969 (425 F.2nd 543). The ruling forced television stations in Mississippi to more accurately represent and reflect the members of their communities, a great majority of whom were black. The ruling also made it clear that stations that don't comply could face the loss of their broadcasting licenses.

Women have also had to go to court to protect their positions. One recent case involved anchor Janet Peckinpaugh at WFSB-TV in Hartford. The station took her off the noon and 5:30 P.M. newscasts because it wanted to maintain a traditional male-female anchor pairing. The jury in the case ruled that the station committed gender discrimination and ordered Peckinpaugh reinstated to her former anchor time slots. Long-time sportscaster Donna deVarona filed a similar age discrimination lawsuit against ABC Sports, claiming the network let her go because of her age. Most women sports reporters still feel they face an uphill battle in gaining respect and credibility, despite the recent success of people like Lesley Visser, Hannah Storm, and Robin Roberts. Sportscasting began as a white, male enterprise and there's still a lot of resistance and chauvinism (see Chapter 13).

Table 12-3 Broadcast News Work Force

	Television	*Radio*
White	80%	84%
Black	10%	9%
Hispanic	6%	5%
Asian	3%	2%
Native American	1%	>1%

Source: Women and Minorities Employment Statistics, *RTNDA Communicator,* October 1998

Table 12-4 Women in Local Television News

	News Staff with Women	*Women News Directors*	*Percentage of Women in the Work Force*
All television	99%	23%	35%
Markets 1–25	100%	16%	34%
Markets 26–50	100%	33%	32%
Markets 51–100	98%	24%	35%
Markets 101–150	100%	13%	39%
Markets 150+	98%	36%	36%

Source: Women and Minorities Employment Statistics, *RTNDA Communicator*, October 1998

Several stations have made a concerted effort to make their news and sports staffs more closely resemble the ethnic makeup of their communities. For example, stations in Miami, south Texas, Arizona, and southern California have lately hired and promoted more Hispanics and Latinos in all areas of their operations. The same can be said for stations in northern California with regards to Asian Americans. Oftentimes, these stations will give preference to bilingual applicants in their job advertisements. Jim LeMay, who worked as vice president of news at WJLA-TV in Washington, D.C. said, "It's not about making rules. If you're not a reflection of your community, you're in trouble. You're not going to have any viewers. They're going to say, 'They don't seem to be like us.'"

To many news directors, it's not a matter of meeting guidelines, but serving the community. Randy Lube, news director at KOLN-TV in Lincoln, Nebraska, said, "We're of the opinion you have to have a diverse newsroom. You have to have a diversity of opinions." According to Will Wright, news director at WWOR in New York, "I believe that every newsroom should be a microcosm of society. How can it be a microcosm of society if it's all white? Or black? It has to represent the environment in which we're broadcasting."

Minorities have made many recent gains. In 2000, ABC and NBC signed separate agreements with the NAACP, which will add more of a minority presence in Hollywood. Key points include adding minority writing positions, hiring more minority directors, and expanding minority scholarship opportunities. NBC also took a major step in February 2000 by naming an executive in charge of diversity. Paula Madison, who also serves as news director and vice president of news at WNBC-TV in New York, will report directly to NBC president Bob Wright.

But many still worry that such gains could be lost. In April of 1998, a decision by the U.S. Court of Appeals set aside rulings by the Federal Communications Commission pertaining to minority representation in radio and television. It's not yet known if that caused minority employment rates to drop from 20 percent to 19 percent in 1999. However, many believe that without the power of legal authority, all of today's forceful talk about minority hiring practices will ring hollow. "I'd like to believe we're all more enlightened, but I don't," said Phil Alvidrez, news director at KTVK-TV in Phoenix. "What I believe will happen is the same as what happened before broadcasters were forced to follow hiring guidelines. Those of us who make our living in it know that television has one of the shortest memories under the sun."

THE GOOD NEWS

Don't give up hope yet. While it's hard to find a job in the sports broadcasting business, it's certainly not impossible. In fact, finding job openings is very easy. Magazines like *Broadcasting & Cable* and *Electronic Media* have weekly classified job listings that include information about the position and where to send a tape. You can get this information for free by going to the local library. Several Internet sites, like tvjobs.com have much of the same information. Of course, none of these job openings are a secret. If you found them, chances are thousands of other job seekers know about them too.

Obviously, some hiring decisions are out of your control. The station may be looking for a male instead of a female, or it may prefer to hire someone locally and save the money it would cost for an extended talent search. Often times, your resume tape could get lost in the stack of hundreds of other tapes competing for the same position. But there are some concrete steps you can take to put yourself in the best possible position to get that first job, which is always the hardest one to get.

The Resume Tape

Without a doubt, the resume tape is the single most important tool you have to sell yourself to a possible employer. A resume tape (or demo reel for radio) is usually a short, 5- to 10-minute presentation of your best material. News directors will look at and listen to thousands of these tapes in a single year and they have developed a quick procedure to weed out undesirable candidates. Because he or she has to go through so many tapes, the news director usually determines in the first few seconds whether your tape is worthy of further consideration. "When I'm in full search mode and hiring for a sportscaster, I usually give each tape about 10 to 20 seconds," says Jeff Kiernan. The trick is to put something on the tape that catches the news director's eye and makes him or her want to keep watching. If you survive this first cut, the next step might be a phone interview to discuss general issues related to the position and your willingness to work. After that, a lucky few (usually three or less) will get called in for personal interviews, at which times specifics about the job and your performance are discussed. But it all begins and sometimes ends with the resume tape.

Do's and Don'ts

There are many companies that make lots of money by consulting to television stations. Places like Frank Magid and Audience Research and Development (ARD) charge hundreds of thousands of dollars to give their input on all aspects of the station's operation. While station management has the ultimate responsibility for all hirings and firings, consultants have intimate knowledge about the stations and what they're looking for when they hire sports personnel. Many companies will work with sports broadcasters on a personal level, acting as an agent for a percentage of the broadcaster's salary. But it's impractical for entry-level sports broadcasters to use such services, for several reasons. Not only because of the expense, but also primarily because small and medium television markets don't rely on agents to find talent. Such services are usually reserved for sports talent in much larger markets.

But that doesn't mean that beginning sports broadcasters can't benefit from a consultant's advice. Don Fitzpatrick Associates routinely provides tips and suggestions on how to make your resume tape stand out from all the others in the news director's office. Some of the suggestions are certainly subjective, but remember, it's a subjective business. No two news directors will react the same way to the same story, much less the same job applicant.

In no particular order, Fitzpatrick has several suggestions for those interested in finding a job in sports broadcasting:

- Show one or two complete sportscasts.
- Give examples of original reporting, including beat reporting.
- Show interaction with other news members, especially a live shot.
- Provide quality sports journalism.

Source: Courtesy Don Fitzpatrick Associates/http://www.tvspy.com

News directors want to see complete sportscasts, because it shows an ability to produce a show without many mistakes. Editing together several different shows (especially if you have several changes of clothes) only makes the news director wonder if you can hold a coherent thought for longer than 60 seconds. In some cases, the news director actually wants to see a mistake, just to know how you will react to it. Overcoming mistakes with a smooth transition or self-deprecating humor can be just as important as a sportscast with no mistakes at all.

It's also important to show as much versatility as possible on your tape. That means including examples of not just anchoring, but reporting, photography, and anything else you've done. Very few people these days get hired strictly as sports anchors, especially in entry-level positions or in small markets. More likely, you'll be asked to write, edit, shoot, produce, report, and anchor your own material. Many people out of college are hired strictly as sports "one man bands," which means they have to do all these things by themselves on a daily basis. Including examples of all the different skills you've learned increases your chances of getting hired because it improves your marketability. News director Ron Lombard, of WIXT-TV in Syracuse, New York says versatility is the number one thing he's looking for. "These days we need sports journalists who can do it all: write, report, produce, and anchor, along with shooting and editing their own material. And the ability to do it all quickly and with attention to detail."

Oftentimes, news directors will want to see how you think on your feet. This is why Fitzpatrick suggests including interaction with other news members or a live shot. These unscripted segments demonstrate your ability to think fast and communicate with the audience, and in some cases can be just as important as the other material on your tape. But it's important not to go overboard. Many sports broadcasters succumb to the temptation of putting dozens of live shots or standups together in a lengthy montage. News directors certainly want to see what you look like, but such montages tell them very little about your ability to report or communicate with the audience.

This tip leads into Fitzpatrick's last point, including some examples of quality sports journalism. Too often, young sports broadcasters load their tapes with scores and highlights, but ignore solid sports reporting. More than anything else, news directors want to see creative, enterprising stories that appeal to more than just the hard-core sports fans (see Chapter 5). They're looking for communicators and storytellers, not just someone focused only on last night's game. Joel Streed of KTTC-TV in Rochester, Minnesota says, "I'm looking for someone who is possibly a cross-over from news. That means you can do more than just read scores and follow highlights. Show me the story you did on the hockey mom who gets up with her child at 4:00 A.M. to get to practice. Or how about the guy pitching horseshoes? I guess the keyword is different." Griff Potter of WQAD-TV in Moline, Illinois says he's looking for "a journalist, not a rip-and-reader. Someone who understands that highlights, runs, and errors are boring television."

Above all, this means you need to demonstrate an ability to write and communicate effectively. It's become something of a disturbing trend on national sports shows to turn the presentation into a comedic sideshow, complete with funny noises, sounds, and impersonations. While a select few sports broadcasters can carry this off, it certainly doesn't appeal to most television news directors. Lombard says he wants someone with "good writing and storytelling and a unique style. Too many sportscasters look and sound alike or try to mimic a particular style."

Even sports broadcasters who have made it to the big time admit the paramount importance of good writing and reading. Kenny Mayne of ESPN says, "I think you have to read in order to write. Read all sorts of things, not just sports. It could be magazines, editorials, or different books so you get different opinions. The more you take in, the more well-rounded you become." That's also the advice from another ESPN figure, Charley Steiner. "I have always believed that the best broadcasters are the ones who are the most literate, the most well-read and not just in sports. I think it's very important to get a liberal arts education—not confine it to sports. The key is to be able to keep sports in some sense of priority and then be able to make judgments on the fly."

Mayne and Steiner seem like tremendous success stories to those just starting out, but just like anybody else, they started small. The key for them, and for you, is persistence and getting lots of experience. "There are very few overnight successes," says Steiner. "When I arrived at Bradley University, the first thing I did was go to the radio station and say, 'Folks, you better get used to me because you're going to see a lot of me over the next four years.' I played records, read news, did play-by-play, and managed the station." Before you graduate from college you should have similar experiences. Do anything and everything you can, including summer internships, even if they're unpaid. The important thing is getting experience and learning about the business. Joel Bernell of WGBA-TV says, "Get whatever experience you can, even if it's in news. Learn to write, edit, and shoot."

FINAL COMMENTS

Even with all this terrific advice, the sports job-hunting process is frustrating and difficult. News directors like Paul Conti admit, "There just aren't that many jobs openings at local TV stations. Be prepared to start very small." And that's probably the most difficult thing young sports broadcasters have to accept. When they finally get that first job, it will probably be at a very small station doing very unglamorous work. Mayne says that the biggest problem job seekers have is impatience. "They get out of college at 21 or 22 and they expect to be in the big time in two years. They get impatient and maybe give up on it too soon because they don't attain whatever goal they set for themselves." Mayne admits he failed several times. He was out of television for five years and it took him three interviews to hook on with ESPN.

   Other sports broadcasters have similar stories. One of the main things that separate them from those who don't make it is persistence and a willingness not to give up. "I've had doors slammed in my face and news directors tell me I wasn't good enough for sports," says ESPN's Rich Eisen. "It's not the most fun activity in the world. But do some research, choose an area where you want to live and go. And keep at it."

OFF-CAMERA POSITIONS

For those students who have neither the desire nor the talent to make it in sports broadcasting, an ancillary field like sports promotion, marketing, or management could be an ideal compromise. Professionals who work in sports promotion, such as university SIDs, have jobs that are difficult and demanding, but also come with certain rewards. Such professionals get to travel a lot, and attend some of the highest profile sporting events in the country. Working for an organization like a college, university, or private company also has the advantage of longevity and job security, especially compared to the typical sportscasting job on radio or TV.

More and more schools now offer courses in sports marketing and management. As we have already noted (see Chapter 2), sports broadcasting is big business involving millions of dollars. Every year, professional teams hire people to negotiate and deal with broadcasting contracts. Media companies need specialists to deal with sports broadcasting schedules, finances, and legal issues. The growing live sports production business needs more executives, producers, and technical crews. Again, many of these jobs offer higher pay and more job security than on-air broadcasting positions. Certainly, working on-camera isn't always the only, or best, way to make a living in sports broadcasting.

REFERENCES

"Careers in Sports: Play-by-play Announcer." ESPN. [Online]. Available: www.espn.go.com/special/s/careers/anno.html, September 7, 1999.

"Careers in Sports: TV Sports Anchor." ESPN. [Online]. Available: www.espn.go.com/special/s/careers/anchor.html, September 7, 1999.

"How to Prepare and Improve Your Television News Audition Tape." Don Fitzpatrick Associates. [Online]. Available: www.tvspy.com, 1999.

Lindner, Ken. "The Diversity Dilemma." *Broadcasting and Cable*. April 3, 1999.

Papper, Bob and Gerhard, Michael. "Starting Salaries: a Crying Shame." *RTNDA Communicator*, May 1999.

"Salary Survey Statistics." *RTNDA Communicator*, May 1999.

Stone, Vernon. "News Operations at U.S. TV Stations." [Online]. Available: web.missouri.edu/~jourvs/gtvops.html, 1999.

Stone, Vernon. "TV and Radio News Careers: Pros and Cons." [Online]. Available: web.missouri.edu/~jourvs/cartext.html, 1994.

Tedesco, Richard. "NBC, ABC Seal Diversity Deals." *Broadcasting and Cable*, January 10, 2000.

Tuohey, Chris. "The Olbermann Factor." *American Journalism Review*, May 1999.

Wang, Karissa S. "NBC Hires for Diversity." *Electronic Media*, February 14, 2000.

"Women and Minorities Employment Statistics." *RTNDA Communicator,* October 1998.

13

Women and Minorities

WOMEN'S WORK

Women have now become highly visible in the field of sports reporting. While men still drastically outnumber women in the field, reporters and anchors like Robin Roberts, Hannah Storm, and Lesley Visser have made tremendous contributions and opened doors for women at all levels of the industry. None of this comes as news to anyone who has followed sports on radio or television, but it represents a dramatic shift in sports reporting within just the past generation.

Up until the 1970s, women had virtually no role as sports reporters on radio or television. Sports were considered a male domain—played, coached, watched, and reported by men. The few female sports reporters, women like Maureen Orcutt of the *New York Times* and Jeane Hoffman of the *New York Journal-American*, were considered rarities who covered obscure women's sports or reported fluff stories. The so-called real sports reporters hung out in bars with ballplayers and the most famous bar of all was Toots Shor's in New York. Author David Halberstam described the place as "a men's club, one that reflected the age. It was white, male and boozy—hard-liquor boozy. Women were most decidedly not welcome."

As women became more empowered in the shifting cultural values of the 60s and 70s, women athletes also became more noticeable and women slowly began to drift into the sports reporting field. Finally, in 1975 Phyllis George broke through the barrier and became the first female sports figure on a national network when she began hosting *The NFL Today* on CBS (see Chapter 16). Just a few years later, Gayle Gardner occupied a high-profile anchor position on ESPN. And in 1990, Robin Roberts became the first black woman to anchor at the network sports level when she also went to ESPN.

"It's something I'm proud of," she says, "and I'll be happy to see more women of color at the network level."

While cultural values certainly played an important part in this process, one cannot ignore the role of legislation. In 1972, the government enacted as federal statute a series of education amendments designed to level the playing field between men and women. Title IX of those amendments prohibited sexual discrimination in educational institutions that received federal funds. Specifically, that meant that schools had to provide equitable athletic opportunities for all students, regardless of sex, in terms of participation, treatment of athletes, and scholarships.

To date, all court challenges and legislative attempts to weaken Title IX have failed. But it has not failed to generate a firestorm of controversy for educators, athletes, administrators, and reporters. Most women's groups contend that Title IX has done exactly what it set out to do: end the domination of athletics by men by opening more doors to women. Before Title IX, only 1 in 27 young women participated in sports, while today the figure is nearly 1 in 2. Many people say the resulting explosion in women's sports has led directly to the success of American women athletes in World Cup soccer and most notably in the Olympics, including the 1996 gymnastics team and the 1998 hockey team. "I could not have been an Olympian without Title IX," said sprinter Evelyn Ashford, who won four medals in track and field. "Title IX allowed me to run on the boys' track team."

Detractors say all this success has come at an unfair price for men's athletics. In an effort to comply with Title IX, several schools have had to reduce or eliminate men's sports (Table 13-1). A survey by the NCAA found that colleges had eliminated 200 men's teams and 17,000 athletic slots in recent years. The College Football Association, led by executive director Chuck Neinas, has joined other groups in lobbying to get Title IX overturned. "It's a quota system, pure and simple," says Neinas, who adds that colleges are trying to get women to participate in athletics in "unrealistic" numbers. Critics also point to the unequal revenue generated by men's and women's sports. In college sports, for example, football is the dominant money-maker at almost every university and at Division I schools it accounts for nearly a third of all athletic revenues (see Table 13-2). The discrepancy becomes less obvious at smaller schools.

The debate has also been a mixed blessing for female sports reporters. One the one hand, it has increased the importance, viability, and popularity of women's athletics, with a corresponding positive effect on women in the media. As female athletes became more empowered, so too did female reporters. Again, the courts played a major role. In 1977, major league baseball refused to let *Sports Illustrated* reporter Melissa Ludtke in the clubhouses at Yankee Stadium. Ludtke and the magazine successfully sued and won the right to gain access, but the fight took its toll. "This crusade has worn me down," she later said. "I'm a little disappointed by my own situation."

Table 13-1 The Effect of Title IX

NCAA surveys conducted in the early 80s and again in the late 90s revealed that Title IX resulted in more women athletes and programs at the college level. But 54% of Division I-A schools said the law forced them to drop some men's programs.

	1981–82	*1998–99*
Women's programs	5,696	9,479
Men's programs	9,113	9,149
Women athletes	90,000	163,000
Men athletes	220,000	230,000

Source: "Colleges cut men's teams." *Chronicle of Higher Education*, March 23, 2001, Vol. XLVII, No. 28

Table 13-2 NCAA Gender Equity Revenues

	Average Revenue	*Percent of Total Revenue*
Division I Men's Sports		
Football	$3,079,380	32%
Basketball	$1,511,710	16%
Other sports	$422,005	4%
Unallocated	$344,487	3%
Division I Women's Sports		
Basketball	$210,123	2%
Other sports	$373,503	4%
Unallocated	$194,336	2%
Unallocated (men and women)	$3,574,714	37%
Division II Men's Sports		
Football	$130,964	11%
Basketball	$102,457	9%
Other sports	$175,126	15%
Unallocated	$449,499	39%
Division II Women's Sports		
Basketball	$74,979	6%
Other sports	$150,572	13%
Unallocated	$44,249	4%
Division III Men's Sports		
Football	$38,481	10%
Basketball	$25,108	6%
Other sports	$89,266	11%
Unallocated	$11,175	3%
Division III Women's Sports		
Basketball	$18,185	5%
Other sports	$70,870	18%
Unallocated	$12,508	3%

Source: NCAA Gender Equity Report, 1997–98

This points out one of the unexpected results of Title IX: a strong and continuing resentment on the part of men who see women as encroaching on their turf. Legislation might have cleared the way for more female sports reporters, but it did not solve the most difficult part of their jobs. Michelle Kaufman wrote for the *Detroit Free Press* in the early 1990s and said she endured constant verbal and emotional abuse in the Detroit Lions locker room. "The locker room isn't a nice place to do business for women or men," she later said. "[But] I have earned the right to do my job without being harassed. When male reporters are treated poorly, it's usually because they wrote something the athlete didn't like or asked a question that the coach didn't like. I wish we had that luxury."

The most infamous incident took place in the fall of 1990 and involved Lisa Olson, a reporter for the *Boston Herald*. Olson claims that one of the players for the New England Patriots exposed himself and made lewd comments to her in the locker room. Olson complained to the team and the league and assumed the matter would be handled and quickly end. Instead, the story became a national referendum on women in sports, with Olson cast as the villain. She received death threats and physical abuse that made it impossible to do her job. She eventually had to leave Boston and the country, and took a job at a newspaper in Sydney, Australia. "How do I describe what happened," she said, "not just the original incident, but the public's reaction and the media circus that followed? It wasn't worth the energy." It's tempting to describe these incidents as ancient history, but a strong undercurrent of resentment remains today.

Criticism has not been limited to athletes. Many male sports reporters resent women's intrusion into "their" business and to a larger extent, the overall effect of the growth of women's sports. In 1998, Sharna Marcus covered college basketball for the *South Bend Tribune*. Marcus said she received better treatment from players and coaches than from male sports reporters. "When I tell people that I cover sports," she said, "they often look as if a dog just told them he can fly an airplane." Robert Lipsyte of the *New York Times* wrote an article decrying the "emasculation" of sports. "[But] what happens when all the women now coming into the game begin exhibiting the same killer instincts as men?" he asked. "Aren't we turning them into a new generation of Bobby Knights and Pat Rileys? Women are already showing the strain: anorexic gymnasts, 15-year-olds burned out by tennis daddies, and swimmers sexually exploited. Is this what everybody meant by equal rights?" ESPN's Jeff Hollobaugh noted, "In a world where women's sports grows in importance daily . . . we have to expect that the media will focus its attention on beauty instead of achievement from time to time. The public wants it."

But the public did not seem to want the bizarre incident that occurred in 1995, involving CBS golf commentator Ben Wright. A female reporter overheard Wright commenting about what he perceived as rampant homosexuality on the women's professional golf tour. Wright did not make the comments on the air and later said they were taken out of context. Nevertheless, the comments were published and Wright became the center of a massive controversy, which led to his suspension and ultimately his dismissal from CBS Sports. LPGA commissioner Jim Ritts later commented, "It's not issues about alternative lifestyles and all the other silly comments that have been made. [It's about] a time in our society when women are given the same opportunities as men; when women are treated equally as a man."

Obviously, women and women reporters still have a long way to go. In late 2000, *Playboy* held a contest called, "Choose America's Sexiest Sportscaster," in which the magazine asked readers to vote on its Web site for the "hottest" among 10 female sports personalities.

The magazine would then invite the winner to pose for a nude pictorial. "We're backsliding," says Fox Sports Net's Jeanne Zelasko. "When I talk to young women about careers in this field, do I advise them to get a solid background in sports and reporting, or do I tell them to enter a beauty contest?" Zelasko was not one of the 10 personalities included in the contest, but according to *Sports Illustrated*, none of the 10 contestants denounced the vote or asked to have themselves removed from the Web site. "We're damned if we do and damned if we don't," says Lisa Guerrero of Fox Sports Net, which seems to sum up the feelings of many women who have struggled to climb the ladder of professional sportscasting.

A PIONEER

You may not recognize the name Heidi Soliday, but in many ways she's blazed as many trails for women sportscasters as Hannah Storm or Robin Roberts. In 1991, Soliday became the sports director at KCCI-TV in Des Moines, Iowa—one of the first women to hold such a position at any station in the country. Soliday started part-time at the station in 1976, and has gone on to cover the Masters golf tournament, the Rose Bowl, the World Series, the Final Four, and many other national sporting events. She shares some of the things she's learned from nearly 25 years in the business.

Q: Were you really the first woman sports director at a local television station anywhere in the country?

A: I'd like to find that out, because I don't know for sure. I know I'm probably the first one ever in the greater Midwest and certainly one of the first in the country. In my travels around the country I haven't seen anyone else in a similar position. It seems most of the women in sports are at the network level, not in local markets. Until recently, a lot of local news directors still believed that guys would not want to watch a female sports director on television.

Q: How did you get into sportscasting?

A: I can't say this is something I always wanted to do. In fact, in college I was pretty sure I wanted to be a film director. But I started watching the Sunday sports one night and thought it really stunk. I figured it couldn't be that hard, so I applied at all three television stations in Des Moines and KCCI hired me the same day.

Q: What has it been like as a woman in what has traditionally been considered a man's position?

A: For me, it hasn't been that big a deal. I'm from Des Moines and that made it a lot easier, because so many people knew me or my family. I'm also not stupid. I realize that in certain ways a woman actually has an advantage over a man in covering sports. A lot of the guys in sports are former athletes and extremely jealous of the athletes they cover. As a result, many of the athletes feel like the men reporters are always on the attack, always out to get them. With women, there's no envy or jealousy. I also think it's easier for a woman to get a story in some situations compared to the men.

Q: You describe yourself as an aggressive reporter. Do you feel like women in sportscasting have to be more aggressive to handle the position and the pressure?

A: If you're a shrinking violet, you're not going to get the story, which is especially true in sports. I made a concerted effort to be that way when I started out. Being a woman and a blonde, there's a great danger that you won't be taken seriously, even today.

Q: How would you describe your style on the air?

A: By nature, I'm sort of a wild person with a bawdy sense of humor. But I'm certainly not a clown and I dislike all the entertainment stuff that's going on in places like ESPN. The trend today in sports, and even in other areas, is toward the wacky and nutty. It's all about look and presentation, rather than substance. I much prefer the straightforward delivery.

Q: Do you consider yourself a role model for aspiring female sportscasters?

A: It's not that I don't want to be a role model, but I'm really uncomfortable with that part of the business. I always get embarrassed when someone comes up and asks for an autograph. I say, "Are you really sure you want one?" I do know that I might have inspired a few people along the way, but I'm not sure my job is really one people should aspire to.

Q: You've certainly had the opportunity or desire to go to a bigger market, or even the networks. Why did you stay in Des Moines?

Figure 13-1 Sports Director Heidi Soliday of KCCI-TV in Des Moines, Iowa

A: I actually did have some opportunities in several other places. I interviewed with CNN for the position that eventually went to Hannah Storm. I also had interviews in places like Chicago, but in a lot of situations it always seemed like a man beat me out. As for the future, what I'd really like to do is work on a news magazine show, where you can really do something in-depth. I'd love to be able to research, write, and develop a story for a show like *HBO Real Sports*. You know, in some respects I actually consider myself a failure, because I never got beyond where I started. But now I feel like I was ahead of my time.

COLOR BLIND?

There has been no single bigger issue in America than race over the past 200 years. Race dominates every facet of American culture and certainly sports is no exception. What makes race relations and reporting so interesting in sports is the fact that while people of color now dominate the sports themselves, they're still underrepresented in sports management, coaching, and reporting.

According to a study conducted by Northeastern University in the late 1990s, there were only three black managers and three black head coaches in the NFL. Black head coaches accounted for only 6 percent of the Division I NCAA football programs. "Today's black athletes are just gladiators," says NFL Hall of Famer Jim Brown. Much of the problem can be traced to lack of minority ownership. Not until the late 1980s did a black hold majority ownership in a major sports franchise (the Denver Nuggets). A decade later, black ownership in professional sports was virtually nonexistent.

The same can be said for minority ownership of broadcast properties. Since the National Telecommunications and Information Administration began keeping records of minority ownership in broadcasting, the totals have never exceeded 3.1 percent, and as of the late 1990s, minority ownership has actually decreased, down to 2.8 percent. Since minority owners have historically hired more minority employees, this represents a downturn for reporters, anchors, producers, and other broadcasters of color. Among evening news correspondents of the major television networks, minorities comprised only 17 percent in 1999, down from 20 percent in 1998. Asians and Hispanics account for less than 5 percent of the total. The situation is slightly better in the sports field, if only because so many former athletes have the opportunity to move from the field to the broadcast booth.

Most sports reporting of race has focused in three main areas: lack of opportunities for minorities off the field, the alleged exploitation of minority athletes, and the continuing battle against racism. The 1980s and 90s saw an increasing unwillingness on the part of the media or the public to defend prejudicial or racist statements in the sports arena. Dodgers executive Al Campanis and CBS broadcaster Jimmy "the Greek" Snyder both lost their jobs after ill-advised on-air comments. Baseball executives suspended Cincinnati Reds owner Marge Schott in the early 1990s for her derogatory comments against minorities, and in the winter of 2000, baseball suspended Atlanta Braves relief pitcher John Rocker for similar comments he made in a *Sports Illustrated* article. "Jackie [Robinson] was always impatient for change," said Rachel Robinson, the widow of the man who broke baseball's color barrier in 1947. "If he were alive today he'd say, 'We've got to do better. We haven't come far enough.'"

Minorities also say they haven't come far enough in representation off the field and for the most part, the major sports leagues agree. "The NFL is on the verge of an awakening," said Carmen Policy, a front office executive with the Cleveland Browns. "We sort of drifted off for a time when we felt there was no overt racism in the league and we got kind of lazy. We realize now there's a lack of opportunity created by a flawed process." Many would argue that the process denies minorities access to coaching, managing, and front office positions, but they don't necessarily see the answer in quotas or affirmative action. Jim Brown advocates a permanent training ground for minority managers at the high school, NCAA, and professional levels. "You shouldn't go to the owner and say, 'Hire some black folks,'" he said. "It's the owner's money. He should hire the most qualified people."

One way or another, much of the debate comes down to the issue of money. Money drives everything in sports, including the race issue. The tremendous amounts of money now available to minority athletes have defused the issue somewhat on the professional level, but it remains a contentious debate in college athletics. "The NCAA is corrupt," says former NBA star Charles Barkley. "There's exploitation of the black athletes and always has been. They use the players to make money for themselves and everybody knows it." NCAA rules prohibit paying a college player for athletic competition, yet the organization makes millions of dollars off the same athletes. Every year, the recruiting process for high school athletes gets more intense, more competitive, and often more illegal. The temptation of money, cars, and women is often too much for even the most well-meaning athletes. In 1989, state football champion Dallas Carter High School in Texas had two All-American football players, Derric Evans and Gary Edwards, who were heavily recruited by schools all over the country. "I was promised money, credit cards, apartments, come home on the weekends when I wanted to," said Evans. "Everybody was promising something. It was just a matter of who promised the most." Perhaps the fame and the attention got to Evans and Edwards, neither of whom ever made it to college. Both were convicted and sentenced to jail for armed robbery.

There's also another side to exploitation, for those who chase the riches from an early age. Several prominent NBA players, including Kevin Garnett and Kobe Bryant, skipped college completely and went right from high school to the pros. In those cases, the players may have given up just as much as the millions of dollars they earned. "People are getting millions of dollars, but not growing up," said Olympic gold medalist Carl Lewis. "Here they are, people who never really learned what it's like to be 20, 21, 25 and have to earn everything. What about important life experiences?" Adds Brown, "The money they're making has no meaning from the standpoint of breaking down barriers or making more opportunities. It's wasted money."

Often the media feeds into this popular perception, by publicizing the latest multi-million dollar contract signing. Author H. G. Bissinger said the only thing more remarkable than the fact that Derric Evans signed his college scholarship offer in a hot tub was the presence of Dallas television and newspaper reporters there to cover the event. Cameras are there en masse when Mike Tyson goes into prison, but very few sports reporters take the time to investigate the underlying issues behind his behavior. The entire sports media focused on John Rocker's crime and punishment, but it had virtually no effect on the racial situation as a whole.

Some media have tried to exert a more positive influence. In the 1990s, the *Portland Oregonian* decided not to include any racially offensive sports nicknames in any of its headlines or stories. The newspaper was widely applauded, but hardly any other media outlets followed suit. What copying has taken place is the preoccupation with sensationalism, celebrities, and scandal. In that sense, minority sports reporting isn't really different from any other reporting and that might be the biggest problem of all.

REFERENCES

Angell, Roger. *Late innings*. New York: Ballantine Books, 1982.
"Clinton Needles Sports World for Not Hiring Minorities." CNN. [Online]. Available: http://europe.cnn.com/allpolitics/1998/04/15/clinton.town.hall/, April 15, 1998.
Davenport, Paula. "Hispanic, Asian Reporters Scarce on Evening News." Southern Illinois University News Release, January 31, 2000.
"Empowering Women in Sports." Feminist Majority Foundation Task Force. [Online]. Available: www.feminist.org/research/sports5a.html.
Giobbe, Dorothy. "Women Sportswriters Still Face Hassles in the Locker Room. *Editor & Publisher*, December 11, 1993.
Gill, Lisa. "Hannah Storm Rocks the Sports World." [Online]. Available: www.cybergrrl.com/fun/.
Halberstam, David. *Summer of '49*. New York: Avon Books, 1989.
Holhut, Randolph T. "Title IX: Leveling the Playing Field for Women." [Online]. Available: www.mdle.com/WrittenWord/rholhut/holhut43.htm.
Hollobaugh, Jeff. "1,500 Runner Not Just Another Pretty Face." ESPN. [Online]. Available: www.espn.go.com/oly/s...ield/columns/hollobaugh_jeff/710008.html, August 30, 2000.
"Hottie Topic." *Sports Illustrated*. December 25–January 1, 2000.
Lipsyte, Robert. "The Emasculation of Sports." *New York Times*, April 2, 1995.
Lopez, John P. "Breaking the Barriers." *Houston Chronicle*. [Online]. Available: www.chron.com/content/chronicle/sports/special/barriers/since.html, 1997.
Olson, Lisa. "Hall of Shame." [Online]. Available: www.theage.com/au/news/ns970123a. htm, January 23, 1997.
Olson, Walter. "Title IX from Outer Space: How Federal Law Is Killing Men's College Sports." *Reason Magazine*, February 1998.
Marcus, Sharna. "Female Sports Writers Unite." *Indiana Daily Student*, March 10, 1998.
Sportscasters: Behind the Mike. [Television show]. The History Channel, February 7, 2000.
SportsCenter of the Century: The Most Influential People. [Television show]. ESPN, February 20, 2000.
"The GolfWeb Q&A: Jim Ritts." [Online]. Available: http://services.Golfweb.com/library/qa/ritts960112.html, January 12, 1996.

14

Global Sports Broadcasting

Ask any American about the biggest sporting events in the world and many will think of the Super Bowl, World Series, Indy 500, or Kentucky Derby. Such events annually attract millions of spectators, with millions more watching or listening at home on radio or television. That kind of interest also generates enormous revenue and profit. As a result, many of the events have transcended the boundaries of sport to become cultural icons. The Super Bowl is no longer a game between the two best teams in the National Football League; it is the biggest sports party of the year played out on the biggest stage in the country.

At least, that is the American perspective. While the Super Bowl reaches an estimated worldwide audience of around 800 million, that's nothing compared to viewing interest in soccer's World Cup, which in 1966 became the first sporting event ever televised on a global basis. It routinely pulls in between two and three billion television viewers. Americans know next to nothing about cricket, except for its kinship to baseball, yet the International Cricket Council World Cup drew more than two billion viewers for its 42-day tournament in 1999. Clearly, there is a great big world of sports broadcasting outside the borders of the United States, which Americans are just now beginning to discover.

OVER THERE

Much like the United States, international sports broadcasting has grown primarily out of powerful national network interests. Just as CBS, NBC, and ABC came to dominate sports broadcasting in the U.S., networks like the BBC in England, Globo in Brazil, and ARD and ZDF in Germany have done the same thing. The size, money, and resources of these networks pushed them to the forefront of sports broadcasting outlets and discouraged almost all serious attempts at competition.

The networks dominance in the U.S. ended as a result of a greater demand for programming and technological advances that satisfied that demand, principally cable television. ESPN started as a bargain-basement operation in 1979, but eventually evolved into the most profitable sports cable operation in the country (see Chapter 15). In much the same way, media mogul Rupert Murdoch challenged established networks like the BBC and ITV in England. Murdoch founded British Sky Broadcasting (BSkyB) and Sky Sports as vehicles to show live sporting events, both over the air and pay-per-view. The two entities don't have nearly the audience as the older networks, but thanks to Murdoch they have much deeper pockets. For example, in 1992 BSkyB paid £304 million for the rights to England's Premier League soccer and four years later upped the ante to £670 million. In the summer of 2000, BSkyB bid £1.11 billion ($1.7 billion U.S.) to retain rights to live games. Murdoch later added more sports channels, including Sky Sports 2, Sky Sports 3, Sky Sports Gold, and Sky Sports Extra. Combined, the Sky networks claimed more than eight million subscribers in the year 2000.

The success of Murdoch's efforts did not go unnoticed by other countries. Some of the more successful challengers to date include DSF (Deusches Sports Fernsehen) in Germany, Teledeporte in Spain, and Torneos y Compelencias in Argentina. All of them have taken programming and money away from more established television networks. "For years and years, the national channels in each country controlled television," says Chet Simmons, a long-time sports producer in the U.S. "Now, the number of channels and stations being built across Europe is going to double in number. Sport throughout Europe is going to have a totally different face. I would be damned concerned if I were the established broadcaster." One thing that helps level the playing field, at least in England, is the International Television Commission. The ITC regulates and licenses commercial television in the UK and has mandated that some sports must be made available for broadcasting by free, over-the-air services.

ITC Exclusivity Rights

England's Television Act of 1954 originally prevented any one broadcaster from obtaining exclusive rights to certain sporting events of national interest. The Broadcasting Act of 1996 further established protections for free, over-the-air broadcasters in relation to pay services. A pay service is not allowed to broadcast a listed or protected event unless rights are also made available to over-the-air broadcasters. Listed events fall in two categories. Category A includes those events in which live coverage *must* be made available to public broadcasters, while Category B includes those events in which live coverage *might* be made available.

> **Category A events:** Olympic Games, FIFA World Cup finals, FA Cup final, Scottish FA Cup final, the Grand National, the Derby, Wimbledon tennis finals, European football championship finals, the Rugby League Challenge Cup final, and the Rugby World Cup final.
>
> **Category B events:** Cricket test matches in England, non-finals play in Wimbledon, all other matches at the Rugby World Cup finals tournament, Five Nations Rugby Tournament matches involving home countries, the Commonwealth Games, the World Athletics Championship, the Cricket World Cup, the Ryder Cup, the Open Gold Championship.
>
> *Source:* ITC Notes, December 1999

Still, the upstarts' ability to take away broadcasting rights poses a major threat to the traditional powers. The BBC had to put up a tremendous fight to retain the rights to the Wimbledon tennis tournament. But it didn't have much left to battle Sky Sports, which won the rights to Ryder Cup golf, rugby league games, and a series of international cricket matches—all live. The acquisition of such rights is the lifeblood of any sports broadcasting enterprise, because it's the only way to satisfy the increasing demand on the part of viewers.

As a result, rights fees for international events have gone through the roof. In 1987, the World Consortium of Broadcasters bought the rights to World Cup soccer tournaments in 1990, 1994, and 1998. The total cost of the deal was $230 million, which seemed like a steal. "The premium value of the '98 World Cup rights were in hindsight, incredibly undersold," said one industry executive. The Bavarian media group Kirch teamed up with the Swiss holding company Sporis to acquire the rights to the tournaments in 2002 and 2006 for $2.2 billion. The escalating fees may seem excessive and even foolish, but global satellite distribution eases the financial strain. For Premier League soccer, Murdoch's channels in Asia and Latin America mean millions more viewers at almost no extra cost.

The staggering cost of rights fees have caused many outlets to form regional partnerships, such as the deal between Kirch and Sporis, which presents another challenge to traditional networks. Murdoch has again been at the forefront, creating a pan-European joint venture with the EBU called Eurosport. Eurosport is one of a growing number of regional conglomerates that also include ESPN-Star Sports and Sportel, an international television operation with ties to more than 250 companies and 40 different countries. Such combinations allow for a pooling of resources and money that make it very difficult for competitors to match. But despite such obvious advantages, there is still room in the marketplace for the established networks. In 1999, India's broadcasting corporation Prasar Bharati won exclusive five-year rights to the country's international cricket matches, beating out competitors such as Sony TV, Zee, and ESPN-Star Sports.

THERE'S NO PLACE LIKE HOME

When Cable News Network launched its CNN International network in the 1980s, it became the first truly global news operation, reaching new audiences all over the world. But despite the tremendous accomplishment, CNN made a near-fatal mistake. It presented an American version of its news to international audiences, which included American anchors, reporters, and story lines. Not surprisingly, audiences dismissed the programming as simply another western import with little or no relevance to their lives or culture, and CNN spent several years trying to rectify its error.

CNN learned the hard way about modern global broadcasting. While technology has made it easy for broadcast signals to cross international boundaries, that same signal is not always welcome. For years, countries have complained about America's domination of the mass media and a resulting cultural imperialism in which the U.S. negatively affects local social values. American movies, music, tapes, recordings and television shows account for more than 90 percent of the world total and that influence can be measured in every country around the globe. Foreign visitors to the U.S. are often surprised to learn that not all Americans act like the guests on *Jerry Springer* and not all teenagers behave like those in MTV's *The Real World.*

International sports broadcasters have seemingly learned the hard lessons of CNN and begun to tailor their programming to the regional flavor of the viewing audience. ESPN now targets its international division to attract niche audiences—a departure from its earlier attempts to focus on U.S. programming aimed at U.S. businesspeople working overseas. So while ESPN Asia has table tennis for the Chinese and cricket for Indians, Orbit-ESPN features horse racing for the Middle East, all delivered in local languages. In total, ESPN reaches more than 150 million viewers in 180 different countries. Another prime example is Eurosport. In 2000, Eurosport had strong ratings in Germany and Scandinavia, but was very weak in England. Thus, in January 2000 the network introduced British Eurosport, its first dedicated national edition. If the offering succeeds, Eurosport will look to do the same thing in other markets, possibly Germany and Sweden. Says David McMurtrie of MediaCom in London, "The challenge is to maintain their very strong global values, while at the same time making the [local] content relevant."

Other organizations also realize the need to emphasize the local flavor and culture. The International Football Channel (TIFC) debuted in March 2000 as a pan-regional, all-soccer programming network targeted specifically to Latin American audiences. The Canadian parent company announced that "all matches will be produced in Spanish by professional sportscasters, bringing a distinct Latin American perspective to the game in keeping with the 'tailored' regional philosophy of TIFC's international coverage." TIFC also planned to provide special programming showcasing sports action in Colombia, Peru, Chile, Brazil, and Mexico. All programming would be produced in Florida or South America.

In a similar vein, Major League Baseball International broadcasts to around 200 countries on a regular basis, but tries to establish as many local arrangements as possible, including using local broadcasters within each country. "Sports is tribal," says Tim Brosnan of MLBI. "People want to root for the hometown guy and this helps position the sports leagues for global growth."

YANKEE GO HOME

Brosnan's attitude represents a significant departure from the traditional American view of international sports. For decades, the predominant view was one of ethnocentrism; with the exception of the Olympics, Americans ignored any international sporting event and instead focused solely within their own borders. The growth of the U.S. in international stature and its success in the Olympics helped fuel the belief that American athletes were the best in the world. Hence, as early as 1903, American professional baseball players competed in a World Series, despite the fact that no teams outside the U.S. were represented.

Much of this attitude still prevails today, although developments in communication and technology have opened the eyes of the American sports public to overseas opportunities. For most professional sports leagues, such opportunities are strictly financial. The NBA in particular has worked hard to expand overseas markets in the wake of domestic stagnation, especially after a disastrous players' strike and the retirement of superstar Michael Jordan (see Figure 14-1).

As NBA merchandise sales and television ratings dropped in the United States, the league projected stable international revenues of $500 million dollars for the year 2000. The league now broadcasts to more than 240 countries in 44 languages and boasts an overseas reach of 650 million households. Starting in 1990, the NBA has also staged a two-game regular season series in Tokyo called the Japan Games. The first games attracted just over 10,000 fans, but games in 1996 had crowds of nearly 40,000 at the Tokyo Dome. "We've seen some explosive growth in the last three or four years," says Heidi Ueberroth of the NBA's international television division. "We just launched our League Pass program in Japan. Fans can have access to all the teams and we can distribute more than 13,000 hours internationally."

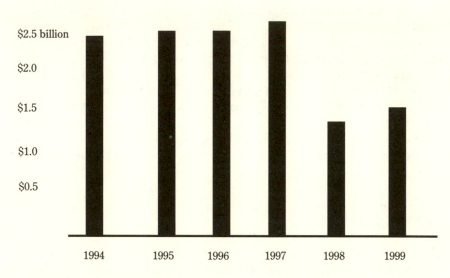

Figure 14-1 NBA Merchandise Sales in the United States (Data from NBA, Nielsen Media Research, and *Sports Business Journal,* as cited in the *New York Times,* March 3, 2000, p. B1)

Other leagues have successfully staged events in overseas markets as a way of increasing visibility and profits. The NFL also plays a game in Tokyo as part of an aggressive international marketing effort. In fact, it was in Mexico City where the Dallas Cowboys and Houston Oilers attracted 112,000 fans in 1995; the largest crowd in league history. The league continues to operate a minor league system in Europe, stocked with American players and coaches. For the first time in its history, major league baseball played regular season games outside of North America when the New York Mets and Chicago Cubs opened the 2000 season in Japan. Major league baseball also continues its Envoy Program, which sends some of North America's best college and high school instructors to teach the game in 32 different countries, and it's Pitch, Hit and Run program teaches fundamentals to more than half a million kids around the world.

Partly as a result, from 1995 to 2000 baseball television revenues outside the U.S. tripled, while worldwide sponsorship revenues increased 800 percent. With retail licenses in more than 50 countries outside the U.S. and Canada, major league baseball projected a 34 percent increase in merchandise sales for the year 2000. And those figures could go even higher if a proposed World Cup baseball tournament becomes reality. By the spring of

2000, discussions for a worldwide baseball championship reached the point that Brosnan declared, "Within the next five years there will be a true world championship."

GLOBAL IMPACT

This mixing of cultures and countries would have seemed unthinkable just a generation ago, but technology has truly shrunk the world into a global village, as trite as that may sound. Sports broadcasting in particular has helped accelerate this process, which has seen the obliteration of traditional boundaries of culture and geography. For example, Malaysia has had a strict policy of controlling access to its airwaves. But cable and satellite technology such as Panamsat's PAS-4 and Hong Kong's Asiasat-2 has almost rendered such restrictions obsolete. In both cases, sports played a significant part, especially ESPN on Panamsat and Star-TV on Asiasat-2. According to a high-ranking Malaysian government official, such intrusions made the country a part of the global television system whether it liked it or not.

But in effect, such technological power may usher in a different type of cultural imperialism. The popularity and profitability of exported American sports programming may eventually push local sports off the screen. Professional American sports have become increasingly attractive to overseas audiences because of the rising influence of foreign players. A heavy influx of Russians into the NHL has resulted in several games being televised to Eastern Europe. In 1999, the NFL video streamed games to Holland and Singapore, focusing mainly on the international hotel market. More than 21 percent of major league baseball players come from outside the U.S., including a substantial number from Latin America, where demand for programming has increased (see Table 14-1). In 2000, Univision and Galavision announced plans to televise major league games for the first time. The Spanish-language networks reach 93 percent of Hispanic households in the U.S., and plan to telecast a limited schedule focusing on teams popular with that audience. The scheduling includes the Arizona Diamondbacks, Atlanta Braves, Houston Astros, and Boston Red Sox, which feature star pitcher Pedro Martinez. Martinez would not be the first player used as a vehicle by an international network. In 1998, major league baseball signed a local television agreement with iTV in South Korea to televise every start of Los Angeles Dodgers' pitcher Chan Ho Park.

The biggest threat may come from the NBA, in light of basketball's tremendous acceptance and popularity in all parts of the world. NBA programming has become increasingly popular overseas, especially in Europe. Michel Denisot of Canal Plus in France says fans of American sports want either pro basketball or the Super Bowl. "We literally started with the NBA,"

Table 14-1 Number of Players from Each Country on 1999 Opening Day
Lineups for Major League Baseball Teams

Country	Number of Players
Dominican Republic	66
Puerto Rico	31
Venezuela	25
Mexico	12
Canada	9
Cuba	8
Panama	6
Japan	5
Australia	3
Colombia	3
Curacao	3
Jamaica	2
Aruba	1
England	1
Korea	1

Source: USA Today, March 17, 2000

he said. "It's part of our history and our identity. It's young, it's modern, it's creative, and those are our ideals." Canal Plus carries about 50 games a year, including the All-Star Game and the playoffs, and has the broadcast rights for Spain and Italy. The 2000 NBA Finals were broadcast to 200 countries in 41 different languages.

Ironically, technological capability may also defeat the great promise of global sports broadcasting, which is the breakdown of traditional geographical and cultural boundaries. As technology becomes more specialized and sophisticated, audiences become more fragmented and nationalized. Author Helen Kelly-Holmes notes that a truly international audience has developed only in the sense of broadcasters becoming more international to serve a predominantly national audience free from the regulatory jurisdiction of government. "Greater choice, greater opportunities, and greater access," she writes, "simply have contributed to the status quo." As the mass audience fragments into smaller groups, those groups tend to focus inward. Natalie Fenton of Loughborough University notes, "In particular, satellite sports channels reinforce traditional gender roles and notions of nationhood."

More technology and more choice also mean a lessened role for the traditional network powers and a shift in the very perception of the nature of television. Researcher Andrew Tolson argues that the multiplicity of channels makes possible a shift from a public service conception of broadcasting to a free-market conception. Europeans in particular have viewed national channels as ubiquitous providers of necessary commodities such as news, education, politics, and sports. Now, broadcasters are considered merely financial brokers to provide specialized programming choices, and this shift has seriously eroded viewership for the previously dominant full-service stations. Official ratings from the British Audience Research Bureau show that over the past 20 years, ITV's audience has fallen from 49 percent to 32 percent, while the audience for BBC1 dropped from 39 percent to 29 percent.

Major American networks have experienced a similar erosion, but on a much smaller scale because they are still the main providers for the country's most popular sports. But the threat of satellite and cable challengers has forced the U.S. networks and sports enterprises to finally look beyond their own borders. Once insulated and isolated, American broadcasters have realized the financial opportunities available in overseas markets and become much more involved internationally. "The key for U.S. leagues looking to entrench themselves overseas is exposure," said David Zucker of ESPN International. That exposure will apparently increase as international sports and athletes become more accepted into American culture. "Reaction can't meet demand and it's all happening sooner rather than later," said Brosnan. "You will start to see worldwide competition. We're already centering on when it will happen." Adds Ueberroth, "We're just scratching the surface as to what we see the opportunities to be."

The very first Super Bowl in 1967 was televised on two television networks (CBS and NBC) to an estimated audience of 65 million people. But the telecast was aired only in the U.S., and not even to all parts of the country. Viewers in Los Angeles (where the game was played) could not see the game because of a local blackout rule. Contrast that to Super Bowl XXXIII in 1999, which was broadcast to more than 800 million people in 180 countries, and in more than 24 languages (see Table 14-2).

Table 14-2 The International Broadcast Schedule for Super Bowl XXXIII in 1999

Country/Area	*Carrier*
Algeria	Fox Sports World
Andorra	Canal + France
Angola	ESPN International
Anguilla	Fox Sports Americas
Antigua	Fox Sports Americas
Argentina	Fox Sports Americas
Aruba	Fox Sports Americas

(continued)

Table 14-2   *(continued)*

Country/Area	Carrier
Australia	SBS/Fox Sports Australia
Austria	ORF/SAT 1/DSF
Bahamas	Broadcast Corp. of the Bahamas/FSA
Bahrain	ORBIT/Fox Sports World
Bangladesh	ESPN International
Barbados	Fox Sports Americas
Barbuda	Fox Sports Americas
Basse–Terre	Canal + France
Belgium	Canal + Flemish/French
Belize	Fox Sports Americas
Benin	ESPN International
Bermuda	Fox Sports Americas
Bhutan	ESPN International
Bolivia	Fox Sports Americas
Botswana	ESPN International
Brazil	Fox Sports Americas
British Virgin Islands	Fox Sports Americas
Brunei	ESPN International
Bulgaria	BNT
Burkina Faso	ESPN International
Burundi	ESPN International
Caicos Islands	Fox Sports Americas
Cameroon	ESPN International
Central African Republic	ESPN International
Canada	Global TV/RDS
Cayenne	Fox Sports Americas
Cayman Islands	Fox Sports Americas
Chile	Fox Sports Americas
Colombia	Fox Sports Americas
Costa Rica	Fox Sports Americas
Dominica	Fox Sports Americas
Dominican Republic	Deportes en la Cumbre/FSA
Ecuador	Fox Sports Americas
El Salvador	Canal Dox/Fox Sports Americas
Fort de France	Canal + France
French Guiana	Fox Sports Americas
Grenada	Fox Sports Americas
Guadaloupe	Canal + France/Fox Sports Americas
Guatemala	Fox Sports Americas
Guyana	Fox Sports Americas
Haiti	Fox Sports Americas
Honduras	Honduvision/FSA
Hong Kong	ESPN International
Iceland	CH. 2

Table 14-2   *(continued)*

Country/Area	Carrier
India	ESPN International
Indonesia	ESPN International
Ireland	Sky Sports
Israel	METV
Italy	Tele + 2
Ivory Coast	ESPN International
Jamaica	CVM-TV/FSA
Japan	NHK/NTV/PPVJ/Gaora
Jordan	METV/ORBIT/Fox Sports World
Kenya	ESPN International
Korea	ESPN International
Kuwait	Kuwait TV
Lebanon	METV/ORBIT/Fox Sports World
Libya	Fox Sports World
Liechtenstein	DSF
Luxembourg	Canal + Netherlands
Macao	ESPN International
Madagascar	ESPN International
Malawi	ESPN International
Malaysia	ESPN International
Maldives	ESPN International
Mali	ESPN International
Martinique	Fox Sports Americas
Matu-Utu	Canal + France
Mauritania	Fox Sports World
Mauritius	Canal + France
Mayotte	Canal + France
Mexico	Televisa/Fox Sports Americas/Radio Acir
Monaco	Canal + France
Mongolia	ESPN International
Montserrat	Fox Sports Americas
Morocco	ORBIT/Fox Sports World
Mozambique	ESPN International
Myanmar	ESPN International
Namibia	ESPN International
Nepal	ESPN International
Netherlands	Canal + Netherlands
Netherlands Antilles	Fox Sports Americas
Nevis	Fox Sports Americas
New Zealand	Sky New Zealand
Nicaragua	Televicentro de Nicaragua/FSA
Niger	ESPN International
Nigeria	ESPN International
Norway	TV 2

(continued)

Table 14-2 *(continued)*

Country/Area	Carrier
Nouvelle de Ledonie	Canal + France
Oman	ORBIT/Fox Sports World
Pakistan	ESPN International
Palestine	ORBIT/Fox Sports World
Papeete	Canal + France
Paraguay	Fox Sports Americas
Papua New Guinea	ESPN International
Peru	Fox Sports Americas
Philippines	TV 23/ESPN International
Qatar	ORBIT/Fox Sports World
Reunion	Canal + France
Romania	Pro TV
Russia	Filmnet
St. Denis	Canal + France
St. Kitts	Fox Sports Americas
St. Lucia	Fox Sports Americas
St. Pierre et Miquelon	Canal + France
St. Vincent & Grenadines	Fox Sports Americas
Saudi Arabia	OES/Aramco Network
Senegal	ESPN International
Seychelles	ESPN International
Singapore	ESPN International
Somalia	Fox Sports World
South Africa	Super Sport (MNet)
Spain	Canal + Spain
Sri Lanka	ESPN International
Sudan	Fox Sports World
Suriname	Fox Sports Americas
Swaziland	ESPN International
Sweden	TV 3
Switzerland	DSF/SAT 1/Canal + France
Syria	ORBIT/Fox Sports World
Tahiti	Canal + France
Taiwan	CTV/ERA Sports/ESPN International
Tanzania	ESPN International
Tobago	Fox Sports Americas
Togo	ESPN International
Trinidad	Fox Sports Americas
Tunisia	Fox Sports World
Turkey	Canal E/Cine 5
Turks and Caicos	Fox Sports Americas
United Arab Emirates	ORBIT/Fox Sports World
United Kingdom	Sky Sports
United States	Fox

(continued)

Table 14-2　*(continued)*

Country/Area	Carrier
Uruguay	Fox Sports Americas
Venezuela	Globovision/FSA
Vietnam	ESPN International
Yemen	Fox Sports World
Zaire	ESPN International
Zambia	ESPN International
Zimbabwe	ESPN International

Source: NFL, http://www.nfl.com

REFERENCES

Boehm, Eric. "Media Pours into World Cup Brew." *Variety*, June 29, 1998.

"ESPN Veteran Surveys Global Sports Arena." *Broadcasting*, September 11, 1989.

"Global Broadcasting at the Finals." [Online]. Available: www.nba.com/finals2000/global_broadcasting_000607.html, June 7, 2000.

Independent Television Commission. "ITC Notes: Sport on Television." [Online]. Available: www.itc.org.uk/about/itc_notes, December 1999.

"India: State TV Awarded Cricket Rights for Next Five Years." *BBC Monitoring Media*, August 23, 1999.

"The International Football Channel Delivers the Most Complete Coverage of the World's Most Popular Sport to Latin America." The International Football Channel Press Release, February 25, 2000.

"It's Here: Major League Baseball Comes to Univision and Galavision." Univision Press Release, February 23, 2000.

Johnson, Chuck. "America's Pastime Crisscrosses the Globe." *USA Today*, March 17, 2000.

Kelly-Holmes, Helen (Ed.). *European Television Discourse in Transition*. Tonawanda, NY: Multilingual Matters LTD, 1999.

Koranteng, Juliana. "TV Goes Local." *Advertising Age*, January 11, 1999.

———. "Sports Wins Around the World." *Video Age International*, August–September 1995.

Marr, Merissa. "BSkyB Scoops Premier League Football Prize." [Online]. Available: http://biz.yahoo.com/rf/000614/l14457229_2.html, June 14, 2000.

"NFL Tests IP Delivery of Football Outside of U.S." *Broadcasting & Cable*, June 12, 2000.

"1999's No. 1 Global Sporting Championship Set to Begin: 'Olympics of Cricket' to Be Broadcast Live in North America." *Business Wire*, May 13, 1999.

Pursell, Chris. "Fields of Competition: American Pastimes Going for Overseas Gold." *Variety*, June 29, 1998.

Ralbovsky, Marty. *Super Bowl*. New York: Hawthorn Books, 1971.

Stoddart, Brian. "Convergence: Sport on the Information Superhighway." *Journal of Sport & Social Issues*, 21 (1), February 1997.

"Super Bowl XXXIII Expected to Be Broadcast in 180 Countries in 24 Languages." [Online]. Available: http://nfl.com/tvradio/990122sbskedintl.html, January 22, 1999.

Tagliabue, John. "Hoop Dreams, Fiscal Realities." *New York Times*, March 4, 2000.

15

The Future

Where exactly is sports broadcasting headed? The answer largely depends on whom you talk to. Many experts predict a healthy future, based on years of continual growth and expansion. However, many others feel that sports broadcasting has "hit the wall" in terms of growth. They believe the industry has reached a peak, financially and otherwise, which threatens its very survival.

THE BIG PICTURE

From a strictly financial standpoint, national sports broadcasting seems on solid ground. Money continues to pour in from all directions, especially from broadcasting operations wanting the rights to air sporting events. In 1998–99, nearly a dozen broadcast and cable outlets paid $29 billion for exclusive rights to major sporting events. In the past 20 years, rights fees for the Olympics have increased 400 percent and NBC will pay a staggering $894 million to televise the summer games in 2008. The network can afford those prices, considering it recouped some $900 in advertising sales for the 2000 Sydney Olympics. Dick Ebersol, chairman of NBC Sports, said, "At first, we were thinking that Sydney would lose money, but now we are already assured of a small profit."

The money seems to reflect the attractiveness of the product and the continuing popularity of sports broadcasting in general. In this age of audience fragmentation and viewer choice, sports programming now attracts more viewers than nonsports programming. It especially attracts the coveted demographic group for advertisers, affluent males ages 18–44. Sports also offers prestige and glamour, not only for events like the Super Bowl, but for *Monday Night Football* and pro wrestling. It also gives the programmer a golden vehicle to promote other programming.

As a result, new sports and new leagues designed specifically for broadcast exposure pop up all the time. In the spring of 2000, Time Warner, Cox Communications, and Comcast each kicked in $5 million in seed money to help start a new women's professional soccer league. The teams in the league will be situated in cities where the three companies own cable systems and can distribute the games. Also in 2000, the World Wrestling Federation announced plans for a new football league called the XFL. The XFL tried to use the popular WWF to help it succeed where other leagues failed. "The only reason this has a chance is because of the promoting and marketing skills of the WWF," said former CBS sports president Neil Pilson. "That's why I give it a slim chance. If it were anyone else, I'd say none." But even with NBC taking a 50% stake and broadcasting games in prime time on Saturday night, the new league lasted only one season. The games averaged only a 3.3 rating on NBC, causing the network and the WWF each to lose about $35 million. The XFL officially folded in May 2001.

But nothing exemplified the phenomenal growth of sports broadcasting better than ESPN. What started in 1979 as a modest sports programming venture has evolved into the world's largest cable TV sports network, with an estimated worth of more than $15 billion. No organization has tapped into the popularity of sports more than ESPN, which has branched out into magazine publication, an Internet site, a radio network, and a chain of sports-oriented restaurants. Its four domestic cable channels (ESPN, ESPN2, ESPN Classic, and ESPNews) deliver more than 10,000 hours of programming each year to 200 million homes. That doesn't include ESPN International, which reaches 150 million households in 180 countries. No wonder that other organizations, like CNN and Fox, have tried to emulate ESPN, with a resulting explosion in sports broadcast offerings (see Figure 15-1).

But there are disturbing signs that the joyride might be ending and not surprisingly, it all starts with money. While the money spent on sports broadcast rights continues to grow, the return on the investment has started to shrink. As sports programming nears a saturation point, ratings have started to flatten and even decline. Ratings for the NBA on NBC fell 19 percent from 1999 to 2000, while the men's NCAA championship basketball game in 2000 pulled in the worst ratings for CBS since the network began televising the event in 1982. That's not good news for CBS, which in November 1999 signed an 11-year deal worth $6 billion to retain rights to the tournament. And the Sydney Olympics Ebersol bragged about? After just four days of coverage, the games had posted the worst ratings in Olympic television history. It's no wonder that Rick Parnell, an economist with Dismal Sciences, Inc., asks, "Will the TV sports craze soon hit a wall of financial losses at the networks?"

Figure 15-1 The ESPN Floor Crew (Courtesy: ESPN/Rich Arden)

Traditionally, advertisers have always footed the bill, especially for major events. In January 2000, ABC demanded and got more than $3 million for a 30-second spot in the Super Bowl. But a few days later, advertisers had to wonder about their investment. Despite a competitive and entertaining game, ratings placed it just 19th among all 34 Super Bowls and 5th in terms of number of viewers. Just two months later, ABC fired *Monday Night Football* commentator Boomer Esiason, along with producer Ken Wolfe and director Craig Janoff. In 1999, the once dominant prime-time package had a rating of 13.7 and a share of 23, the lowest numbers in its 30-year history. "I'm not sure ratings suggest you'll have a never-ending flow of advertising dollars," says Mark Mitchell, a financial adviser to sports teams for Business Valuation Services. (Ratings are a percentage of the audience based on total television households; a share is a percentage of the audience based on who's actually watching.)

Much of the advertising done on the Super Bowl was for new Internet companies, which creates an interesting problem. Such companies are the fastest growing category among advertisers in most media, with an estimated $1.2 billion for 1999. The growth of the Internet threatens to siphon off viewers from traditional broadcasting services, such as the current situation with major league baseball. In March 2000, major league executives began talks to collectively negotiate audiocast rights for all teams, a move that would threaten revenues from traditional over-the-air broadcasts. "The radio rights are escalating every year and it's very difficult to make money on the play-by-play," said Bobby Lawrence of Clear Channel Communications. "If baseball's going to sell our audio, we think that's a real issue."

We touched briefly on the impact that the Internet has already made on sports broadcasting (see Chapters 1 and 2). If viewers or listeners can't get a particular game in their area, they can get radio or real-time coverage free of charge on the Internet; a move that could draw customers away from their television sets and radios. The 2000 PGA Players Championship included online coverage of the famous 17th green, completely surrounded by water. Microcast of New York streamed continuous coverage of the hole over the first two days of the tournament and reported five million hits. Over the first weekend of the 2000 NCAA men's basketball tournament, CBS *SportsLine* received more than 93 million page views, many of them game clips. "The Internet provides a way for a lot of content to reach an audience that isn't well served by the broadcast medium," says Dan O'Brien, Internet analyst for Forrester Research. That seemed to be especially appropriate for fans of the 2000 Montreal Expos. Without any games on local TV and no English radio outlet, the only way for fans to hear the games was to listen to the broadcasts through their computer on the Web site majorleaguebaseball.com.

But the net can also be used as a complimentary medium, because it adds the extra benefit of customer interactivity. For the first time, sports fans can actively participate in a game telecast instead of being merely passive viewers. ESPN vividly demonstrated this in the winter of 2000 with its "NHL Rules!" concept. It combines ESPN, ESPN2, and ESPN.com to get non-hockey fans more interested in the game. While analysts and commentators explain the action on the two networks, net users can ask online questions and get real-time answers during the game. Net users can also vote on players that they would like to see interviewed online between periods.

Technology has made possible the convergence of video, telephony, home computing, and cable. In the short term, that means interactive television, which will be a $20 billion business by 2004 according to Forrester Research. Dozens of media outlets have begun streaming together television and Internet services, including INTERVU, which worked with Time Warner to deliver video highlights to the official Web site of the 2000 Winter Goodwill Games. At the same time, Fox Sports Net launched new programming in New England called "Gameface" that allowed viewers face-to-face live interaction with players, coaches, and other fans through the use of Web cams over broadband. The NFL has established its interactive programming overseas, streaming games to Holland and Singapore. "Besides streaming the games, we conducted online polls related to the 2000 season," says Desmond Ang Ban Seng of Singapore's SingTel Corporation. "We also created chats and forums so that subscribers could talk to each other about the NFL."

Other technology also threatens to take away ad revenues. For years, VCR owners have had the capability to speed through or skip commercials. New technology coming into the home will allow viewers to program their favorite game and automatically skip the commercials. TiVo Personal TV Service allows viewers to shift the schedules of their favorite shows and create a customized viewing lineup. The technology will allow consumers to pause, rewind, instantly replay, and play back in slow motion any live television broadcast.

There are signs that networks are turning to nontraditional sources of revenue to make up for shrinking ad dollars. In 1999, local ABC affiliates agreed to pay the network $45 million a year to help offset the $550 million cost for *Monday Night Football*. Now, CBS has prepared to sell to Host Communications of Kentucky the right to market sponsorships of the NCAA basketball championships. That deal would provide CBS with $700 million over 11 years.

No one is suggesting that national sports programming faces extinction. As long as the demand exists, programmers will find a way to deliver the product. But it certainly appears the economics will change. Experts can't yet gauge the impact of digital technology, which will almost quadruple the number of broadcasting outlets. Digital will allow programmers to compress their current signal and show up to four channels on the same amount of bandwidth. How will all those extra stations affect sports programming? If advertisers don't like the ratings they see now, what happens when the audiences become even more fractured and fragmented? And how can stations make a profit on four different channels when it's so hard to do it now with just one?

One of the major reasons for the rush to develop digital technology was the attraction of sports programming. Viewers may not want to see their local news or favorite soap opera in crystal clear detail, but there is a great interest in the World Series or other major sports events. In fact, sports programming has become the testing ground for digital implementation. WRAL-TV in Raleigh, North Carolina claims the first commercial high-definition television signal in the country on July 23, 1996 and a short time later it premiered a high-definition college football game. Sports action dramatizes the single biggest selling point of digital: the ability to provide the picture bigger, sharper, and larger than life.

But this new digital technology will cost billions of dollars and could make current industry models obsolete. Each television station in the United States will have to pay somewhere between $1 million and $8 million to covert to digital, which will put a serious strain on current economic models. According to Jim Yaeger of Benedek Broadcasting, "This is the first time anyone has ever asked us to make this size investment upfront without knowing or being able to project revenues generated off it that will eventually offset those costs." Many media analysts say advertisers will not pick up the slack. "The advertiser won't pay any extra to get on [digital]," says Christine McPike of KOLN-TV in Lincoln, Nebraska. "To them, it's about delivery, frequency, and the number of eyeballs getting the message. Picture quality is very much a secondary issue."

Ultimately, it appears the consumer will end up with the bill. Initially, that means very expensive digital television receivers. Current prices for such sets run from about $5,000 on the low end to more than $50,000 or more. The price will come down as the technology becomes more widely accepted, but that's still major sticker shock for consumers used to spending around $100 for a set. Higher cost could also come in the form of subscription fees, limited access, or pay-per-view. The popularity of pay-per-view boxing and the NFL's *Sunday Ticket* demonstrate that sports viewers will pay for programming. It seems as if the only question left is "How much?" David Smith, chairman of Sinclair Broadcast Group says, "It's very easily done in today's digital world. You'll be charged 5 cents, 10 cents, 50 cents, $10, or $20 each month to watch television. It will absolutely happen today." Adds Jamie Kellner, CEO of Warner Brothers Television, "I think our business has to evolve to be competitive against other platforms. Seventy to 80 percent of the people are paying for what they're getting today (from cable) and they seem to have no problem doing it."

The issue of pay-per-view in sports has been around for a long time. Sports providers say as long as free, over-the-air broadcasting continues to deliver big audiences, that's where the events will remain. But as audiences continue to dwindle and fragment, the possibility of more pay-per-view programming increases. Currently, the four major professional sports leagues in the U.S. each have some sort of pay-per-view service, such as *Sunday Ticket*. As more and more programming moves away from free TV, Congress continues to take a harder look at the issue. Some legislators, notably Sen. John McCain of Arizona and Rep. Edward Markey of Massachusetts, have fought for years to ensure sports' survival on free television. The courts have also weighed in on the issue. In April of 1999, a U.S. Circuit Court ruled in *Shaw v. Dallas Cowboys* that the *Sports Broadcasting Act* does not include satellite and pay-per-view events. If the ruling stands up through trial, it would seriously damage sports leagues in regards to making money from subscription services (see more on this issue in Chapter 17).

Even if the pay-per-view issue gets settled, dozens of questions still remain. Experts still can't agree on a single, industry-wide digital standard. According to tests run by NBC, it could be 2005 before digital systems deliver reception as good as consumers get with standard analog broadcasting. With prices for digital sets still high, consumers haven't responded enthusiastically to the new technology. And if no one buys the sets, how will the programming get delivered? That problem has escalated fears that digital penetration may not reach a profit-making level for a dozen years or more. According to Josh Bernoff at Forrester Research, "High definition will be a terribly expensive flop. When you look deeper, no one really wants it."

That statement sounds suspiciously like what critics said before radio boomed in the 1920s and right before television took off in the 1950s. In both instances, sports programming helped the struggling media grow from infancy to established power. It seems sports programming has the potential to do the same in the new electronic age.

ON THE HOME FRONT

While experts and analysts try to figure out what local sports broadcasting will look like in the near future, at least one industry veteran has a bold prediction. "There's no future in local TV sports," says Chuck Dowdle, longtime sports director at WSB-TV in Atlanta, Georgia. "In 10 years, sports won't even be a part of the local newscast."

Why the dire warning? Sports has been a staple on local news for decades. Even in an age of dozens of cable channels and alternative media, most viewers can find highlights of their hometown team in only one place—the local television station. And the proliferation of media has only made stations more eager to cover the local team and distinguish themselves from the competition.

But local television sports faces a serious crisis that has nothing to do with new technology or distribution systems. Most stations and news directors have come to the conclusion that not enough people watch sports to justify its position in the newscast (see Table 15-1 and Table 15-2). Sports ranks

Table 15-1   Interest in Local Television Elements

Element	Percentage of Viewers Expressing Interest
Weather	94%
Local crime	91%
Community events	91%
Education	91%
World news	88%
Local government	86%
Environment	86%
Health and fitness	83%
Sports	63%
Religion	58%

Source: Center for Survey Research and Analysis/University of Connecticut (as cited in RTNDF Journalism Ethics and Integrity Project)

Table 15-2 Main Reason for Watching Local News

Reasons for Watching Local News	*Percentage of Respondents*
To stay informed	28%
Local coverage	20%
Weather	12%
Like/trust news anchors	6%
Convenience/time	5%
Habit	2%
Sports	2%
No other choices	2%

Source: RTNDF Journalism Ethics and Integrity Project

near the bottom in almost every research poll of why people watch local television news. In a 1998 poll conducted by the Radio and Television News Directors Foundation, the percentage of people who watched local news because of sports exactly matched those that said they watched because there were no other choices on television. That same poll asked similar questions of television news directors. Only 71 percent of that group felt the viewers were "very or somewhat" interested in local sports.

Numbers like those have prompted some stations to take drastic action. KVBC-TV in Las Vegas has almost completely eliminated the sports block within its newscast. The station will still do sports on an as-needed basis, such as when a big story breaks. Otherwise, it's strictly national scores and nothing else. Says news director Mike George, "Right now, sports has three minutes to fill, even if they have nothing to fill it with." In a similar move, WTSP-TV in Tampa discontinued sports reports in its 5:00 and 5:30 P.M. newscasts in April 2000. News director Jim Church said, "The audience at that time is heavily female, and there's not much interest among female viewers for sports."

And women are one of the big reasons behind the "tune out" factor. Television began as a medium predominantly watched in taverns by white, middle-aged men. But according to the RTNDF survey, viewers who watch local television news are now predominantly female (52 percent to 48 percent) and young (53 percent under the age of 44). All of that spells trouble for the traditional sports audience. Audience Research and Development (ARD) president Jim Willi says, "Sports skews heavily male," which research also confirms. It's a combination that just doesn't work, especially with newscasts that come right after the late-afternoon television lineup geared particularly toward women. As a result, several stations have cut back or eliminated sports in their newscasts at 4:00 and 5:00 P.M. The time allotted for sports segments also continues to dwindle, down to just a minute or two in several major markets. News directors have found it works better to take the extra time and give it to another segment in the newscast. Or better yet, use the time to "tease" upcoming stories. One news director at a station in Texas said that on a routine day he simply hopes to get through the sports segment without losing too many viewers. ARD, a leading consulting firm in the industry, advises its clients to run an interesting story after sports, so viewers won't tune out.

Another obvious reason for cutbacks is the proliferation of other sports media. Viewers have no trouble finding national scores and highlights on ESPN, CNN, Fox, or the Internet. And these sources offer the information faster and in greater detail. Many news directors don't want to waste time in their local show with a pale imitation. "Real sports fans aren't going to wait until 11:30 at night to get sports highlights from us," says Clark of KVBC-TV. Ron Bilek, a former news director and now television consultant, says too many sports reporters do little besides present scores and video highlights of games taken from satellite feeds—information the viewer can easily get somewhere else.

As a result, sportscasts have had to make tremendous concessions. We have discussed at length the role of entertainment in sports programming and reporting (see Chapter 3). One reason sports has migrated towards entertainment is an attempt to attract and maintain a female audience. Almost every news director now wants reporters who can deliver the nontraditional sports fan. News director Joel Streed of KTTC-TV in Rochester, Minnesota admits he wants "someone who can do more than just read scores and follow highlights. There are so many sports outlets out there geared for the hardcore sports addict, that you need to bring sports into the mainstream news to keep your viewers." If that means doing sports stories on a dog that can shoot a basketball or a football player taking ballet lessons, then so be it. "I try to reach the housewife who doesn't care about sports," says Bernie Smilovitz. Smilovitz has built a successful 15-year career at WDIV-TV in Detroit. "My slant on sports is that I do sports for everybody and I do anything to get them to watch."

But not everyone is joining the revolution willingly. Many traditional sportscasters object to watering down their product to suit a nontraditional audience. Mike Clardy, a former sports anchor and reporter at KRIS-TV in Corpus Christi, Texas said he resented having to condense actual sports coverage in favor of offbeat stories. And many knowledgeable sports fans have tuned out as a result. There's also the problem of too much of a good idea. When the nontraditional sports movement started several years ago, it was fresh and entertaining. But like anything successful on television, it has become copied to death. Almost every market in America has someone doing blooper plays, funny voices, or quirky editing. Critics used to complain that local television sports was all the same—highlights and locker room interviews. Now, it's in danger of becoming wall-to-wall comedy shtick. KPIX-TV in San Francisco says it's returning to a more traditional sportscast after a failed attempt with a recent hire. The sportscaster ignored scores and highlights in favor of a comedy approach, with resulting criticism from viewers and local media. "Most of the resume tapes I look through have the same day-to-day garbage," says sports director Cory Curtis of WOLO-TV in Columbia, South Carolina. "But that doesn't mean that I'm looking for sports packages for the nontraditional fan."

There's also been a backlash from traditionalists who see sports losing ground in the daily newscast. Cutting sports time or eliminating it completely changes the very nature of the local newscast, which has always catered to the widest possible audience. Targeting a newscast for groups like women or the young makes it more of a niche program, like much of the content on cable. Then there's the credibility issue. Television stations have a mandate from the FCC to operate in the public "interest, convenience, and necessity." Is completely eliminating an entire segment of the newscast in the public interest? And can viewers take such a station seriously? Mark Effron, vice president for news at Post-Newsweek Stations, wonders what would happen to a station like KVBC-TV if Las Vegas got a professional sports team. "In an attempt to be a full-service newscast," he says, "it's a little foolish to eliminate sports. You don't want to give people a reason not to watch you."

THE FUTURE IS THEN

Former college and pro football coach George Allen had a saying, "The future is now." But for sports broadcasting, the saying could be, "The future is then." In other words, many experts believe that whatever ails sports broadcasting can be cured by going back to the traditional fundamentals—good reporting, good writing, and good broadcasting. Technology has become so sophisticated, that modern broadcasting has become more smoke than fire. As a result, sports broadcasters have become captives of overnight ratings, demographic breakdowns, make-up artists, computer graphics, and satellite technology. Freedom may be found in the fundamentals.

To many sports broadcasters, that essentially means good, solid, local reporting. Who won and how? And why does it make any difference to the viewer? The main focus of sports broadcasting today is no longer content, but delivery and presentation. There is no doubt sports has followed the trend of broadcasting in general and become more entertainment-oriented (see Chapter 3). This shift has been much debated in the industry, but it poses only a significant problem when it comes at the expense of journalistic fundamentals. And there is serious evidence that such fundamentals have eroded in recent years.

Lou Prato runs a television consulting firm and says the quality of broadcast writing has fallen dramatically, and he's not alone. "I continue to be disappointed and appalled about the state of broadcast writing, no matter what the market size," says Merv Block, a former CBS newswriter and now broadcast writing coach. "Too many reporters and anchors are deficient not only in basic grammar but in common sense and knowledge." Block and other industry experts cite a variety of reasons, including the deadline pressure of the business, lack of training in schools, and inadequate time to train young on-air talent. And again, there's the constant focus on style over substance in the newscast. "One hates to generalize," says Bill Slatter, a former NBC news executive who is now a talent agent, "but I don't think too many news directors pay much attention to the writing. They're more caught up in the cosmetics" (see Chapter 4).

The entertainment focus of sports broadcasting has also caused the industry to tilt away from solid reporting. Today's sports reporting usually focuses on "serious" topics only when they are lurid, sensational, or involve criminal activity. Sports broadcasters have also followed the lead of news in focusing more on celebrities and the celebrity culture. The result, according to former sports reporter Gene Collier is that "sports journalism in America . . . remains the culture's virtually omnipotent Department of Hero Maintenance and Disposal, hourly separating the worthy from the flawed, polishing and immortalizing the best, degrading the worst for entertainment's sake." Collier covered sports for 22 years for newspapers in Pennsylvania, until the indiscriminate hero-worship made him walk away. He now writes features for the *Pittsburgh Post-Gazette*.

It certainly won't be easy to break out of the mold in today's bottom-line world, where financial pressures have reduced much of sports broadcasting to a copycat industry. "Virtually all of the aspiring sportscasters today are clones," says Bruce Lang, news director at KHSL-TV in Chico, California. "They're ESPN wannabes with some high-energy-manic-standup-comedy shtick that's obnoxious to all but about two percent of young males." In this case, imitation may not be the sincerest form of flattery, just the quickest and easiest way to get the job done. But there are some people willing to do things the hard way. More and more news directors say they're looking for storytellers and communicators, rather than would-be comedians. "I'm looking for good writing and storytelling," says news director Ron Lombard at WIXT-TV in Syracuse, New York. "We like to see people who are natural communicators and do it with their own style." News director Joel Streed at KTTC-TV in Rochester, Minnesota says he wants someone "who can shoot, edit, and above all, write." And adds Cory Curtis, "The candidate has to show me creativity. I'm looking for someone who can tell a story and tell it in a way I haven't seen before. I've seen plenty of packages about disabled athletes or extraordinary people. That's not what gets it done."

Perhaps sportscasters could take a lesson from WBBM-TV in Chicago. Mired in last place in the ratings, the CBS affiliate decided to reinvent its local newscast in the winter of 2000. That meant no entertainment-type stories, glitzy graphics, or happy talk. Instead, WBBM went to a single anchor, made time for clarifications and corrections, and added places for viewer comments, and put no time limit on stories. It also meant rethinking local weather and sports, which had to earn the time they got each night with relevant content. "I think everyone will be watching," said Carl Gottlieb of the Project for Excellence in Journalism. "In focus groups, people tell us they're sick and tired of the happy talk approach." Said Chicago reporter John Callaway, who contributed to the show, "We've all been sitting around and moaning about the 10 o'clock news, and now someone comes along who wants to fix it." But after some initial viewer interest, the audience began to fade and WBBM finally pulled the plug in November 2000. "[It] was billed as what news could and should be," wrote *Electronic Media*, "[but] the viewers didn't agree. They were never turned on and eventually dropped out." Perhaps the problem wasn't so much the attempt as much as the format. Critics called the show "PBS on CBS" and said WBBM ran too many long stories that didn't seem to connect to audiences.

Connecting to the audience—writing, storytelling, and creativity. That's about all Edward R. Murrow had in the 1950s when he became the most revered figure in American broadcast journalism. The primitive technology of the time did not allow Murrow to lean on fancy graphics or throbbing music, yet he remains arguably the most influential broadcaster in history. Charles Kuralt carved out his niche in broadcasting history not with rapid-fire jokes or funny voices, but with simple and dramatic storytelling. No one who ever watched or listened to Kuralt or Murrow could ever forget their work. The same cannot be said for today's sports broadcasters.

REFERENCES

"ABC, CBS Might Soon Make Bids." Associated Press. [Online]. Available: http://www.espn.go.com/mlb/news/2000/0626/605429/.html, June 27, 2000.

Alm, Richard. "Networks Will Pay Any Price for TV Spots." *Dallas Morning News*, December 4, 1999.

"Broadcast TV's Future Not Free." *Electronic Media*, January 10, 2000.

Brodesser, Claude, Freeman, Michael, and Katz, Richard. "The Revolution Will Not Be Televised." *Mediaweek*, April 14, 1997.

"BSkyB and TiVo Strategic Alliance to Offer United Kingdom's First Personal Video Recorders." TiVo, Inc. Press Release, February 29, 2000.

Carman, John. "Super Bowl Ratings Were Not Bad, Not Great Either." *San Francisco Chronicle,* February 1, 2000.

Carter, Bill and Sandomir, Richard. "NBC's Ratings for Olympics Are Worst Ever." *New York Times*, September 20, 2000.

Collier, Gene. "The Ex-sportswriter: 'I Was Looking for Heroes in All the Wrong Places.'" *Columbia Journalism Review*, January–February 2000.

Deggans, Eric. "WTSP Is the Latest to Cut Regular Segments out of 5 and 5:30 Newscasts." *St. Petersburg Times*, April 27, 2000.

Duffy, Shannon P. "Sports Fans' Class Action Over 'Sunday Ticket' May Proceed." *The Legal Intelligencer*, April 13, 1999.

"Fox Sports Net to Unveil Plans for Live Interactive Sports Programming Featuring Multiple Web Cam Participation." *BW Sports Wire*, February 15, 2000.

Gammons, Peter. "Winning Cures All Problems." ESPN. [Online]. Available: http://www.espn.go.com/gammons/s/update/0420.html, April 20, 2000.

Gottlieb, Carl and Chinni, Dante. "Taking an Honest Look at Serious Local News." *Electronic Media*, November 20, 2000, p. 8.

Hall, Lee. "Not a Pretty Picture for HDTV, Study Says." *Electronic Media*, December 14, 1998.

Halonen, Doug. "GE Test Blows Hole in DTV." *Electronic Media*, February 14, 2000.

Higgins, John M. "Women's Pro Soccer Gets Cable Kick-start." *Broadcasting & Cable*, February 21, 2000.

James, Steve. "NBC Sees Nearly $1 Billion in Olympic Ad Sales." Reuters. [Online]. Available: http://dailynews.yahoo.com/h/nm/20000628/en/television-olympics_1.html, June 28, 2000.

Johnson, Steve and Kirk, Jim. "Channel 2 Experiment a Newsworthy Gamble." *Chicago Tribune*, February 5, 2000.

"Journalism Ethics and Integrity Project." Radio Television News Directors Foundation. [Online]. Available: http://www.rtnda.org/issues/survey.htm, 1998.

McAdams, Deborah D. "Xtreme Bedfellows." *Broadcasting & Cable*, April 3, 2000.

———. "Leveraging 'Raw' Power." *Broadcasting & Cable*, February 7, 2000.

"NFL Tests IP Delivery of Football Outside of U.S." *Broadcasting & Cable*, June 12, 2000.

"NHL Rules! Takes Everyone a Step Closer." [Online]. Available: http://www.espn.go.com/nhl/s/rules/primer.html, January 24, 2000.

Prato, Lou. "The Business of Broadcasting." *American Journalism Review*, 1995.

"Ratings Drop 18 Percent from Previous Low." Associated Press, April 4, 2000.

Schafer, Alison. "Sports Report." *RTNDA Communicator*, February 2000.

Schneider, Michael and Dempsey, John. "ABC's Super Spots: $3 Million for 30 Seconds." *Variety*, December 2, 1999.

Shea, Jim. "The King: How ESPN Changes Everything." *Columbia Journalism Review*, January–February 2000.

Tedesco, Richard. "These Games Won't Stream, but Others Do." *Broadcasting & Cable*, April 3, 2000.

———. "A Whole New Web Ball Game." *Broadcasting & Cable*, February 28, 2000.

"Time Warner Selects INTERVU to Deliver Video Highlights of Winter Goodwill Games over the Web." INTERVU Press Release, February 16, 2000.

16

Legends of Sports Broadcasting

A chapter entitled "Legends of Sports Broadcasting" is guaranteed to cause controversy. There are always arguments about what a "legend" really is and who qualifies for a list of sports broadcasting's all-time greats. And someone will no doubt complain about a name left off the list or maybe even a name on the list.

This listing does not pretend to be a comprehensive account of history's great sportscasters. Many of the men and women not on this list have all contributed to the industry in some important way, but these people stand out for one reason or another. Some excelled for their ability, others for their longevity, and some for their contentiousness. But all of them left their mark and became the most recognized names of their era.

BEFORE THE MICROPHONE

It's hard to talk about the greatest sports broadcasters without mentioning the pioneering print journalists who paved the way. The American sporting press in the first two decades of the twentieth century was a colorful and extremely talented group. Men like Damon Runyan, Ring Larnder, and Hugh Fullerton covered sports in a poetic and entertaining style, but were also true journalists. In fact, Fullerton helped expose the Black Sox scandal of 1920, despite enormous pressure from the conservative baseball establishment to stay silent.

The most notable figure during this era and the man who helped bridge the transition to the electronic media was Grantland Rice. Rice often wrote sports in a flowery, Shakespearean style that to modern readers seems almost ridiculous. But his words perfectly matched the sports culture of the

239

1920s and they have become a permanent part of the American sports land-scape. It was Rice who came up with the nicknames, "The Galloping Ghost" and "The Bambino." And his description of a football backfield as "The Four Horsemen" helped transform Notre Dame from an unknown Catholic school into legend.

Rice also made his impact felt in other ways. He is credited with turning the Masters golf tournament into a huge event, because Rice would encourage his sports writer friends to stop off in Georgia for the event after they left spring training in Florida. And unlike many of his colleagues, Rice had no trouble adapting to the new electronic media. He was behind the mike for the first World Series broadcast on radio and also hosted a series of sports-related newsreels.

THE EARLY ERA: 1920–1950

Write down a list of sportscasting firsts, and chances are Graham McNamee or Harold Arlin were involved. Arlin is credited with the first-ever broadcast of a major league baseball game, on August 5, 1921 from Forbes Field in Pittsburgh. Arlin became radio's first-ever full-time announcer at KDKA in Pittsburgh, where he also did the first college football game on radio, again at Forbes Field in 1921 between Pittsburgh and West Virginia.

McNamee announced the first network World Series game, describing the action for WGY and WJZ in 1922. In 1927, he broadcast the first coast-to-coast Rose Bowl game, and then in 1932 he was behind the mike for the first national radio broadcast of a NFL game. Like many of the radio announcers of his era, McNamee had no initial interest in sports. He auditioned at NBC as a singer, but was soon converted to an announcer and began working at WEAF in New York City. He would later recall the passions his broadcasts could evoke, as evidenced by the mountains of mail he got from listeners. One of his best qualities was his strong voice, which was so important in the early days of radio. McNamee's broadcasting credits included 12 World Series, 3 Rose Bowls, and 8 heavyweight championship fights.

Another would-be singer with a strong voice rivaled McNamee as the dominant sportscaster in the early days of radio. Ted Husing had a rapid-fire delivery once measured at 400 words per minute. But he also brought thorough preparation into the broadcast booth for the first time. Another great radio sportscaster, Ernie Harwell, said Husing was the first sportscaster who really studied his business. Along with preparation, Husing also brought controversy. Highly outspoken, he was once banned from broadcasting Harvard football games for calling the play of the school's top quarterback "putrid." A few years later, baseball commissioner Kennesaw Mountain Landis suspended Husing during the 1934 World Series for second-guessing umpires. Husing eventually left sports in 1946 to become one of radio's first disc jockeys.

If Ted Husing brought preparation to the broadcast booth, Red Barber turned it into an art form. "He was a journalist," said talk-show host Larry King. "He would get to the ballpark three hours before the game and take notes to intersperse in his broadcast. He was the best sports announcer I ever heard." Barber originally wanted a career in vaudeville and went into broadcasting very reluctantly. His first big job came with the Cincinnati Reds in 1936, then he moved to the Brooklyn Dodgers in 1939.

It was with the Dodgers that Barber's true genius flowered. Born and raised in the south, he broadcast games with a down-home, soft-spoken style that included endearing expressions. "Rhubarb," "catbird seat," and "tearing up the pea patch" all became part of baseball terminology and opened up the game to countless new fans. His poetic descriptions particularly appealed to women, who started coming to games in larger numbers after Barber's arrival. Barber was also an extremely thoughtful and intelligent man, who won several awards in his later years for a series of weekly conversations he did on National Public Radio. "Red Barber did for broadcasting what the great writers did for newspapers," said author Charles Fountain. "He allowed people to see a game in ways that even fans in the stands couldn't see."

Barber's rival for the heart and soul of New York was Mel Allen. Born Mel Israel (he later took his father's middle name), he grew up in small Alabama towns and received two degrees from the University of Alabama. He did his first announcing in college, doing football games on radio. But his real dream was to work in New York and broadcast for the Yankees. On a lark, he went to CBS in New York in 1936 and got a job. Four years later, he had become the Yankees number one announcer.

Allen stayed with the team for 25 years and earned a reputation as a dedicated performer. "Mel taught me preparation, word, and attention to detail," said sportscaster Curt Gowdy, who became Allen's broadcast partner in 1949. "He was a master and I couldn't have had a greater mentor. There was no more decent man than Mel Allen." During his tenure, Allen's trademark calls of "How about that?" and "Going, going, gone!" became known all across the nation. He eventually broadcast 20 World Series and 24 All-Star games, and with Red Barber became the first broadcaster inducted into the Baseball Hall of Fame.

If Allen had one flaw, it was that he loved the Yankees too much. When the team let him go in 1964, Gowdy said, "It broke his heart. Nobody understood it. It hurt Mel deeply and he was a sensitive guy." Allen revived his career in the 1980s by becoming the voice of the syndicated television show, *This Week in Baseball*.

Unlike Mel Allen, Bill Stern did not grow up a sports fan and knew very little about sports. During broadcasts of the Masters golf tournament in the

1940s, he talked about the golfers "points" instead of strokes. But Stern's relative lack of knowledge never seemed to bother him or anyone else, judging from his tremendous popularity. He came to broadcasting from the stage, where he had been stage manager at RCA Music Hall in New York. Maybe that's why his broadcasts always seemed to have a theatrical, dramatic quality and his voice inspired so many imitators. "Bill Stern is to my mind the greatest," said Hall of Fame broadcaster Bob Wolff. "He had a beautiful voice and called the games well." Others must have agreed, for Stern was voted the nation's most popular sportscaster for 13 years.

Rarely has a sports broadcaster been so identified with a mistake as has Clem McCarthy. In 1947, McCarthy accidentally called the wrong winner of the Preakness Stakes, giving the race at first to Jet Pilot before finally correcting his error and identifying the real winner, Faultless. It was one of the few mistakes McCarthy made during a 32-year career in which he became the most famous radio voice in horse racing history. He was the first person to broadcast the Kentucky Derby, announcing the event from 1928 to 1950, and his rapid-fire delivery and trademark greeting, "R-r-r-r-r-acing fans!" inspired countless imitators.

THE MIDDLE AGES: 1950–1980

While McCarthy concentrated on horse racing, Ernie Harwell stuck with baseball. Early in his career, Harwell covered a variety of events, including the Masters golf tournament. But principally, he served as the radio voice of the Detroit Tigers for nearly half a century. When new owners took over the team in the early 1990s, they forced Harwell out of the radio booth because they considered him too old. Harwell worked on the Tigers television network, but a public outcry demanded his return to the radio booth. In 1998, the criticism got so heavy the Tigers finally relented. At the age of 80, Harwell was once again the Tigers full-time radio announcer. "My idea was to do whatever the Tigers wanted me to do, whether it was TV or radio. But I love being on radio."

If anyone can match Ernie Harwell for longevity, it's Vin Scully. In 2000, Scully celebrated his 50th anniversary with the Dodgers organization, going back to when he started broadcasting games in Brooklyn in 1950. Scully joined the Dodgers fresh out of Fordham University and learned his craft at the side of Red Barber. Barber's professionalism, his attention to detail, and his demanding preparation all left an impression on Scully, who later referred to Barber as his other father. "He remembered this kid who had worked in CBS, and I had played baseball at Fordham University and he called up there—typical of Red—to check on me, and he talked to my coach," Scully said. "Then he asked me if I would do football. So I did two football games, and that's really how it started."

Scully picked up much of Barber's descriptive, poetic style and combined it with his own warm and sincere personality. As a result, he has touched three generations of baseball fans and become one of the most beloved figures in broadcasting. "There was a gift given to him—no one could ever argue that point," said Sparky Anderson, former manager for the Detroit Tigers and Cincinnati Reds. Anderson also did some commentating work with Scully on World Series CBS Radio broadcasts and said, "You couldn't possibly work at becoming that good; you have to start with a gift, and he did." Pat Lute, publicity director of the Baseball Hall of Fame in Cooperstown, New York, said Scully "brings poetry to the airwaves with his fluid descriptions of what's going on out on the field."

Scully has been so identified with the Dodgers that it's easy to forget all his other accomplishments in broadcasting. He worked eight years as an announcer for CBS, doing play-by-play work for the NFL and covering the PGA Tour. His resume also includes three World Series and four baseball All-Star games for NBC, just a small part of his total of 25 World Series and 12 All-Star games as an announcer. He was elected to the broadcasters wing of the Baseball Hall of Fame in 1982. "He's the best that ever was," said Anderson.

Like many of his colleagues, Marty Glickman was an athlete before turning to sportscasting. But he was no ordinary athlete. As a sprinter, Glickman qualified for the 1936 Olympic Games in Berlin, only to be denied a chance to run because of anti-Semitism. He later became a football All-American at Syracuse and had a brief professional career in football and basketball. But the Brooklyn native gained even greater fame in the broadcast booth, where he stayed on the air from 1939 to 1992. Glickman became the voice of New York sports, calling games for the Knicks, Jets, and football Giants, as well as horse racing. He also gained a reputation as one willing to help other broadcasters break into the business. Upon hearing of Glickman's passing in January 2001, Madison Square Garden Network broadcaster Bill Daughtry said, "He was a friend and mentor to just about everyone in New York sports."

They called him Cowboy Curt Gowdy because of his Wyoming heritage and his love for the outdoors, two things he never outgrew. Gowdy popularized outdoor sports reporting with his ABC series *The American Sportsman*. He also has a state park named after him in his home state.

Gowdy admits that luck played a big part in his rise from obscurity to one of the most recognizable sportscasters in history. "I was discovered while working for a radio station in Cheyenne and it was like a Hollywood movie script," he said. The general manager of a station in Oklahoma was on vacation in Wyoming and looking for a new broadcaster for University of Oklahoma football games. Gowdy was hired on the spot and just four years later was broadcasting for the New York Yankees. He spent 17 seasons doing games in New York and Boston.

Gowdy's career took several twists and turns from there, most notably as a principal announcer for the fledgling American Football League. He was behind the mike for the infamous "Heidi" game in 1968, when NBC pulled the plug early on the Jets-Raiders game and missed one of the most dramatic comebacks in football history. Gowdy also broadcast Hank Aaron's 715th home run and Carlton Fisk's dramatic homer in the 1975 World Series. His totals include 16 World Series, 8 Super Bowls, and 8 Olympic games. But he says his most memorable assignment came in Super Bowl III, when Joe Namath's Jets upset the favored Baltimore Colts. "The sight of Joe Namath jogging off the field, holding his hand in the air with one finger extended in victory, is something I'll never forget," he wrote. "Sports memories do indeed last a lifetime."

If Gowdy has a rival in his Olympic experience, it's Jim McKay. McKay became the voice of the Olympics on ABC for nearly 30 years, most notably in 1972 when he won Emmy awards for his coverage of the massacre of the Israeli Olympic team. During the crisis, McKay was on the air for 16 straight hours with only a single, static shot of the Olympic village to help him. "Simply put, you have to remain a reporter," he said. "You have to make sure what you say is accurate and it's a little more important than whether the 100 meters was run in 10.4 or 10.3 seconds."

McKay also earned his place in history as the pioneering host of ABC's *Wide World of Sports* where he brought personality into sports reporting. "Jim McKay was to a sports event what Walter Cronkite was to news," said former ABC producer Terry Jastrow. "Every event he covered was a little motion picture, a beautiful narrative." According to Jastrow, it was McKay who came up with the program's signature line, "the thrill of victory and the agony of defeat," which he wrote on the back of a used envelope.

McKay won 13 Emmy Awards and a Peabody Award during his long career, which as of 2000 still included work in golf and horse racing. "Sports at its ultimate expression," he once said, "must function on three levels: man against the environment, man against his opponent, and man against himself."

With his trademark plaid sport jackets, Lindsey Nelson always stood out on the air. But of all the sportscasting greats, he had perhaps the quietest and most overlooked career. Nelson was an extremely versatile and durable broadcaster, joining NBC in the early 1950s and occupying the national stage for the next 30 or so years. "What was most impressive about Lindsey was his staying power in broadcast journalism," said Kelly Leiter, dean emeritus at the University of Tennessee, Nelson's alma mater. "Once he took off, he stayed up there and never came down until his health forced him to retire. In a field as quixotic as broadcasting, he remained a major star of radio broadcasting and then television broadcasting."

Unlike many broadcasters, Nelson never got pigeon-holed with one particular sport or team. He did baseball's game of the week for NBC in the 50s, then had long stints as a baseball play-by-play man with the New York Mets and San Francisco Giants. He also did work for golf tournaments, horse racing events and Notre Dame football. But perhaps he's best known as the Voice of the Cotton Bowl, where he broadcast the New Year's Day game for 26 years. His awards include four years as the Sportscaster of the Year, a Life Achievement Emmy award, and induction into the American Sportscasters Hall of Fame. After his retirement, Nelson returned to Tennessee and worked with his alma mater to help future broadcasters. "He was one of the nicest human beings I've ever met in my life," Leiter said. "He was kind, considerate, and he was a gentleman. Fame never seemed to go to his head. He was the same the first day I met him as he was the last."

If fame never seemed to go to Lindsey Nelson's head, the same cannot be said for Howard Cosell. Cosell was generally considered loud, bombastic, obnoxious, and supremely egotistical. He was also courageous, defiant, articulate, intelligent, and a man of principle. And no sportscaster, before or since, generated more passion and emotion from the audience than Howard Cosell. You either loved him or hated him and there was no in-between.

Cosell started out as a lawyer but fell into sports while doing a case involving Little League baseball. He got his start in radio and later gravitated to television, which made him a national star. He and Muhammad Ali seemed to burst together upon the national stage and his fair treatment of Ali surrounding Ali's refusal to undergo induction in the Army earned him a reputation as a sportscaster of integrity.

Cosell was just about the exact opposite of every sportscaster of his day. He didn't particularly care for the games themselves and certainly wasn't a fan. He often decried the "jockocracy" of sports broadcasting, where former athletes were given prominent positions in the broadcast booth over more trained journalists. And he always pushed for more solid and serious sports reporting, instead of the "gee-whiz" stories typical of the era. "What poses for sports journalism on television," he wrote, "too often comprises a cursory sideline interview with an athlete or a critical comment here or there." In many ways, Cosell was proudest of his ABC show *Sports Beat,* which attempted to address very serious issues in sports and society.

None of this made him very popular with his peers and a great majority of the fans. Bob Costas once said that if you cut open Cosell, you'd find a nest of snakes. Several critics ridiculed his statement that "he just tells it like it is," pointing to the fact that he changed his last name (from Cohen) and wore a toupee.

Cosell probably reached the height of his notoriety on *Monday Night Football*, where millions listened to his every word and his caustic comments became a lightning rod for controversy. Thousands of fans wrote angry letters to ABC, demanding the network take him off the air. "I don't like crowds to begin with," said his long-time *Monday Night* partner Don Meredith, "but to walk through one with Howard Cosell—man, people shout all kinds of things at him. And they're not kidding around. People can be violent toward Howard."

But despite all his flaws, Cosell remains perhaps the most important and influential sportscaster of the last half of the twentieth century. He redefined the concept of sports broadcast journalism in his generation, while becoming the single most recognizable and imitated figure in the industry. "One time in the late 1970s, some fan began one of those frequent get-Cosell-off-the-air campaigns," said sports writer David Kindred. "I defended Cosell as the very model of what a journalist ought to be: a finder of facts, a thinker, incisive, enthusiastic, entertaining, and principled."

It's almost impossible to mention Howard Cosell without also talking about Don Meredith, for the careers of the two men went hand-in-hand during their tenure together on *Monday Night Football*. While their act worked together so smoothly on the air, in real life Meredith was everything Cosell was not: shy, insecure, and, most of all, fun-loving. During his all-pro quarterback career with the Dallas Cowboys, Meredith never took football or life too seriously. He often joked or sang songs in the huddle during games.

Meredith brought that same kind of attitude to the broadcast booth when he joined ABC in 1970 for the premiere season of *Monday Night Football*. "When *Monday Night Football* was first offered to him, he almost didn't take it," recalled friend and former teammate Pete Gent. "He said he'd rather do weekend games on CBS with Frank Gifford. I told him, 'Don, on Monday night you're going to be the only game on. If you're any good, you're going to make a fortune.'"

Meredith was a natural and *Monday Night Football* skyrocketed in popularity. He brought the same carefree attitude he had about life into the broadcast booth, telling jokes and singing, "Turn out the Lights, the Party's Over," whenever a game was clinched in the final minutes. Meredith became a star simply by being himself, and his down-home Texas folksy-ness made for the perfect contrast to Cosell's ego and erudition. Meredith left ABC for a while to pursue other projects, including some TV work on the dramatic show *Police Story*, but eventually returned, if only for a short time. And even though *Monday Night Football* is still going strong after 30 years on the air, many observers say it just doesn't have the same feeling as when Dandy Don was in the booth. "When was the last time anyone stood around the water cooler discussing what the announcers said on *Monday Night Football*?" asked writer Dan McGraw in 1998. "In the glory years of the 1970s, Cosell and Meredith called each game as if it were a morality play or an epic drama."

Just as Meredith walked away from football at an early age (31), he also left broadcasting at the peak of his career. Always insecure and full of self-doubt, Meredith has become something of a recluse. His home in Santa Fe, New Mexico lists only a fax number and there's no address, just a post office box. "He has become football's Joe DiMaggio," says author Peter Golenbock. "He makes ceremonial appearances, but fiercely guards his privacy."

With all respect to Meredith, no one made a better career out of being himself than Harry Caray. For three generations of baseball fans, Caray came to symbolize the simple joys of the game, whether broadcasting from the centerfield bleachers, leading the crowd in a chorus of "Take Me Out to the Ballgame" or using his favorite exclamation, "Holy Cow!" "We are all fans," he said during his induction speech at the Baseball Hall of Fame, "and that is whom I represent. The fans are responsible for my being here. They are the unsung heroes."

Caray had a special relationship with the fans because he put them first and believed the game should be entertaining. Growing up in St. Louis, he loved attending Cardinals games, but didn't get the same feeling of excitement listening to the games at home. "When I stayed home and listened to the radio broadcasts, what I heard was as dull and boring as the morning crop reports. I decided there had to be a better way." That prompted Caray to call KMOX radio and land himself an audition. He started in Joliet, Illinois but returned to St. Louis to do Cardinals games in 1945. Caray probably never would have left the Cardinals except for some very personal problems that pitted him against team owners. Fans knew he liked women, caroused, and probably drank too much. But that only endeared him to them even more. Harry Caray was one of them.

After St. Louis, Caray finished out his career with the White Sox, the Athletics, and most notably the Cubs, where he became a national icon. His passing in 1998 generated an outpouring of affection from peers and fans all over the world. Before Caray died, Chicago sports writer Bernie Lincicome wrote, "[He] is nothing less than the pure joy of baseball, a clear, uncomplicated devotion to the game, his reactions honest, his anticipation urgent, his disappointment obvious. Baseball is never more compelling than when seen through Harry Caray's eyes." Baseball author Curt Smith added, "He was baseball's Falstaff: how sweet it is and away we go."

THE MODERN ERA: 1980–PRESENT

Rarely has a sportscaster been more closely identified with one sport than has Keith Jackson. For nearly three decades, Jackson called college football games for ABC, becoming as much a part of the college scene as pep rallies, falling leaves, and walks across campus. No wonder that after Jackson temporarily retired after the 1998 season, broadcast partner Bob Griese said, "It's like losing a part of Americana."

Jackson put a permanent imprint on fall Saturdays with an easy-going style that introduced America to a slew of down-home phrases. Ironically, Jackson says he never really said the one phrase for which he's most remembered—"Whoa Nellie!" His southern style seemed to make things looks easy, but Jackson worked hard to become a talented and versatile performer. "Here's a play-by-play performer who actually understands what's going on down on the field," said former University of Iowa football coach Hayden Fry. In 1992, Fry presented Jackson with the Amos Alonzo Stagg Award, one of the highest awards given out by the American Football Coaches Association.

Jackson's work in college football obscured his diverse career. He broadcast in the Olympic games and also served as the lead announcer for network NBA telecasts. Few people remember that Jackson also served on the very first *Monday Night Football* crew along with Howard Cosell and Don Meredith. But college football was Jackson's first love, so much so that he cancelled his retirement in 1999 and returned to do regional games for ABC. "The idea of going through life not having tasted the flavor of a college football afternoon, I can't imagine, because I've been involved with it for so long," he said. "The feeling of the fiesta on Saturday afternoon is so special. Nothing else in the world is like it, there really isn't. It's so refreshing, and so redundantly so."

When Jackson relinquished the lead role on the college football telecasts, ABC already had a distinguished national performer ready to take his place. But the network did not give the job to Brent Musburger, a sign of how dramatically his career changed from its peak in the 1970s. After sportscasting jobs in Chicago and Los Angeles straight out of college, Musburger shot to stardom with CBS Sports. With Phyllis George and Irv Cross, he helped turn the *NFL Today* into the premier pre-game show on television. His other assignments included the Masters golf tournament, NCAA Final Four, U.S. Open tennis, and the NBA.

All of that work may have hurt Musburger's career, as critics and fans began complaining of overexposure. He claimed the criticism never bothered him, saying, "I know the barbs are going to be sent my way. Once you're a public figure, you're in the spotlight and there's going to be opinions about you." Whether or not the opinions bothered Musburger, he shocked the sports world with his departure from CBS in 1990 to accept a much more limited role with ABC. Instead of doing the high-profile games, Musburger now worked on halftime shows and track meets. ABC even replaced him as the lead host on golf coverage. Yet, Musburger did not complain. He called his role one of "quality over quantity" and said he enjoyed his work as much as ever. "This is a passion for me, even if I weren't doing it for a living."

Musburger's partner on the *NFL Today* didn't have the same journalistic or professional pedigree, but Phyllis George probably had a greater impact on the industry because she opened doors for aspiring female sportscasters to follow. George doesn't qualify as a sportscaster in the technical sense of the term; her work on the show was mostly features and short interviews. But she occupied a prominent place on the national sports stage and presented sports in a way that attracted new fans, both women and men.

George came into the national spotlight in 1971 when she won the Miss America pageant. That opened the door to a position as a cohost on *Candid Camera* and eventually led to CBS in 1975, where she became the first female sportscaster with a national audience. After 10 years on the *NFL Today,* she tried her hand on the *CBS Morning News,* with disastrous results. She left broadcasting for a while to start her own business, but returned in the 1990s to host her own cable television show focusing on women's issues.

Many critics complained of her work on the *NFL Today,* dismissing her studio work and the stories she did. But millions of viewers loved her and she helped the show dominate the NFL pre-game ratings for a decade. She also influenced the careers of countless young women who saw her and realized they could also have a career in sports broadcasting.

Marv Albert also disappeared from the national sports scene for a while, but not by his own choosing. The versatile play-by-play man made scandalous headlines in 1997 with tabloid reports of a bizarre sexual encounter with a woman in a Virginia hotel room. By the time the smoke had cleared, Albert pleaded guilty to a sexual assault misdemeanor and lost his high-profile jobs at NBC and the Madison Square Garden network. A year later, a judge cleared Albert's record, but his national reputation had still suffered major damage. "The gossip pages are great, as long as your name isn't in them," he said. "I went through a nightmare."

The incident obscured what had been one of the most prolific and successful careers in the business. Albert built a solid reputation calling games in New York for the Knicks and Rangers, which led to national assignments for the NHL, NBA, NFL, major league baseball, and the Olympics. During his 30-year career, he has won six cable awards for outstanding play-by-play announcer and been named New York state Sportscaster of the Year 20 times. He also built something of an entertainment career, appearing several times on late night talk shows to discuss sports or narrate video clips.

Albert began to rebuild his reputation and his career in 1998, when he returned to the MSG network. Just a year later, he joined Turner Network Television as a play-by-play man for NBA telecasts and even got his old job back at NBC. Long-time fans and listeners felt Albert had paid his dues and no longer should have to sit on the sidelines. "Thirty years of sparkling work as a New York sportscaster should give him the right to a second chance," said sports writer Adrian Wojnarowski. "His voice is a song of sports memories for millions of metropolitan area fans."

As Marv Albert returned to NBC, the network's most recognizable sportscaster was preparing to leave. Dick Enberg spent 24 years at NBC, covering a wide variety of assignments. But when the network lost its NFL package in 1998, Enberg became restless. And when his contract expired, he joined CBS in a move that stunned many in the sports broadcasting industry. "Those who know me know I'm emotional to a fault," said Enberg. "I'm guilty of being a romantic and all those things." Sentiment had much to do with Enberg's decision to leave. As the clock wound down on NBC's last game in 1998, Enberg noted that the network was ending a 32-year affiliation with the NFL. "From Joe Namath to John Elway . . . and from Curt Gowdy to all of us who had the honor of bringing you this game."

Enberg's move to CBS sparked some fond memories of his days doing college basketball with Billy Packer and Al McGuire. Once the nation's most popular basketball announce team, the three reunited for a game in February 2000. It must have seemed like old times for viewers, as Enberg, McGuire, and Packer argued back and forth for what seemed like the entire game. But as Enberg said afterwards, "We really do like each other."

Enberg's career at NBC included eight Super Bowls, NCAA college basketball, Notre Dame football, and work on the network's Olympic telecasts. He has presided over some of the most memorable moments in sports with unflagging enthusiasm, punctuated often with his trademark exclamation, "Oh, my!" His self-described sentimentality helped him earn four Emmy Awards and recognition as Sportscaster of the Year eight times from two different organizations.

Much like Dick Enberg, Bob Costas has a romantic and nostalgic view of sports and sports broadcasting. "It was a combination of loving sports and being exposed to great announcers," said Costas, who grew up on Long Island. "The 1950s and 60s was a great era in New York broadcasting, with Red Barber, Mel Allen, Marty Glickman, and Lindsey Nelson. For me, sports and broadcasting were inseparable."

Fresh out of Syracuse University, Costas made a name for himself as one of the youngest play-by-play men in the country, calling games for the St. Louis Spirits of the ABA. That eventually led to NBC, where Costas quickly became the network's rising young star. During his tenure at NBC, Costas covered major league baseball, the NFL, the NBA, college basketball, and the Olympics. He also gained a reputation as insightful, intelligent, and interested in more than just sports. Costas hosted a late-night interview show for the network, which won him an Emmy Award for Outstanding Informational Series and he also became a frequent contributor to NBC News.

But sports remained his first love, just as it was when he read the sports sections of the New York papers as a seven-year-old boy. When Costas signed a six-year contract extension with NBC in 1996, he noted, "Without comparing myself in terms of ability, this will allow me to do what Brooks Robinson and Carl Yastrzemski did—spend my entire career with one team."

While Enberg and Costas built their styles on emotion and eloquence, Dick Vitale used high-speed energy to become one of the most successful basketball broadcasters in history. Throughout his career, spent entirely with ESPN and ABC doing college basketball commentary and play-by-play, Vitale has been passionate, excitable, and controversial, but never dull. "I may not always be right," he said, "but no one can ever accuse me of not having a genuine love and passion for whatever I do" (see Figure 16-1).

Figure 16-1   Dick Vitale (Courtesy ESPN/Ray Martin)

Vitale had a successful career as a pro and college coach before joining ESPN in 1979. Since then, he has broadcast more than a thousand college games in his trademark high-energy style and introduced dozens of new terms into the game. Fans across the country instantly recognize such Vitale-isms as "T-O" (timeout), "PTP'er" (prime time player), and "diaper dandy" (freshman star). His popularity led him to branch out into other media, where he writes basketball newspaper and magazine columns, does games on radio, and hosts his own Internet Web site.

Critics complain about Vitale's sometimes grating style and his growing overexposure. But Vitale can answer with his numerous awards, including Sports Personality of the Year from the American Sportscasters Association and the Curt Gowdy Media Award from the Basketball Hall of Fame. To his peers and to millions of fans, Vitale symbolizes the passion and enthusiasm of college basketball. "My mom and dad told me that if you gave 110 percent all the time, a lot of beautiful things would happen," he once said. "And I'm living the American dream."

The same could probably be said for John Madden, who has much in common with Vitale. Both came to broadcasting from the coaching ranks, both have energetic and unusual styles, and both helped make the sports they covered more interesting to watch. Madden won 103 games and a Super Bowl as a NFL coach and admitted he never really wanted to go into broadcasting. He turned down the first offer from CBS before finally giving in. "I never thought coaching would satisfy my need for playing, but it did," he said. "And I never thought television would satisfy my need for coaching and it did. If it hadn't, I would have been back."

Millions of football fans are glad he didn't return to coaching. Madden combined a unique style and entertaining wit to become the most popular football analyst on television, due in great part to his ability to explain complicated football concepts in simple and understandable ways. Fans loved his humor and quirkiness, witnessed by the fact that he hated to ride in airplanes and always traveled to each game in his Madden Cruiser bus. His ability to communicate with the audience made Madden a natural for endorsements and he has become one of the most recognizable pitchmen on television. He also branched out with a series of four books and his football video game, Madden '98, is the number one selling sports game of all time.

All of this has not gone unnoticed by his peers. Madden has virtually retired the Emmy Award for Outstanding Sports Game Analyst, winning it for a 13th time in 2000. He has also been named Sports Personality of the Year by the American Sportscaster Association and won the Golden Mike award from the Touchdown Club of America. "I would put Madden as a commentator in the same category as Howard Cosell," said ABC sports executive Don Ohlmeyer.

Madden spent the first 15 years of his career with CBS, but when the network lost its NFL contract after the 1993 season it also lost Madden and his broadcast partner Pat Summerall. It's almost impossible to talk about one without the other, for they have formed one of the most popular and long-lasting teams in the history of sports broadcasting. Since their first game together in 1981, Madden and Summerall have worked nearly 400 games together. "It would surprise anyone in the TV business to stay together that long without someone saying it's worn out," said Summerall. "But I haven't heard anyone say that yet."

Like Madden, Summerall came to broadcasting from the NFL, where he starred with the New York Giants. Summerall principally stayed with football as a broadcaster, but his smooth voice and reassuring delivery helped his career branch out in other areas. For years, Summerall was the leading network presence at the Masters golf tournament and the U.S. Open tennis tournament, until he and Madden left CBS to join Fox. At first, the veteran announcer was reluctant to get in the booth with Madden. "I made it known that I didn't agree with the pairing and it made for some hard feelings," he said. "I didn't think we would work together as well as I did with [Tom] Brookshier."

Summerall went through a highly publicized bout with alcoholism in the mid-1990s, but returned to the broadcast booth seemingly better than ever. Heading into the year 2000, Summerall had worked 15 Super Bowls on television and showed no signs of slowing down. "I think it's the closest thing you could ever come to playing," he said. "I don't think you can match it in any other profession. I would have quit long ago if I didn't enjoy it."

OTHER NOTABLES

Al Michaels quietly built a broadcasting career that ranks with the greats of all-time. After joining ABC in 1976, he broadcast major league baseball, *Monday Night Football*, and the Super Bowl. He's also built a reputation for honesty and integrity, and lost his job as the Cincinnati Reds lead radio broadcaster when he refused to announce phony attendance figures. But he's perhaps best known for his call of the 1980 Olympic hockey match between the United States and Soviet Union. "Do you believe in miracles? . . . Yes!" Michaels also won respect for his coverage of the San Francisco earthquake, which interrupted a live broadcast of the 1989 World Series. "This is what sportscasters do," he said later. "To me, it requires knowledge of sports, but you have to know about a lot of other things as well." Said former ABC producer Dennis Lewin, "He was fully prepared, not just as a sportscaster but as a journalist."

Marty Brenneman succeeded Michaels in 1974 as play-by-play announcer for the Cincinnati Reds and stayed there more than a quarter century. He has called numerous World Series games on radio for NBC, none more memorable than the 1975 series between his Reds and the Boston Red Sox. Brenneman was named Ohio Sportscaster of the Year a dozen times and was honored in 2000 with induction into the Baseball Hall of Fame. Just as Brenneman's son Thom followed him into the business, Joe Buck followed his legendary father Jack Buck. Jack Buck's career included work in several Super Bowls and a one-year stint hosting the NBC program *Grandstand*, but he's most known for his work as announcer for the St. Louis Cardinals. Buck started doing Cardinals games in 1954 and took over the lead announcing role when Harry Caray left in 1970. He's a member of the Baseball Hall of Fame, the Broadcaster's Hall of Fame, and the Radio Hall of Fame.

Harry Kalas has smoothly described the baseball action in Philadephia for decades. His unique baritone became identified with the Phillies and allowed him to do narration work for NFL Films. "It's so much of a business now," Kalas once said, perhaps remembering his childhood listening to Cubs and White Sox games on the radio. "But once it starts between the white lines, I still love the game."

Long before Cubs fans ever fell in love with Harry Caray, there was Jack Brickhouse. Brickhouse was the voice of the Cubs for four decades starting in 1941 and he also did play-by-play for the Chicago White Sox from 1940–67 and for the Chicago Bears for 24 years. He was even behind the microphone in the early days of the Chicago Bulls. No wonder he loved Chicago as much as the city loved him. "I have traveled the globe meeting dignitaries every-where," he once said, "but without hesitation, Chicago and all its people comprise my favorite town."

Most Yankee fans remember Phil Rizzuto more for his broadcasting than his Hall of Fame career as a shortstop. "The Scooter" played and broadcast during the Yankee glory days and to him the game was always some-thing to get excited about. "Rizzuto's openness and [his quality of] saying anything that comes to his mind is his most endearing quality," said baseball author Bob Marshall. "He retains a kidlike enthusiasm for the game." Much the same could be said for Bill King, a sports broadcasting institution in the Bay area. At one time, King served as play-by-play man for Oakland Athlet-ics, Golden State Warriors, and Oakland Raiders, describing each game with a unique style that combined excitement and poetry. His longest stint was with the Raiders, where he lasted 26 years and broadcast four Super Bowls.

It's almost impossible to think about the NBA without talking about Johnny Most and Chick Hearn. To many Boston fans, Most was the heart and soul of the Celtics. His gravelly voice broadcast Boston games for some 30 years and his enthusiasm and love for the Celtics never waned. Nearly two generations later, NBA fans still remember his dramatic call that "Havlicek stole the ball!" in the 1965 playoff series with Philadelphia. While Most built a loyal following on the east coast, Hearn was doing the same on the west coast. During his career with the Lakers, Hearn witnessed the feats of Baylor, West, Chamberlain, Magic, Abdul-Jabbar, Worthy, and Shaq, un-abashedly backing the team through thousands of broadcasts. Basketball writer Joe Jares referred to Hearn as, "The frenetic Lakers broadcaster who roots, coaches, and referees while he's smoothly describing the action."

Unlike most of his contemporaries, Jack Whitaker could also report news and at one time worked in both the news and sports divisions at ABC. During his 50-plus year career, Whitaker covered the Super Bowl, the Olympics, major league baseball, did play-by-play work for two NFL teams, and hosted the CBS Sports Spectacular. But he's best known for his work in horse racing's Triple Crown and golf's major championships, where his in-sightful commentaries became a fixture. Media writer Rudy Martzke once observed, "With his eloquent opening and descriptions of St. Andrews, [Whitaker] reminded everyone he's as treasured as the storied course he was reporting."

Ray Scott did football and baseball play-by-play for several teams and also broadcast in the World Series, but he's forever linked to the Green Bay Packer dynasty of the 1960s. As the Packers lead announcer for a dozen years, Scott was a first-hand witness to Lombardi, Starr, and the Ice Bowl.

"He had a voice that resonated," said Packers public relations director Lee Remmel. "Everything he said sounded like it was chiseled in stone."

Dan Kelly and Fred Cusick chiseled their careers over thousands of NHL games, becoming hockey broadcasting legends in their respective cities. Kelly spent most of his long career in St. Louis, where his son carried on the tradition calling Blues games for KMOX radio. Cusick finally retired at age 78 in Boston, where he worked for 45 years and broadcast more than three thousand hockey games. Both men are members of Hockey's Hall of Fame.

And what Kelly and Cusick did for hockey, Chris Schenkel did for bowling. In a 46-year career, Schenkel called more than 600 college and pro football games, but he's best known for his work on ABC's Pro Bowlers Tour. The popular series lasted 36 years, with Schenkel behind the mike much of the way. Before the last televised match in 1997, the veteran sportscaster could barely hold his emotions. "I'm sorry to see it going off the air because we had so many highlights," he said.

REFERENCES

"ABC's Jim McKay Knew the Feeling of Despair." Cox News Service, 1996.

"ABC's Jim McKay to Receive 2000 PGA Lifetime Achievement Award." [Online]. Available: www.pga.com, 1999.

Barnes, Brandi. "Lindsey Nelson Always Found Time to Help UT." *The Daily Beacon*, (University of Tennessee), June 20, 1995.

"Broadcaster Jack Brickhouse Bidden Goodbye Under 'Hey, Hey' Wreath." Associated Press, August 10, 1998.

"Broadcaster Marty Glickman Dies." Reuters, Janaury 3, 2001.

Caray, Harry and Verdi, Bob. *Holy Cow!* New York: Villard Books, 1989.

Carlisle, Jim. "Musburger Adjusts to Quality over Quantity." Scripps Howard News Service, January 1, 2000.

Catsis, John. *Sports Broadcasting*. Chicago: Nelson-Hall, 1993.

Cosell, Howard and Boventre, Peter. *I Never Played the Game*. New York: Morrow, 1985.

Crowe, Steve. "Harwell Confirms Return to Radio Booth." *Detroit Free Press*, December 4, 1998.

———. "Enberg Won't Fall into Super Farewell Sap Trap." *Detroit Free Press*, January 23, 1998.

de Turenne, Veronica. "Dodgers and Scully Still Moving On." Scripps Howard News Service, October 1, 1996.

"Dick Vitale." [Online]. Available: www.espn.go.com/espninc/personalities/dickvitale .html, October 4, 1999.

Golenbock, Peter. *Cowboys Have Always Been My Heroes*. New York: Warner Books, 1997.

———. *Bums*. New York: Pocket Books, 1984.

Harwell, Ernie. "Days of Noteworthy Voices Long Gone." *Detroit Free Press*, April 10, 1998.

Hertzog, Bob. "Bob Costas, Commack." [Online]. Available: www.lihistory.com/specgrow/costa.htm.

Hiestand, Michael. "Packer, McGuire, Enberg Reunited." *USA Today*, February 7, 2000.

Hlas, Mike. "Retiring Jackson Is 'Part of Americana.'" *Cedar Rapids Gazette*, October 24, 1998.

————. "Hayden Throws, and the TV Guy Picks Him Off." *Cedar Rapids Gazette,* December 31, 1997.

"Interview with Don Meredith." *Playboy,* February 1978.

Jares, Joe. *Basketball: The American Game.* Chicago: Follett Publishing, 1971.

Kent, Milton. "Schenkel's Saturday Bowling Reaches End of the Lane at ABC." [Online]. Available: www.sunspot.net/columnists/data/kent/061997kent.html, June 19, 1997.

Kindred, Dave. "Top 5 Ornery Charmers: No. 1, Howard Cosell." *The Sporting News,* July 7, 1999.

Lyson, Katarzyna. "Musburger Reflects on Changes in Sports." *Daily Northwestern,* October 20, 1997.

"Madden and Summerall Remain Constants in NFL Booth." Associated Press, September 20, 1998.

Marshall, Bob. *Diary of a Yankee Hater.* New York: Franklin Watts, 1981.

Martzke, Rudy. "Albert's NBA Schedule Filled with Traveling Calls." *USA Today*, April 28, 2000.

————. "A(verage) B(ritish) C(overage)." *Detroit News*, July 25, 1995.

McGraw, Dan. "How to Save *Monday Night Football*." *U.S. News and World Report,* December 12, 1998.

"NBC Signs Costas into 21st Century." *Cowles Business Media*, June 18, 1996.

"Packers, Twins, Vikings Announcer Ray Scott Dies." Associated Press, March 24, 1998.

Patton, Charlie. "A Game Worth Viewing: NBC Ends Its NFL Broadcasting with Class." *Florida Times-Union*, January 26, 1998.

Sportscasters: Behind the Mike. [Television show]. The History Channel, February 7, 2000.

SportsCenter of the Century: The Most Influential People. [Television show]. ESPN, February 20, 2000.

Wade, Don. "Between the Lines, It's Still the Best Game in the World." *Evansville Courier-Press*, May 20, 1997.

Wojnarowski, Adrian. "Repentant Albert Gets Second Shot." *The Record,* Bergen, NJ, July 16, 1998.

"Yankees Broadcaster Allen Remembered at St. Patrick's Cathedral." Associated Press, November 4, 1996.

17

The Commissioners' Perspective

On April 24, 2000, the Museum of Television and Radio in New York hosted a unique seminar featuring the commissioners of the four major league sports in the U.S. They gathered as part of the Leonard H. Goldenson University Satellite Seminar Series to discuss how the electronic media have impacted their respective sports. A partial transcript of the seminar appears below, courtesy of the Museum of Television and Radio, the Isabelle and Leonard Goldenson Foundation, and a grant from Loreen Arbus. The seminar participants included the following people.

Gary Bettman assumed the duties of NHL commissioner in 1993. Bettman helped the league negotiate its first network television contract in more than 20 years and increased NHL deals with ESPN and ESPN2. He spent 12 years as a senior vice president of the NBA before coming to the NHL.

David Stern was elected NBA commissioner in 1984 and has worked with the league since 1966. Under his leadership, the NBA has quadrupled revenues, added six franchises, and established offices overseas.

Allan H. "Bud" Selig became commissioner of Major League Baseball in 1998, after six years as chairman of the league's Executive Council. Selig has pushed hard for interleague play, additional playoff rounds, and realignment.

Paul Tagliabue became NFL commissioner in 1989, after more than two decades as the league's outside counsel. Tagliabue oversaw league expansion and helped the NFL secure the largest television contracts in entertainment history.

MT&R President Bob Batscha served as moderator for the discussion.

Question: *Let's first begin with your roles. How has television changed your role as commissioner?*

Bettman: The role of the commissioner today is like the CEO of a major entertainment company in relation to setting television policy, formalizing national television contracts, and establishing the rules and regulations for local television. I think it's important for all of us to make sure we create a platform to provide the greatest number of games to the fans.

Selig: Our job is not only negotiating television contracts, but improving the relationship between television, radio, and the sport that keeps the intrinsic integrity of the sport, yet benefits the sport and the fan.

Stern: On the one hand, you have to protect the game. But it's important to realize, the average fan doesn't attend the game; he or she experiences it electronically, whether that's in Berlin or Bozeman. You have to put yourself in their place and in the place of the fan in the arena, then do the best you can.

Tagliabue: We're in a unique situation because we're the only league that schedules all its games for television. We don't have any individual team contracts and we also share all television revenue equally. That has a tremendous ripple effect in a variety of ways, including competitive balance.

Question: *You mentioned protecting the integrity of the game. What are the challenges for television sports with all the new developments such as the Internet?*

Stern: You get involved with the pace of the game. What do television time-outs do to the game? What about commercials between innings or between periods? I think we've all found our games stretched for time by television, but we have to adjust. Don't go overboard, but realize the importance of television to the sport.

Selig: There's no question television has changed the composition of the game. We need to be sensitive to scheduling, because we've all heard the complaints about how television schedules games at bad times. We try to determine the maximum number of people who can reasonably watch the game without compromising the integrity of the sport. It seems to get harder to do each year, but I think we're all doing quite well.

Bettman: I agree, but would like to look at things a little differently. Television technology has enabled us to "get it right" more often, in terms of integrity. Our officials are now subject more and more to replays, which can help us make the right calls about 99.999 percent of the time. We can see the same plays over and over again. Was it a legal play or an illegal play? Was the puck in the net or did it go in the side? Obviously, it's a human game and you'll never have it right 100 percent of the time, but because television can cover things so well, the expectation is that we should be right 100 percent of the time.

Tagliabue: It's really in the eye of the beholder. Some think instant replay violates the integrity of the game, which after all is played by humans and officiated by humans, but we're better off having it. It's a great entertainment factor, plus it's one of the earliest forms of television interactivity. Soon, technology will allow you to choose your own replay, and that's when it will really become interactive. But we still have to make sure we preserve the game's integrity.

Question: *Talk a little bit about the role of Roone Arledge, who is credited with introducing personality into television sports. How did he fundamentally change things and what impact did he have?*

Selig: It was a huge change, especially when you consider the way sports were covered in the 40s and 50s. Today, players, teams, coaches, and the commissioners are under much more scrutiny and pressure than ever before, but I think that's helped sports. Each year the technology gets better and the channels multiply, which makes the glare that much greater. Roone changed the way all of us live.

Bettman: Roone added the idea of storytelling, not just what happened in the game, but who and why. That provided fans an emotional connection with the sport, which made things better for everyone.

Tagliabue: Gary's right in that Roone told a story and went beyond the game. But people have always found a way to connect with sports, like Ken Burns showed us in his *Baseball* series. Radio and newspapers play a big part in that, but only television has the ability to take the sport to tens of hundreds of millions of people on a worldwide basis. That's something the other mediums can't do.

Question: *Talk a little bit about sports announcers, who have become such an important part of the game.*

Stern: Their importance is really for historical purposes. People don't really tune into a game because of the announcer, but because they want to hear the event or see their favorite team. Only later does the event become connected in people's minds with the announcers, such as when Russ Hodges called Bobby Thomson's home run or Johnny Most's call of Havlicek stealing the ball. The announcers are great and they add a flourish, but more and more I'm persuaded that fans don't really tune in just for them.

Bettman: I agree with David. When *Sports Illustrated* ranked the greatest sports moments of the century, I think the reason hockey was number one was because of Al Michaels' call "Do you believe in miracles?" We can all remember where we were when that happened. Something like that is a rare exception because it evokes such emotions. And I do think many people tuned into football games just to hear Howard Cosell, and listened to hockey because of Foster Hewitt. The same thing probably happens today with John Madden, but those instances are few and far between.

Selig: Life is so much different today. The role of the local announcer, people like Harry Caray, Bob Prince, and Vin Scully, has changed in recent years. Years ago, the local announcer played a more dominant role in the life of a franchise as compared to today.

Question: *How has the development of ESPN changed things for you?*

Bettman: With the innovation of sports 24 hours a day, seven days a week, people can get sports all the time. That's a plus for us in terms of getting our product out, but we're also under much more scrutiny. Things that were never mentioned years ago, we now see over and over on television and become defining moments. But overall, I think ESPN has been a blessing.

Stern: In 1979, when I first heard the idea I thought it was ridiculous. Who would watch college badminton or even the NBA 24 hours a day? And what about the cost? The fact is, ESPN helped create a new genre we now see with CNNSI, Fox Sports, and the like. Now, it's "You name it, you can see it around the clock." And now, for better or worse depending on your point of view, we're going to push that even further with the Internet. We haven't yet tested the limit of the ultimate fan.

Question: *We hear a lot today about how viewers are watching more specialized channels and aren't watching the national networks as much. Is that a threat to national sports?*

Tagliabue: It's not a threat, it's a reality. We have to share viewers not only with other sports, but other cable outlets. I can go home and watch 50 or more channels, and not just on sports. More significant for us rather than ESPN, was *Monday Night Football,* because it took our game to a different audience with different demographics. Things have now come full cycle and we're all in prime time, sharing the audience across the spectrum. The key is to keep our audience bigger than other audiences on a relative basis. I think all four of us are doing that, which is why sports has become such a critical part of television.

Stern: The drama of live sports is only going to enhance the value and importance of sports programming, wherever it appears. It doesn't matter whether you're a NHL fan, a NBA fan, or a badminton fan. We'll probably test the limits with the upcoming Olympics, when viewers can see events on cable or satellite and simply go wherever they want. Certainly it will have an impact, but as long as we're all out there hustling for fan base and promoting our sports, all sports are winners and it's good for all of us.

Question: *In today's media environment, it's generally assumed that the consumer has control and can jump from event to event. Does that change your thinking in how you present your sports?*

Stern: All of us have some version of [pay-per-view events]. The games are there for the fans if they don't happen to like the game shown in their area. But if fans have all this choice, it also fragments our audience. The challenge for us is whether we want to get involved with "channel conflict," or in effect, competing with ourselves. That will lower the ratings for individual games, but not the overall number of people watching. You still have the same number of people consuming the collective program.

Selig: All of this has created more popularity and more viability. People talk about declining ratings, but the fact is, more people than ever are watching—they're just watching in different forms, like on a superstation or whatever. On balance, you have to consider the benefit to the individual franchise versus the sport as a whole, and I think all four of us have done a remarkable job in an era when technology and consumer habits change so drastically.

Bettman: Because there's so much fragmentation and so many options out there, we need to do more to compete with other forms of entertainment. From a narrow perspective, that's more difficult for hockey since we haven't had a network television contract for the past 20 years. That makes it harder to grow that fan base when you're going upstream against the market. For us, maximum exposure means giving the fans what they want.

Tagliabue: All sports have two key elements. First, is the "us versus them" quality. We've talked about the U.S.-Soviet Union hockey game and the Dodgers-Giants rivalry in New York. The second element is the idea of the "superhuman," someone like Gretzky, McGwire, Jordan, or Payton, who are superhuman compared to the rest of us. Maybe that's where you draw the line between us and other sports. Are sports putting humans on the field, or superhumans, who have always been the main attraction?

Question: *What is your Internet strategy and how does it incorporate fan loyalty?*

Bettman: Our Internet strategy is to give the fan as much in-depth knowledge as possible, plus the ability to hear from them. It's not just about broadband, convergence, or seeing video highlights, but clubs doing business by interacting with fans. Our ability to fill arenas and stadiums will be a function of fans talking directly to teams and vice-versa. Long term, the big screen in your home will eventually have everything you could ever want in connection with the game, such as statistics, video, and history. But there's also the element of connection to the community, which you can do through the Internet.

Selig: If done properly, the Internet will increase the relationship between the fan and the sport, and increase popularity. It has an enormous potential and could develop an even more intimate fan relationship.

Stern: There are obviously enormous revenue possibilities, because sports is the killer application of the Internet. People talk about the Internet in terms of commerce, content, and community. Sports has extraordinary commerce and we've seen the great content, but the real application is community. Projections show that by the year 2003, there will be 600 million people hooked up, with 400 million outside the United States. That presents a tremendous opportunity to talk to like-minded people, buy or trade tickets, and let their views be known. The ability to communicate with the fans will be extraordinary and will only allow us to serve them better. It will enhance our relationships and build generations of new fans.

Tagliabue: For the avid fan, the Internet will do certain things, but it will also allow us to make avid fans out of those not even in touch with the sport. We video-streamed games in Holland last year [1999], so fans in Europe were able to watch NFL football. I guess it depends on what kind of fan you're talking about, but it could be phenomenal if developed the right way.

Stern: I also have a theory that when people are totally hooked up to their home electronics, ordering pizzas or getting medical advice online, that's when they want to be connected in a physical way and that's what will drive them to the arena. It's the last place to get a sense of actual community, which substitutes for the electronic community. In that sense, sports becomes even more important to reinforce how people are brought together by the Internet.

Selig: Back in the 50s and 60s, many baseball owners were very reluctant to put their games on live television for fear of losing attendance. They only allowed maybe 18 or 20 games a year, all on the road, and convinced themselves it was the right thing to do. But in time, they realized how television was an effective tool in promoting the game and now look at the figures: an average attendance of 13,000 in the 50s compared with 30,000 today. I agree with David and think it can be the same thing with the Internet.

Bettman: Free television is the best advertising for the game, short of people actually watching in the building. And the owners realize that if we get people to watch on television, a percentage of them will want to come and see the games in person.

Question: *Could you explain the role of women in sports as it relates to radio and television?*

Selig: I believe the role will hopefully increase. We've initiated the Women in Baseball program, which is now well underway. Years ago, it was unheard of to have women in the front office or in radio and television. That has gone out in the past two or three decades and I hope in the next decade, we make as much progress as we have in this last one.

Bettman: There's more interest than ever before in women's sports, when you consider things like the WBNA, Women's World Cup Soccer, and women's hockey. And because of ESPN and Fox, there's an opportunity to expose these sports to more than the people who go to the games. Certainly, interest will help fuel growth, but it's going to take some time to reach the same level as the male-dominated sports. It's been 80 or 90 years in the making, but it's coming.

Stern: The last male bastion is sports, but in the front office the woman's role has increased dramatically. We couldn't run some of our operations without that. The sports themselves will struggle to a degree, but that's another issue for another time—the lack of appropriate female voices.

Question: *Could you explain the role of pay-per-view? Given the current market situation of smaller audiences and rising costs, are we getting to the point where we might have to pay to watch any sports on television?*

Tagliabue: Obviously, the viewer is going to have more choice and more options, and some people will pay for those options. But as long as network television is healthy, the games will be on network TV because that's the primary way to reach fans. The fundamental question is how long the broadcast network system will remain healthy and continue to deliver a mass audience for all of us. There are also other issues involved, such as how much advertisers will spend in other areas, including the Internet.

Selig: This issue has actually been around a long time, because back in the 50s some people complained that the Dodgers and Giants were moving to California because of the promise of pay television out there. Here it is 43 years later and we haven't seen it yet. I agree with Paul that as long as the delivery systems stay unchanged, things will continue as they are.

Bettman: I think there's more to it than delivery systems and economics. Especially for our crown jewel events, it's important to reach the broadest possible audience. Right now, over-the-air national network television delivers that audience, but that could change. But as long as networks remain the most effective vehicle for reaching our audience, that's where you'll see us.

Question: *Much has been said about athletes as role models. What is your take on that and what part does the media play?*

Selig: Life has changed in recent years and athletes are under much more intense pressure. Being a professional athlete today is far more challenging than it was years ago. But I still believe the athlete has a social responsibility, not just to the individual community but to the country as a whole. Often times, we blame the media for things they didn't create, and we also have to recognize their role in the tremendous growth of sports.

Stern: In reality, the stars are teachers to the young. They teach by example such things as, how to get tattooed, how to wear your hair, or how to wear your pants. That's a good thing. We have enormous opportunities to deal with things like the digital divide, volunteerism, and illiteracy, and I think we as athletes, teams, and leagues are responsive to that. It's true that [dysfunction] plays better in the media. You never hear much about people like David Robinson, Steve Smith, or Jayson Williams for donating millions of dollars to causes. But some sort of incident will define a player in a negative way. That's the way it is, that's life and that's the responsibility of being a professional athlete at the highest level.

Question: *One of the big issues recently was putting microphones on coaches. What do you think about that and does it alter the reality of the events?*

Stern: We first miked a coach in 1981, so we've been doing it forever. The issue is not about the media, but how to engage and involve the fan to hear and experience something new. I think in five years, we'll all look back at this issue and laugh, especially when you see in NASCAR they put a camera on every car and you can pick what car to follow, or when the XFL puts a camera wherever. This wasn't the networks, but me trying to get us ready for what we have to face.

Bettman: Our players and officials have been very receptive to the idea. The only thing they have asked for is some type of cutoff switch, so they can be off mike when they lose it.

Tagliabue: We're 100 percent in favor of miking coaches, players, owners, and commissioners, except when players and coaches tell us it cuts into their ability to play or compete without undue interference. It's a great enhancement to let the fans see the pain or exhilaration of the game.

Stern: This issue got away from us, and I take full responsibility. It's not quite the issue it was made out to be. One day, I'll be featured with this episode in Chapter 1 of a book on how not to deal with a subject.

Selig: Some baseball people think it compromises the integrity of the sport, but I think we should pursue it aggressively. It increases enjoyment and can create lasting memories. Some feel it's a burden, but we have to overcome that.

Question: *To what degree does the media dramatize violence and what can be done about it?*

Stern: Don't hold your breath about doing anything about it. The reality is in the First Amendment world of news, the networks will incessantly emphasize things they think appeal to the fans. And to them, there's nothing as appealing as good, old fashioned fisticuffs, as sad as that may be. I think it will continue because it's a fact of life. I wish it weren't so, but I don't see any change.

Selig: I can't fault Fox or ESPN for picking up brawls. Our responsibility is to deal with the causes, instead of feeling sorry for ourselves and worrying about what the media do or don't do. That won't change, so we need to deal with the root causes and make sure it doesn't happen again.

Bettman: I'm not going to complain and say "poor me" on this, but the real issue here is perspective. For example, the incident between Marty McSorley and Donald Brashear was shown over and over, and some people wanted to see it. But to suggest that's representative of the league or happens on a regular basis crosses the line.

Question: *What upcoming new technology will drive your sports?*

Bettman: Television is able to bring home the excitement of the arena and help attendance. After 20 years with no national television contract, we're still catching up in that area. We believe we have the fastest, most exciting sport around, but we have trouble translating that excitement to television.

I shouldn't say we have trouble translating to television, but rather in bringing the excitement of the arena into the home. Once we get that issue solved, our ratings will go up.

Tagliabue: The most important technology is the one that enables the viewer to experience what the player on the field experiences. We experimented with the helmet cam 10 years ago. Other things include the umpire cam, isolated camera, and miniaturization. Whatever enables the viewer to experience the game in 3-D and full speed to feel the pain and exhilaration of the game. When high definition television finally comes to full flower, I think it will have an enormous impact.

Stern: We're trying to recreate the courtside experience in high definition, Dolby Surround Sound, and where the fan has the opportunity to pick whatever camera angle is most appealing. That is an extraordinary opportunity.

Selig: We want to do anything that will make the game more interesting to the fans, whether that's camera angles or whatever, because it makes the game more popular. We know that as television has become more sophisticated, sports have become more popular, and I think that will continue.

INDEX